BENEATH THE SURFACE
OF WHITE SUPREMACY

Stanford Studies in

COMPARATIVE RACE AND ETHNICITY

BENEATH THE SURFACE OF WHITE SUPREMACY

Denaturalizing U.S. Racisms

Past and Present

Moon-Kie Jung

Stanford University Press
Stanford, California

Stanford University Press
Stanford, California

Printed in the United States of America

Library of Congress Cataloging-in-Publication Data

Jung, Moon-Kie, author.
   Beneath the surface of white supremacy : denaturalizing U.S. racisms past and
present / Moon-Kie Jung.
      pages cm — (Stanford studies in comparative race and ethnicity)
   Includes bibliographical references and index.
   ISBN 978-0-8047-8938-7 (cloth : alk. paper)
   ISBN 978-0-8047-9519-7 (pbk.   )
   1. Racism—United States. 2. United States—Race relations. 3. Minorities—
United States—Social conditions. I. Title. II. Series: Stanford studies in
comparative race and ethnicity.
E184.A1J86 2015
305.800973—dc23
                                                              2014037753

ISBN 978-0-8047-9522-7 (electronic)

To Minja Ahn
and
to the memory of Juliana Kwija Yang

CONTENTS

ACKNOWLEDGMENTS

For fourteen years previous to the present one, I taught sociology and Asian American studies at the University of Illinois, Urbana-Champaign. Probably typically, surely not uniquely, this public university changed significantly over that span, on the whole for the worse. To my great good fortune, graduate students and fellow faculty I personally worked and interacted with carried on being their wonderful selves. No doubt their stimulating company and scholarship made this book better. The staff—administrative, clerical, janitorial, technical—were kind and capable, two of whom I would like to acknowledge by name: more than helping me good-naturedly for thirteen and fourteen years respectively, Shari Day of sociology and Mary Ellerbe of Asian American studies are just good people. I thank my new coworkers at the University of Massachusetts for warmly welcoming me.

Fellowships and grants from the following institutions provided material and intellectual support for research and writing: Center for Comparative Studies in Race and Ethnicity, Stanford University; Center for Advanced Study and Campus Research Board, University of Illinois; School of Social Science, Institute for Advanced Study; and James Weldon Johnson Institute for the Study of Race and Difference, Emory University. Faculty, fellows, staff, and librarians at these places and at the University of Hawaiʻi were terrific, all too frequently indispensable.

I am immensely grateful to colleagues, many of whom perform double duty as trusted friends, for taking the time and effort to read and comment on drafts. I subjected most of them to a selected chapter or two: Julia Adams, Larry Bobo, Adrian Cruz, David Eng, Didier Fassin, Behrooz Ghamari-Tabrizi, Neve Gordon, Tom Guglielmo, Monisha Das Gupta, Alison Isenberg, Moon-Ho Jung, J. Kēhaulani Kauanui, Amanda Lewis, Tim Liao, George Lipsitz, Hazel Markus, Anna Marshall, Monica McDermott, Charles Mills, Erin Murphy, Michael Omi, Naomi Paik, Hyun Ok Park, Nicola Perugini, Jemima Pierre, Leland Saito, Sandy Schram, Gillian Stevens, Eddie Telles and the students in his graduate workshop, Manu Vimalassery, Robert Warrior, Robert A. Williams, Howie Winant, Edlie Wong, and Mina Yoo. I burdened several volunteers and pushovers, as generous as they are brilliant, with all or nearly all of the manuscript: Sara Farris, Tyrone Forman, Dave Roediger, Catherine Rottenberg, Joan Scott, João Vargas, and Caroline Yang. Jae-Kyun Kim supplied skillful research assistance on two of the chapters and the bibliography. At Stanford University Press, I have been spoiled by the always excellent editor-in-chief Kate Wahl and a superb production team.

As I age, the line between family and friends among my loved ones loses meaning, while the one encircling them all takes on more. Compounding my profound regret and apology to many of them for not staying in closer touch, I mention here only those who have suffered and supported me the longest and deepest: parents Woo-Hyun Jung and Minja Ahn, grandma Kwon Soon-Ok, brother Moon-Ho and sister-in-law Tefi Lamson, nieces Mina and Seri, BFAMs Eric Bennett and João Vargas, godson Toussaint, and, above all, partner Caroline Yang. I dedicate this book to my mother and my late mother-in-law, each of whom confronted cancer with courage and grace.

Chancing future lawsuits, I blamed the unruly errors of previous books on unsuspecting, preliterate children. As my nieces and godson have grown and, alas, learned to read, I feared I would have to face up to my own failings this time around. Mercifully, my newborn nephew-in-law Matthew storked in to save the day. I will post his email address as soon as possible.

BENEATH THE SURFACE

OF WHITE SUPREMACY

PART I
DENATURALIZING
COMMON SENSE

But this cowardice, this necessity of justifying a totally false identity and of justifying what must be called a genocidal history, has placed everyone now living into the hands of the most ignorant and powerful people the world has ever seen. And how did they get that way? By deciding that they were white. By opting for safety instead of life. By persuading themselves that a black child's life meant nothing compared with a white child's life.

James Baldwin, "On Being White . . . and Other Lies"

CHAPTER I

INTRODUCTION: RECONSIDERING RACISM AND THEORY

COMPLETELY PENETRATED HEART

On a cold, drizzly morning in the fall of 2009, Kiwane Carrington woke up at the home of his longtime friend I. Thomas. The house, a modest rental, sat on the southern edge of a predominantly Black area on the north side of Champaign, Illinois, not far, but far removed, from the university on the city's east side.[1] Carrington had been staying there for a few weeks by then, as he had for much of the prior summer. With the Thomases, the fifteen-year-old, who had lost his mother to pancreatic cancer the year before, found a home away from home. Both I.T.'s mother, Deborah Thomas, and her boyfriend would later describe him as "like a son."

On October 9, a Friday, Ms. Thomas, a student at the local community college, had left early for a seven o'clock English class. In the next hour and a half, fifteen-year-old I.T., her oldest, and her three younger kids made their way to school. When Ms. Thomas returned home, she saw Carrington in the kitchen, fixing himself breakfast, and briefly chatted with him; he attended a different high school than I.T. and did not need to be there until ten. Sometime while she and her boyfriend were in their room, Carrington departed. By noon, the house was empty, with Ms. Thomas gone to her psychology class and her boyfriend to work at Wendy's.[2]

By a little after one o'clock, Carrington, along with one of his best friends, J.M., was back at the Thomas residence. They might have looked for an open door or window; Ms. Thomas disapproved but was aware that I.T. and Carrington occasionally used one of the windows, if unlocked, to get into the house when no adults were home to let them in.[3] Likely, Carrington and J.M.

sought shelter from the weather, still chilly with intermittent rain.[4] Unlikely, Carrington intended to turn on and rob his surrogate family.

A neighbor next door happened to spot the pair and telephoned the Champaign police. He knew Ms. Thomas and was concerned that the two "young guys"—"black males" when asked by the police—were trying to "find a way inside the house." He did not recognize Carrington or his friend, obscured as they were by the "hoodies on their heads."[5] A radio dispatch for a burglary in progress went out. The first two police officers to arrive were Robert T. Finney, the Champaign police chief, and Daniel Norbits, a fourteen-year veteran of the force. According to the dispatch printout, Finney noted at 1:30:07 p.m. an "OPEN DOOR IN BACK"—just the screen door, as it would turn out; the main door remained shut and locked. Forty-four seconds later, someone at the scene transmitted, "SHOTS FIRED ON VINE [STREET], 1 SUSP DOWN"; the Illinois State Police-led multijurisdictional investigation of the shooting later determined that a single shot had been discharged.[6] The downed "suspect" was Carrington. An ambulance arrived on the scene at 1:36 p.m. By the time the paramedics checked six minutes later, the "[patient] was pulseless and was not breathing."[7] All efforts to revive him on the way to and at the hospital failed, and Carrington was pronounced dead. The attending physician told a police investigator, "it appeared that a bullet had completely penetrated the patient's heart."[8] The autopsy later concluded, "The death of this 15-year-old, black male, Kiwane Carrington, is from a Gunshot Wound of the Left Arm with Reentry Into the Chest, involving the lung, heart, diaphragm, vena cava and liver. A large-caliber, copper-jacketed bullet was recovered from the right upper abdominal quadrant behind the liver."[9]

There were four people who could have directly seen and heard the fatal incident: Carrington, J.M., Finney, and Norbits.[10] As his friend lay dying next to him, J.M. was at once arrested and hauled away. At the police station, in a windowless interrogation room, he decided alertly, on his own, not to waive his Miranda rights and answer questions.[11] He was subsequently locked up in juvenile detention over the weekend. With the initial burglary charge untenable, he would face a felony count of "aggravated resisting a peace officer" for many months, throughout which he did not give a statement. Of the four, only Finney and Norbits related to investigators their accounts, which, by law, could not be used against them in any subsequent criminal proceedings.[12] Finney told his story within four hours of the shooting. Meanwhile, speaking to two ranking Champaign police officers, including a deputy chief, approximately three and a half hours after the shooting, Norbits's union lawyer "advised that Officer Norbits was not able to give a statement to the investigative team at that time"[13] and/or "requested that the interview with Officer Norbits take place at another time. . . . [because] Officer Norbits was having some memory issues with the event."[14] About an hour afterward, at a meeting attended by Norbits, the attorney, two state police investigators, and one of the two Champaign police officers, Norbits's wish to postpone the interview was granted, and it would not transpire until four days later. Perhaps irregularly and patently unwisely, the two from the Champaign force appeared to have the most and final say in the decision, injecting suspicion of favoritism and undercutting the independence of the investigation.[15]

According to the investigation, Finney had arrived at the Thomas residence before the other officers, just moments ahead of Norbits.[16] He drove an unmarked Toyota Highlander, and he was dressed in street clothes: blue jeans, a University of Illinois sweatshirt emblazoned with the officially abandoned "Chief Illiniwek" logo, and a black leather jacket with his police badge affixed to it.[17] Finney walked around the adjacent house from which the neighbor had called in. With the two teens by the backdoor, Finney approached from the side, advancing toward the lone, narrow opening, between the Thomases' house and detached garage, to the otherwise fenced-in backyard. Norbits took a more direct route, up the driveway. Finney had the better angle on the scene. He recalled seeing an open "storm door," which he radioed in. Then, to his left, he "saw Officer Norbits . . . moving up" the drive. Venturing "a little bit closer," Finney "observed two individuals right at the door."[18]

His vision blocked by the house to his left, Norbits eyed, on his right, Finney walking toward the backyard opening. Norbits described what happened next *before* he himself made visual contact with Carrington and J.M.: "I see Chief Finney emerge along the fence [of the neighbor's house] . . . and all of a sudden I see Chief Finney draw his gun and say, 'stop or I will shoot you.'"[19] Going over the point multiple times during his interview, Norbits did not waver from this account. Perhaps concerned that Norbits had inadvertently left out a crucial detail, an investigator queried, "Dan, do you recall anybody specifically saying 'police or Champaign Police'? . . . Do you remember that at all?" Norbits replied, "I don't have any recollection of that."[20] Keep in mind that Finney, unlike Norbits, was not in uniform but in casual attire; particularly if he raised his arms to point his gun at the kids, would his small badge, at chest level according to investigation photographs, have been readily visible and decipherable by the startled, doubtless scared, youths?

Set on "heightened" alert by and taking his cue from Finney's abrupt threat and actions, Norbits unholstered his own gun and joined the confrontation.[21] The officers instructed the teens to get down, as corroborated by the neighbor, who did not see but heard what was happening; the staff person at the police station, who overheard through the phone while on the line with the neighbor; and a third officer, who arrived right after Norbits and only heard, from the far side of the house. Finney concerned himself with J.M., while Norbits engaged Carrington. Many words have been used by the police, the state's attorney, the media, and the public to characterize what occurred during the short span of less than three quarters of a minute preceding the deadly shot, most of which gave the impression of a two-sided fight. None of those words were Carrington's or J.M.'s.

Physically, the two pairs were unevenly matched: the police officers were larger, most likely by a sizable margin. Carrington and J.M. were slight: police documents varied in their estimations, but the two adolescents were decidedly smaller than the average adult male.[22] Finney happened to mention that he was 6 feet 1 inch tall, and Norbits was sure he was taller than Carrington but did not want to "guess" beyond that; in police photographs taken after the shooting, Finney and Norbits appeared to be at least of medium build.[23]

Finney and Norbits described the youths as having actively resisted. Rather incongruously, both officers portrayed them as having been silent throughout, unintentionally calling to mind shock or fright more than belligerence. Whatever resistance there was, it did not include attacks on the officers, even in their stories to investigators. According to Finney, J.M. tried to move past him, and Finney pushed him back. J.M. allegedly made another attempt, and Finney applied physical effort to take him down to the ground; Finney's minor injuries—scrapes to knee and hand, stretched shoulder ligament—were from this exertion, not blows inflicted by J.M. Norbits did not see Finney's dealings with J.M. He himself was trying to force Carrington down. Like Finney, he did so, at least initially, with only his left hand, the one without his pistol.

Norbits supposedly expressed concern about Carrington's hands, possibly reaching into a pocket, which Finney recounted, too. (Neither Carrington nor J.M. had weapons, in their pockets or elsewhere, raising the specter of Amadou Diallo but not a bit of the police investigators' inquisitiveness.) While he may or may not have gone down immediately, Carrington did not appear to have been particularly active in his "resistance." Prompted by a police investigator with a seemingly leading question—"And um, is he [Carrington], he's fighting back with you, or?"—Norbits reined in the rhetoric, "I mean, I, I can't say he's throwing punches but he's clearly resisting."[24] Similarly, to the question "Was he [Carrington] physically resisting Norbits?" Finney answered, "As far as I could tell he was still . . . I mean he wasn't going along with the program either."[25]

With Carrington "in a sitting position," according to Finney, Norbits's gun fired;[26] in Norbits's version, Carrington fell after the shot.[27] A sitting position would seem to be more consistent with the "downwards" trajectory of the bullet.[28] Belying the impression of tight spacing between Carrington and the gun—"I remember trying to get him down on the ground, er, yea and the gun goes off"[29]—the autopsy concluded "without evidence of close range firing."[30] Norbits fully acknowledged that he was trained to keep his "fingers indexed" off of the trigger.[31] His gun, a Glock 21, featured "internal safeties to prevent accidental discharge" that become "deactivated" only "when the trigger is pulled." Since the gun was found to be in "proper working condition," and there was no evidence or allegation that Carrington himself reached for the gun, the clear implication was that Norbits had to have squeezed the trigger.[32] Finney "didn't see the shot being fired."[33] His memory of shooting Carrington "a real vague recollection," "a blur," Norbits stated repeatedly and incoherently that he did not remember.[34]

Norbits was placed on administrative leave during the ensuing investigation. Without interruption or sanction, however, Finney continued in his duties as the police chief. Further, within a month of Carrington's death, Steve Carter, Champaign's city manager and Finney's boss, who arguably wielded more power than the mayor or the city council, declared his unflagging support for the police chief. At a city council meeting, Carter proclaimed that Finney had done nothing wrong and that he was an "excellent police chief."[35] At the time, the state police-led investigation was in progress, and the prosecutor presumably had not made any determinations on the case. Evidently, nobody seriously entertained bringing charges against Finney, or credibly could have, given his undisrupted tenure in office.

On December 8, 2009, Julia Rietz, the state's attorney for Champaign county, issued a fourteen-page report, concluding, "Although Carrington's death is tragic, the evidence provided by the Illinois State Police investigation does not support the filing of criminal charges, and rather supports the conclusion that the shooting was accidental."[36] Among the charges Rietz ruled out was involuntary manslaughter. According to Illinois statute 720 ILCS 5/9–3, "A person who unintentionally kills an individual without lawful justification commits involuntary manslaughter if his acts whether lawful or unlawful which cause the death are such as are likely to cause death or great bodily harm to some individual, and he performs them recklessly," and per 720 ILCS 5/4–6, "A person is reckless or acts recklessly when that person consciously disregards a substantial and unjustifiable risk that circumstances exist or that a result will follow, described by the statute defining the offense, and that disregard constitutes a gross deviation from the standard of care that a reasonable person would exercise in the situation."[37]

Rietz's decision turned on two choices. First, she opted to believe Norbits and Finney wholesale. There was no part of their, or their colleagues', narratives that her report doubted, much less contradicted. No indication of scrutiny or skepticism. Crucial irregularities (e.g., four-day delay before interviewing Norbits), disagreements in accounts (e.g., Finney's first words to the teens; bodily position of Carrington when Norbits shot him), and potential discrepancies in the physical evidence (e.g., autopsy finding of no evidence of "close range firing") were unnoticed, uncommented upon, or explained away. Her report also showed no effort by her or her office to question Norbits and Finney further, despite the fact that their interviews with the police investigators had been conducted in a congenial, collegial manner and were legally shielded against self-incrimination.[38] Given Rietz's credulity, it was of little surprise she deemed "that Norbits acted reasonably when he engaged in a physical altercation with Carrington with his weapon drawn."[39]

Second, Rietz chose to fill in a crucial blank, Norbits's partial amnesia, with a restrictive application of the law and charitable speculation. Concerning the act of shooting itself, she determined that "there [wa]s no evidence that Norbits made a conscious decision to disregard a substantial risk when the weapon discharged."[40] Comparing this statement against the law's wording, we can see that she severely limited what was subjected to the test of "gross deviation from the standard of care that a reasonable person would exercise in the situation": it was confined to "when the weapon discharged," the very moment the trigger was pulled. All of Norbits's actions between his decision to physically subdue Carrington with his weapon drawn and his pulling of the trigger—like the placement of his finger on the trigger while physically engaged with Carrington, a practice self-admittedly at strict odds with his extensive training and knowledge—were thus subtly pushed out of consideration. What about Norbits's consciousness? Rietz judged that "the evidence indicates that Norbits pulled the trigger accidently [sic], most likely as a reflex when he was struggling to hold Carrington with his left hand."[41] As far as I could gather, no such evidence existed: it was pure conjecture that plugged Norbits's utter and, one would logically have to suspect, convenient gap in memory.[42] On this point, Norbits's responses included, "I, this is where, and I'm not trying, I just, this is where I get a real vague recollection"; "I don't have a complete recollection of what exactly . . . "; "I, I'm drawing a blank at this point"; "I just, at this point, I, to be honest with you, just don't remember"; "I wish there was something else I could tell you but . . . "; "Right now that is a blur"; "Something had to happen for the gun to go off. . . . And that's where the piece, the puzzle's missing for me too." The last two were replies to questions about whether he "remember[s] consciously pulling" the trigger and whether he "remember[s] if [his] finger was on the trigger or off."[43] To Rietz, this fuzzy recall "sound[ed] like a reasonable explanation": "I find that very credible."[44]

Scrutiny and skepticism were reserved for Carrington, J.M., and those who might have registered the slightest empathy toward them. Although Norbits and Finney had no previous contact with or knowledge of Carrington and J.M. before the fateful day and therefore could not have been prejudiced by it, Rietz detailed their juvenile records, which police investigators had exhaustively assembled; by contrast, only the last five years of Norbits's (and none of Finney's) personnel records were forwarded to Rietz, critically leaving out Norbits's central involvement in the beating and consequent heart-attack death of a developmentally disabled man nine years earlier.[45] Rietz further disclosed that J.M.'s "MySpace page indicates that he associates with the North End Gorillas, a Champaign street gang," without confirming its existence, its actual character, or J.M.'s association; when asked about the so-called gang, in relation to Carrington, Ms. Thomas dismissed the notion as silly: "That's not a gang. That's a little neighborhood kids. . . . Ain't no gang. (laughs)."[46] Punitive and paternalistic, the prosecutor would not drop the felony charge against J.M. for four more months, and then only upon his and his mother's completion of a six-week "Parenting with Love and Limits" program.[47] Leaving no stone unturned, the state's attorney's report also duly summarized Carrington's school record, including attendance.[48] No official word, however, on whether he made his bed every morning.

While withholding information about Carrington's death, police investigators had conducted lengthy interviews of the Thomas household, including two of the children, right after the shooting.[49] One of the manifest objectives was to set in black-and-white, unambiguous terms that Carrington did not have permission to be at the house when he was killed, as if this could prove a legal violation and rationale. Although it became clear that Ms. Thomas's initially telling investigators that Carrington did not have permission was akin to a parental house rule applicable to her own kids and that she definitely would not have considered Carrington a burglar or trespasser, Rietz not only found the issue germane for her report but also gratuitously opined that some of Ms. Thomas's clarifying statements were inconsistent and "were not considered to be credible."[50]

The overall impression incised by the prosecutor was that the ultimate focus of the criminal investigation had not been Carrington's death but his life, not Norbits's and Finney's conduct but Carrington's and J.M.'s. Opening with an absolution—"In this case, there is no evidence that Officer Norbits acted recklessly"—a paragraph near the report's end coiled into a rebuke: "Significantly, the interaction between Norbits and Carrington was largely dictated by Carrington's behavior. By not complying with the officers' lawful commands to get down on the ground, and by physically resisting Norbits' efforts to get him to comply, Carrington put in motion a series of events that were entirely avoidable."[51] In effect, Carrington committed police-assisted suicide, proximately through his regrettable choices in attracting Norbits's bullet and more generally through his regrettable choices in life.

Carrington, J.M., and the Thomas family are Black. Every state actor named above is white.

RETHEORIZING RACISM

A longtime resident of Champaign, I was, and am, convinced that had Carrington and J.M. been white kids having done exactly the same thing in a neighborhood a half mile, or mere blocks, to the south, both would still be alive. Based on what I and other heretics have read and heard, and also not read and not heard, around town, most of our fellow denizens did not share our belief. But our uncommon sense was in step with existing research: for instance, according to a study of 170 largest U.S. cities, Blacks were 5.25 times more likely than whites to be victims of police homicide and constituted a *majority* of them (Jacobs and O'Brien 1998).[52] More broadly, Blacks have fared worse than whites in every facet of their dealings with law enforcement (Alexander 2010).

Circumstantial evidence on Champaign also raised racial doubts. Compared to the country as a whole, economic inequality between Blacks and whites, a robust predictor of police killings (Jacobs and O'Brien 1998), has been much more pronounced in Champaign: in 2006–2010, the Black-to-white ratio of median family income was 0.41 for Champaign and 0.62 for the United States.[53] Of the 125 officers in the Champaign Police Department, fewer than 5 percent (6) were Black, while over 90 percent were white;[54] by contrast, according to the 2010 census, 15.6 percent and 67.8 percent of Champaign residents were Black and white, respectively.[55] Not subject to a residency requirement, between two-thirds and three-quarters of the city's police force lived in predominantly white rural areas outside the "twin cities" of Champaign and adjoining Urbana.[56] Based on available evidence, from 2006 through 2008, Blacks filed over 60 percent of all complaints against the police, but the department tended to be much more dismissive, sustaining only 10 percent of them in contrast to 35 percent of complaints made by whites.[57] Over 80 percent of the over 80 arrests made per year in Champaign public schools were of Black students; in a joint effort by the school district and the police department, specifically assigned police officers, armed with guns, operated full-time in the city's middle schools and high schools.[58] In Champaign county, Black juveniles were 25 times more likely than their white counterparts to be charged with a crime. On charges of "resisting arrest and/or obstructing justice"—which Carrington, like his friend, might well have faced, had he survived—Black youths accounted for a mind-boggling 92 percent.[59]

Yet the possibility of racism, however defined, had no legitimate place in the dominant discourse on the Carrington case. Less than two weeks after the shooting and more than a month and a half ahead of the state's decision not to prosecute Norbits or Finney, an editorial in the *News-Gazette*, the daily with a practical monopoly on local print news, primed its readers for the eventual outcome: "Police said Carrington and another juvenile ignored their commands and tried to flee. It was during the struggle to restrain the youths that Carrington was shot. Circumstances point to an accidental shooting, that Officer Daniel Norbits did not intentionally discharge his service weapon during his struggle with Carrington."[60] Around the same time, in line with the sentiments of his colleagues, city council member Kyle Harrison agreed with the city manager that the case was a "defining moment for the community": "This is all of our problem. It's not a black thing or white thing. It's a community thing."[61] The report of the state's attorney contained no hint of a racial analysis, even to dismiss the possibility of its warrant. This emboldened the *News-Gazette* to editorialize, "Although the Champaign Police officer involved, Daniel Norbits, is white and the youth who was shot, Kiwane Carrington, is black, the facts do not suggest race was a factor in what happened." Mirroring the prosecutor's explanation that it had anticipated and maybe influenced, the newspaper could not resist a dig, what it regarded as "obvious—that this nightmare could have been avoided if the youths had submitted to proper police orders."[62] In their effort to preempt negative reactions to the decision by the state's attorney, city officials acknowledged the need to repair relations between the police and the Black community but refrained from any talk of racism possibly being implicated in those strained relations, the prosecutor's assessment, the investigation, and the shooting itself.[63] After the city administratively slapped Norbits on the wrist months later with a thirty-day suspension for failing to maintain control of his weapon, the police union released an astonishingly spiteful statement: "How unfortunate and disappointing to see Officer Norbits become the 'victim' for doing exactly what he was trained to do in the name of making someone other than Carrington himself accountable for Carrington's long-standing reckless behavior."[64] If Norbits, and not Carrington, was the true "victim"—the word strangely, ambiguously spotlighted with quotation marks—how could racism have been involved? At least the union had the decency to stop short of crying reverse racism.

Beyond inscribing the case to memory, I begin this book with the legitimated police killing of Kiwane Carrington because, though particular, it was not exceptional but eminently expectable. Though unique in concrete details, it wended its way more or less predictably to more or less unsurprising outcomes.[65] Though not generalizable, it enables and compels theoretically and politically far-reaching questions about racism that I grapple with in this book. Most fundamentally, did racism impinge upon this case, and if so, what do and should we mean by *racism*? Is it an *ideology*? A *structure*? What do and should we mean by those concepts?

No evidence, or allegation, has surfaced that any of the police officers—or investigators or city government officials or prosecutors—uttered "racist" words. Although such expressions might have proved decisive and damning, rightly or wrongly, their absence is unremarkable: even when their interactions with Black male youths blatantly bespeak racial bias, the police rarely resort to racist speech during them (Brunson 2007; Brunson and Miller 2006). How should we make sense of this ordinary lack? Would, and should, racist words serve as compulsory, conclusive proof? What are the implications for how we conceive of racism? What are racist words beyond the few that most would agree on?[66] Was Finney's "stop or I will shoot you" racist? What about Rietz's invocation of "North End Gorillas"? How much theoretical weight should we assign to *discourse*, to what people say and write? What about the related notion of *intentionality* that words are usually supposed to represent?

One of the first things the police did, when the neighbor called in, was to categorize Carrington and J.M. by race, as well as gender, and various officials noted and reproduced the classification subsequently without hesitation or trouble, as did the media and the public. Nobody lived up to the common, often defensive, refrain "I don't see race" in any literal sense. Yet none of the people directly implicated in the shooting and its legitimation explicitly talked of race beyond registering the adolescents' being Black or disclaiming its relevance. If asked, they would all have undoubtedly denied that race affected their perceptions, judgments, or actions in any way. But even if indeterminate or unknowable in this particular case, race must somehow factor in policing practices that lead to Black youths making up over 80 percent of those arrested in Champaign public schools or over 90 percent of those charged with resisting arrest or obstructing justice in the county. How should we reconcile such apparent contradictions between "colorblind" discourse and racist practice? Is there a contradiction? Is it a matter of people hiding their true attitudes and feelings, of political correctness? Is "colorblindness" the dominant form of racism today, as is often argued, and if so, in what sense? If this incident had happened in the middle of the twentieth century rather than at the break of the twenty-first, what would have been similar or different? Would it have been somehow more straightforwardly racist? In other words, what are, and how do we account for, the continuities and discontinuities between the eras preceding and following the Civil Rights Movement?

As among state actors and local mainstream media, there was among the general public an unequal distribution of scrutiny, skepticism, and blame on the one hand, and of empathy, credence, and exculpation on the other. There were exceptions, but Blacks' and whites' views were noticeably divergent, again consistent with current research (Hurwitz and Peffley 2005). At almost all public forums that dealt with the Carrington case—vigils, memorials, protests, city council meetings, court hearings, press conferences—Blacks were far overrepresented and voiced, variously and to varying degrees, criticisms of the structures, cultures, and practices of the police department, city government, and other state institutions. In reaction to the nonprosecution of the police, Carol Ammons, a member of the progressive Champaign-Urbana Citizens for Peace and Justice, distilled and conveyed the underlying sentiment of this movement: "If white children were being murdered in this country the way we have experienced [young] African-American men being murdered, we would not have to demand justice in this case."[67] On the whole, white public opinion, quieter overall, was more liable to side with the police and the state's attorney and blame Carrington, J.M., their families, Blacks, and activist organizations. Not atypically, one letter to the News-Gazette rejected the idea that Carrington should not be blamed for his own death, referring to "predators burglarizing houses" and "just a couple of delinquents." It closed, "The black community must assert itself by demanding their offspring be law-abiding and prosperous citizens, not delinquent criminals dealing in drugs and the stolen property of others."[68]

In this age of colorblindness and multiculturalism, when almost nobody identifies as a racist and almost everybody condemns racism, why do Blacks and whites hold such disparate viewpoints? Do discourses that are produced by dominant institutions and individuals aligned with them, predominantly though not exclusively white, perform the same work that critical subaltern discourses do? Are they two conflicting positions that are functionally equivalent, if substantively opposed? If not, how should we conceptualize their difference in relation to operations of power? In relation to "truth"? In relation to potential and actual transformations? Further, how do we comprehend dominant actors' routine *ignorances*, the ignoring of opinions of their racial others and, more paradoxically but no less mundanely, the ignoring of their own knowledge about racial inequality and domination?[69] What are the assumptions, implications, and consequences?

Solely based on this case, Champaign, like many places, might falsely look as if it were populated entirely by Blacks and whites: Asians and Latinas/os, respectively making up 10.6 percent and 6.3 percent of the city's residents, were seldom a visibly significant presence at most events related to the Carrington homicide.[70] Asians and, to a lesser degree, Latinas/os have not been disciplined and punished by the police and the courts as harshly as Blacks. Yet, when they did become involved, they were disapproving of the police and other state agencies; except for one fulsome testimonial by an Asian small business owner at a city council meeting, I cannot recall any Asian or Latina/o sticking up for the police. How do Latinas/os and Asians fit into the racial picture? Is the principal racial line shifting from nonwhite/white to Black/non-Black, as many now speculate?[71] What are the historical roots of anti-Latina/o and anti-Asian racisms, and how do they relate to anti-Black racism? Many Asians and Latinas/os in Champaign, as elsewhere in the United States, are migrants or children of migrants. How does "immigration," past and present, figure in the racial politics of belonging?

Even less visibly present than Latinas/os and Asians were Native Americans, who compose only 0.3 percent of Champaign's population.[72] In this context, was Finney's "Chief Illiniwek" sweatshirt meaningful? Only in the face of external sanctions, imposed by the National Collegiate Athletic Association, did the University of Illinois finally, after many years of controversy and protest, abandon its racist mascot in 2007. Nonetheless, the fictitious caricature remains popular among large segments of alums, students, and local residents and can still be seen everywhere around Champaign-Urbana. Given the highly politicized nature and salience of the figure, donning anything with references to it is always more than a sartorial choice and cannot but be a political one. How do we apprehend the omnipresence of a fictional "Indian chief," which so many of the nonindigenous proudly hail, together with the fact that the 0.3 percent was once 100 percent? Is this presence-absence still recognizably tied to the genocidal history of European and U.S. colonialism? How does the history of anti-Native racism, if rooted in empire building, articulate with those of anti-Black and other racisms? How does *imperial subjection* structure *racial subjection*, and vice versa? Is it possible and desirable to construct a unified theoretical framework to study the multifarious histories of racisms of the vast but frequently denied U.S. empire? If the United States has been an empire, how far does its imperial history reach back, and what are the limits and possibilities of antiracism?

In the Carrington case and countless other instances throughout the history of the United States, the *legitimacy* of racial state violence is rarely threatened, its naked brutality and inequality rendered acceptable and justifiable, habitually without notice. How is this legitimation achieved? How do we theorize the *racial state*? What is the basis for arguing that the United States is one? Is it compatible with the liberal concept of *nation-state*, which almost everyone, including social scientists, implicitly and explicitly assumes the United States to exemplify? How do the racial state and the nation-state relate to empire?

SCOPE OF THE BOOK

Matters of racism are not and have never been simple matters. They were not contemporaneously more transparent in the past, before the Civil Rights Movement, and they are not consistently less powerful now. The premature death of one fifteen-year-old in a small city in central Illinois during the inaugural year of the age of Obama can bring up so many weighty issues because it, like most phenomena racial, is embedded in a dense web of meanings, practices, and structures of different depths, scales, and histories.

With a distinctive set of problems, approaches, and empirical foci, *Beneath the Surface of White Supremacy* is guided by a number of organizing principles. First and foremost, I seek to devise and hone more effective conceptual tools, unsettling common sense and pushing our collective understanding beyond received theoretical and political boundaries. The emphasis is on innovation, novel ways to expose and shine more light on racial inequalities and domination. Second, the book targets those aspects of racism—for lack of prior attention or entrenched debates, as well as no doubt my idiosyncratic curiosities—that I find especially misunderstood, overlooked, and puzzling. The aim is not comprehensive breadth. I do not touch on the many aspects of racism that are ably researched by others. Third, the book implicitly argues against methodological chauvinism and for eclecticism and aptness, not hewing to a single mode of analysis or a particular type of evidence. I draw on archival, legal, media, and statistical investigations. Finally, with the exception of one chapter, the book builds on theories and concepts I admire. For my and the readers' sake, I make little effort to summarize the relevant literatures. Instead, I think with and through a select set of inspired and inspiring works that invite and promise further development. Of course, I critique and transform, but always with the common collective goal of advancing antiracist research and praxis in mind.

The book is divided into three parts. In the first, "Denaturalizing Common Sense," I take measure of the whole. This introductory chapter attempts to defamiliarize what appears to be all too familiar—the legitimated slaying of a young Black male by the police—through close description, aiming to discern the dominant racial common sense that prevailed. In the opposite direction, the defamiliarization of this particular event opens up a multitude of more general questions about the workings of racism that I take up in the rest of the book. Chapter two is the broadest in scope, as well as the most abstract: it outlines a new theory of *racism*, an indispensable, if deeply fraught, concept in the social sciences. I build on two of my favorite theories: Eduardo Bonilla-Silva's structural theory of racism and William Sewell Jr.'s theory of structure. The former goes a long way toward denaturalizing commonsensical views on racism, both lay and scholarly, by stressing its structural character. Insightful in myriad ways, it is held back by an unsatisfactory concept of structure. Integrating, critiquing, and extending Sewell's more cultural and historical understanding of structure, I address a number of thorny issues, including scale, meaning, consciousness, and change. To do so, I prune the overgrown concept of ideology and distinguish between dominant and subaltern positions, discursive and nondiscursive practices, and performative and reflective discourses. Foregrounding the *practical* over the *representational*, the restructured theory allows us to square a host of contradictory theories and findings in the social-scientific study of racism.

Parts two and three are less broadly abstract, and each comprises two empirical cases, one historical and one contemporary. The second part, "Denaturalizing the Nation-State," brings into question what, to great distortion, is almost always assumed. The United States is the specific "nation-state" under scrutiny, but the arguments are, with due modifications, applicable to other states of the West and beyond. Chapter three flatly disputes the universal assumption that the United States is and has been a nation-state. I contend that the United States has always been an *empire-state*, positing a conceptual shift with potentially sweeping implications. Foremost, it provides a firmer basis for understanding the United States as a racial state, a state of white supremacy, requiring none of liberalism's contortions of the past and false promises for the future. For empirical analysis, I turn to constitutional law of the long nineteenth century. I show how U.S. state formation has always entailed the racial construction of colonial spaces. Tracing the strange career of *Dred Scott v. Sandford*, the notorious Supreme Court case on slavery almost never associated with empire, I argue for a unified framework to analyze the different but linked histories of racial subjection, including those of Asians/Asian Americans, Blacks, Latinas/os, Native Americans, and Pacific Islanders.

Chapter four undermines the taken-for-grantedness of the nation-state from a completely different direction. The empirical object of analysis is the current social-scientific literature on immigration and immigrants. Since the 1990s, immigration scholars have revitalized assimilation theory to study the large and growing numbers of migrants from Latin America, Asia, and the Caribbean in the United States. Neoclassical and segmented assimilation theories seek to make sense of this ongoing wave of migrants and their offspring that differs in significant ways from the last great wave at the turn of the twentieth century. They also recognize and try to overcome the limitations of earlier assimilation theories. Yet the new theories continue to misconstrue race, badly, by assuming precisely what should be dissected: the "nation-state" and structures of inequality and domination. Shifting the focus from *difference* to *inequality* and *domination*, I propose a fundamental reorientation in our theoretical approach, from *assimilation* to the *politics of national belonging*.

The final part, "Denaturalizing Ignorance," fixes on symbolic domination. Chapter five investigates a mostly forgotten massacre that took place in Hawai'i on September 9, 1924. During a protracted strike of Filipino sugar workers, the police shot and killed sixteen strikers on the island of Kaua'i. But the incident hardly registered, arousing among non-Filipinos little sympathy and little questioning of the legitimacy of the actions of the police or the courts that punished dozens of the surviving Filipinos but none of the police. How is such immediate consensus in defense of state violence formed? Incorporating W. E. B. Du Bois's concept of *double consciousness*, I rework one aspect of Pierre Bourdieu's social theory, challenging his overreliance on the tacit consent of the oppressed as the source of legitimacy. Exposing clear evidence of Filipino strikers' oppositional discourse and practice that went ignored, I propose the concept of *symbolic coercion* that refers to the *tacit nonrecognition* by the dominant. The chapter explicates how racial symbolic coercion made possible and legitimate the state's lethal use of physical coercion against Filipino working-class men.

It is one thing for the dominant to routinely ignore the dominated's express knowledge of racial inequalities and domination, but it is quite another for the dominant to routinely ignore their *own* express knowledge. Chapter six explores this paradoxical phenomenon, which I label *symbolic perversity*. Contrary to the prevailing liberal notion that the dominant, like all people, would act justly if they knew about this or that injustice, I underscore the ideas that the dominant *know* plenty and that the knowledge is not hidden away in the buried recesses of their unconscious or some arcane archive. Rather they tacitly ignore this knowledge that they produce, have ready access to, and consume. This deeply patterned ignorance, a depraved indifference, follows a racial logic that devalues the suffering, indeed the lives, of certain categories of people. To illustrate, I undertake statistical and textual analyses of the *New York Times*, an irrefutably dominant institution, and its handling of unemployment data produced and made widely available by the federal government, another irrefutably dominant institution. The findings on Black unemployment and its news coverage fly in the face of conventional wisdoms that racism in contemporary United States, since the Civil Rights Movement, is hard to detect (and therefore hard to combat) and that nearly everybody believes in racial equality in principle (even if not in any particular strategy of living up to it). The concluding chapter draws out some of the book's main implications for progressive antiracist theory and politics through a reflection on the social thought of James Baldwin.

The blacks have a song which says, *I can't believe what you say, because I see what you do.*

James Baldwin, *The Devil Finds Work*

CHAPTER 2

RESTRUCTURING A
THEORY OF RACISM

In recent decades, the concept of *racism* has come under intense critical scrutiny. With little agreement on what it referred to or how it was analytically useful, some called for wholesale abjuration. Though no less dissatisfied, others opted to rework the concept. I choose the latter strategy. The very ubiquity of the term in the social sciences renders doubtful its successful removal. Moreover, even if we could somehow get rid of it, doing so would likely set off a proliferation of neologisms that abound already, for, however variously and imprecisely, racism refers to a social reality of oppression that is far from fading and hardly obeys the rhetorical practices of social-scientific discourse.

One of the most compelling and influential reconceptualizations is Eduardo Bonilla-Silva's "structural theory of racism." Surveying existing approaches, he identifies a common failing: racism is reduced to ideas. Against this "idealist" consensus, he proposes an alternative theory that grounds racism in a "racial structure" of a "racialized social system." The merits of the theory are many and far-reaching, and therefore it provides a productive basis for further "rethinking" (Bonilla-Silva 1997: 465, 467, 470).[1] It also raises a number of questions that stem from a consequential choice: this structural theory's underlying theory of structure. After introducing Bonilla-Silva's theory, I discuss and critique a more robust conceptualization of structure and delineate its implications for rebuilding a structural theory of racism. I then clarify the perpetually muddled and frequently inflated concept of ideology and relate it to the other components of the theory, using contemporary anti-Black racism in the United States as an extended example. The chapter concludes with a synopsis of the reconstructed theory and methods for the critical study of racism.

RACISM AS THE IDEOLOGY
OF A RACIALIZED SOCIAL SYSTEM

Although Bonilla-Silva has published prolifically since "Rethinking Racism: Toward a Structural Interpretation," the 1997 article remains the fullest elaboration of his theory and anchors his subsequent, and many others', research.[2] In this generative piece, he writes that "most analysts regard racism as a purely ideological phenomenon" (p. 466). He argues that social psychology defines racism as "a set of ideas or beliefs," which may lead to prejudicial attitudes that may, in turn, elicit discriminatory behavior. Although he concedes that Marxists, unlike social psychologists, may not see racism as *purely* ideological, Bonilla-Silva contends that they "ultimately subordinat[e] racial matters to class matters" (p. 467). He finds more promise in institutionalist, internal colonialist, and especially racial formation theories but, again, criticizes them for not fully developing a "structural" account. For example, the highly regarded racial formation theory of Michael Omi and Howard Winant (1986, 1994) is said to overemphasize "ideological/cultural processes" (p. 466).

Upon casting the otherwise divergent theoretical approaches as "idealist," Bonilla-Silva (1997: 467–69) explains how idealism undermines the social-scientific understanding of racism. Applicable to most of the aforementioned theories, in assorted combinations, idealism leads analysts to reduce racism to an individual "psychological phenomenon"; to subscribe to a "static," unchanging view of it; to characterize it as "irrational"; to seek and find it only in "overt behavior"; to deemphasize its contemporary causes in favor of historically distant ones; and to analyze it, as both explanans and explanandum, "in a circular manner." Above all, idealism "exclude[s racism] from the foundation or structure of the social system." That is, racism is not moored to a social base that is itself racialized. For example, however materialist they may be, Marxists tether racism, according to Bonilla-Silva, to the workings of a class structure, not a racial one.

To remedy this state of affairs, Bonilla-Silva (1997: 469) offers the concept of *racialized social system*, which denotes a "societ[y] in which economic, political, social, and ideological levels are partially structured by the placement of actors in racial categories or races." In such a society, "its 'normal' dynamics always include a racial component" (p. 473), and racial categorization entails, echoing Marx on class, "some form of hierarchy that produces definite social relations between the races" with "different social rewards" and "life chances." These racialized relations at the different levels together constitute "the racial structure of a society," and the differential economic, political, social, and psychological rewards form the basis for the development of "dissimilar objective interests." However, while the racial structure may shape interests and make "racial contestation" inevitable (p. 475), there is no a priori correspondence: interests "are related to concrete struggles rather than derived from the location of the races in the racial structure" (p. 470). The dominant ideology of this structure is what Bonilla-Silva calls *racism*: "I use the term *racism* only to describe the racial ideology of a racialized social system" (p. 467; emphasis in original). In the end, what he finds objectionable and seeks to emend is not that racism is conceptualized as an ideology per se but as one without reference to a specifically racial structure.

As Bonilla-Silva points out, there are a number of advantages to his approach. It explains "racial phenomena" as the "'normal' outcome of the racial structure," rather than as the effects of a "free-floating [racial] ideology" or of extra-racial structures. Historical change happens through "specific struggles at different levels among the races, resulting from differences in interests." Driven by interests, racial practices are assumed to be "rational," regardless of whether they are overt or covert, consciously or unconsciously "motivated." Keyed to contemporary interest-based struggles, the theory also obviates the need to hearken back to "a long-distant past" to explain the present. Finally, as racism functions as the ideological component of the racial structure, racial stereotypes, once formed, tend to reflect the relative social positions of racial categories (Bonilla-Silva 1997: 475–76).

For all of its undeniable gains or, more accurately, *through* them, Bonilla-Silva's theory directs us to a number of crucial follow-up questions.[3] Is racial structure sufficient for explaining "racial phenomena"? How do extra-racial structures matter? Does significant change with regard to racism occur only through "racial contestation"? Is the nation-state, which appears to be what "social system" and "society" signify, always the appropriate unit of analysis? What about more local or transnational scales? With its focus on "objective interests," how does the theory account for meaning or culture? Is it confined to the ideological level? Even if "racially motivated behavior, whether or not the actors are conscious of it," is rationally based on interests (p. 475), how do we attend to varying levels of consciousness? To address these and other questions that it enables, I propose that we retool Bonilla-Silva's structural theory.

AN ALTERNATIVE THEORY OF STRUCTURE

Culture as Apart from Structure

Given its centrality to his theory, what does Bonilla-Silva mean by *structure*? In a footnote (Bonilla-Silva 1997: 469n5), he reveals that he employs Joseph Whitmeyer's (1994: 154) concept of structure: "the networks of (interactional) relationships among actors as well as the distributions of socially meaningful characteristics of actors and aggregates of actors." In the article that Bonilla-Silva draws on, Whitmeyer continues, "The latter would include distributions of membership categories (e.g., race), wealth, power, and roles, as well as distributions of organizational and societal characteristics." What is explicitly left out is "culture." Noting that others such as Anthony Giddens (1979) and William Sewell Jr. (1992) integrate culture into their theories of structure, but neither agreeing nor disagreeing with them, Whitmeyer (1994: 154–55) consciously chooses to keep the two concepts discrete. Bonilla-Silva (1997: 469n5) likewise cites Sewell (1992), and Pierre Bourdieu (1984), as points of contrast, finding their theoretical renditions of structure "more relational" and attentive to "agency." He is also no doubt aware of the exclusion of "culture" from Whitmeyer's and thereby his own concept of structure. Given Bonilla-Silva's focus on social systems, or societies, and his insistence on the "collective," not the "individual," I would sum up his Whitmeyer-based *racial structure* as the network of relations among a given society's racial categories of actors with unequal material resources, over which they struggle at various levels—economic, political, social, and ideological.

Bonilla-Silva's (1997: 469n5) theoretical choice is intriguing, for he, unlike Whitmeyer, actually seems to prefer Sewell's and Bourdieu's "more complex conceptions" of structure. Perhaps the economy of Whitmeyer's formulation is the appeal. However, along with other drawbacks discussed later, the untenable exclusion of "culture" argues against parsimony. It is simply hard to see how the ties that form "networks of (interactional) relationships" could avoid being, at least partly, cultural: for the ties to be able to tie, they must be socially *meaningful* in some way.[4] But, even if we were to grant that networks could be analytically bracketed to be structural but not cultural, the second part of Whitmeyer's definition would surely breach the partition between structure and culture: "the distributions of socially *meaningful* characteristics of actors and aggregates of actors" (1994: 154; emphasis added). In addition to inheriting these contradictions, Bonilla-Silva's theory itself suggests the need to incorporate culture: one of the four levels of his proposed racial structure, the one in which racism is placed no less, is the ideological. To be sure, ideology, like culture, has many possible definitions, but to see them as mutually exclusive does not seem to be a viable or fruitful option. In any case, I do not think Bonilla-Silva (1997: 467) endorses such a view, as the fused term "ideological/cultural" he invokes in his criticism of Omi and Winant indicates. In fact, arguing against epiphenomenal theories of racism and positing the ideological level as constitutive of, rather than external to, the racial structure, Bonilla-Silva's theory cannot but overflow the concept of structure he borrows from Whitmeyer.

Culture as a Part of Structure

For a more suitable theory of structure, I turn to Sewell, the theorist and historian mentioned by both Bonilla-Silva and Whitmeyer. For Sewell (1992: 27), structures are "constituted by mutually sustaining cultural schemas and sets of resources that empower and constrain social action and tend to be reproduced by that action." Not limited to cognitive-psychological notions of them (Howard 1994; Neisser 1976), Sewell's *schemas* refer to "not only the array of binary oppositions that make up a given society's fundamental tools of thought, but also the various conventions, recipes, scenarios, principles of action, and habits of speech and gesture built up with these fundamental tools." Not to be confused with rules or laws, these are "not formally stated prescriptions but the informal and not always conscious schemas, metaphors, or assumptions presupposed by such formal statements" (1992: 7–8). In short, schemas constitute the "semiotic" (i.e., meaningful, cultural) dimension of social life. Supplying the "materialist" dimension, *resources* are of two types: human and nonhuman. Human resources are "physical strength, dexterity, knowledge, and emotional commitments that can be used to enhance or maintain power," whereas nonhuman resources designate "objects, animate or inanimate, naturally occurring or manufactured, that can be used to enhance or maintain power" (Sewell 1992: 9). Structure is the reiterative, practical articulation—or jointing—of schemas and resources through human agency.[5]

Though to widely varying degrees, structures tend to reproduce themselves, because, as Sewell contends, resources are the effects of schemas, and schemas are the effects of resources. That is, the schemas and resources of a structure are "mutually sustaining" (Sewell 1992: 27).[6] A taxi company, to take a mundane example, would be but a motley collection of persons, cars, and garage if a particular set of schemas—including driving and mechanical techniques, governmental licensing of cars and persons, wage labor, commodification of transportation, and collection of fares—were not applied to turn them into resources. Conversely, we could say that the assembled resources—trained drivers and mechanics, licensed vehicles, fare meters, garage—evoke and instill the schemas of a taxi company.[7]

Structures do change, of course, which Sewell's theory is exceptionally adept at explaining. Rather than resorting to exogenous factors, he proposes that the very processes involved in structural reproduction also generate structural transformation. It is through agency—the articulated enactment of schemas and mobilization of resources—that structures exist and persist, and it is through agency—the *rearticulated* enactment of schemas and mobilization of resources—that structures change. A structure is transformed when agents apply its schemas to different resources or when they mobilize its resources through different schemas. The former describes what Sewell calls the *transposability of schemas* and the latter the *polysemy of resources* (1992: 17–19). In fact, the transposition of schemas and the remobilization of polysemous resources are one and the same process of rearticulating schemas and resources viewed from different analytical angles.

Rearticulations of schemas and resources occur, in part, because there is a "*multiplicity of structures* . . . which exist at different levels, operate in different modalities, and are themselves based on widely varying types and quantities of resources." Their heterogeneity ensures that structures are hardly all homologous and mutually compatible and that agents have mastery of countless schemas and access to numerous resources. Structures do not only come in innumerable forms but also intersect with each other. Since structures exist only through them, agents at the "*intersection of structures*" can recombine schemas and resources in creative ways, and different agents applying different schemas to the same resources can produce conflict and change. The "resource consequences" of a structure are never fully foreseeable, which opens up the possibility of unanticipated changes. The stock market crash of 1929 would be a spectacular example of the "*unpredictability of resource accumulation*" (Sewell 1992: 16–19; emphases in original).

Social life is saturated with structures, from a casual conversation to global capitalism. Sewell proposes two dimensions along which we can sort them: *depth* and *power*. Depth refers to the degree to which schemas are unconscious or conscious. They can range from the syntax of human language, much of which is hard-wired in our brains, to Bourdieu's *habitus* or Giddens's *practical consciousness*, which apply to bodily dispositions and tacit knowledge, to deliberate choices like attending an antiwar demonstration. Deeper schemas tend to be more "durable," less vulnerable to transformations. They may also be more extensive, since they can manifest themselves in myriad "surface" structures.[8] Power varies according to how much and what kinds of resources are implicated (Sewell 1992: 22–26). For example, the U.S. military entails resources of a different order and magnitude than a friendship between two school children or, for that matter, any other military on earth.

Dualities of Structure

With his theory of structure, Sewell sets out to destabilize and reconcile three ingrained binary oppositions that undergird social-scientific reasoning: structure vs. agency, structure vs. change, and structure vs. culture. As discussed above, he ingeniously demonstrates the first two pairs to be false oppositions: structures do not exist without or apart from agency, and change is not something that is introduced from outside structures but rather presupposes and is enabled by them. There is one major caveat, however. Perhaps because structure is so widely counterposed to agency and change, Sewell tends to stress the *enabling* character of structure and ignore its *constraining* aspect.[9] While he briefly acknowledges that "occupancy of different social positions . . . gives people knowledge of different schemas and access to different kinds and amounts of resources and hence different possibilities for transformative action" and offers illustrative glimpses, the asymmetrically relational character of social positions and the ordinary condition of disagreement and conflict, potential and actual, are not pivotal to his theory (Sewell 1992: 20–21). In this regard, Bonilla-Silva's insistence on the centrality of hierarchical relations and of struggles, in particular those initiated from below, presents a welcome counterbalance, on which I elaborate later.

Sewell is likewise largely convincing in trying to "overcome the divide between semiotic and materialist visions of structure," which is often posed by sociologists and others, in contrast to anthropologists, as the divide between "culture" and "structure" (Sewell 1992: 3–4). He attempts to do so by making both visions equally essential to his concept of structure: all structures are the articulations of *cultural* schemas and *material* resources. He also takes great care not to give either side theoretical priority: schemas are the effects of resources as much as the reverse.

Two interrelated missteps, however, ultimately thwart Sewell's efforts: the strict conceptual segregation of schemas and resources and a residual carry-over from Giddens's theory of structuration. According to Sewell, schemas are semiotic, and resources are material. And one does not overlap with the other. This compartmentalization is reinforced by his reading of Giddens. Throughout his article, Sewell makes much of Giddens's ambiguous and contradictory pronouncement that structures are "virtual." Sewell then, rightly, dismisses this notion: if resources are a part of structures, a view shared by Giddens, structures cannot be virtual. Nonhuman resources are self-evidently not virtual, "since material things by definition exist in space and time." Human resources are similarly "actual as opposed to virtual," for they also "exist in what Giddens calls 'time-space'" (Sewell 1992: 10). But when it comes to schemas, Sewell affirms Giddens's claim that they are indeed virtual. Thus, by positing resources as "actual" and schemas as "virtual," Sewell keeps these two components of structure separate, albeit equal.

In my view, Sewell does not "overcome the divide between semiotic and materialist visions" so much as interiorize and reproduce the divide within the concept of structure itself. I suggest, instead, that schemas and resources share a common ontological status: they are both actual. Like resources, schemas exist in space and time.[10] What is the alternative? To state that they "cannot be reduced to their existence in any particular practice or any particular location in space and time" is only to restate the idea that schemas are iterable and transposable, as Sewell (1992: 8) himself points out. It does not mean that they do not actually exist—that they exist only as ideal-typical principles outside history. I would insist that schemas, like resources, are formed and transformed through practices *in* history (i.e., in space and time). They are present in human bodies, not only but including brains, and they are present in—and in conjunction with—resources, which are, after all, "instantiations or embodiments of schemas," and include, most obviously, texts (Sewell 1992: 13). Only by artificially suspending time for synchronic analysis do schemas seem to vanish into virtual reality.

Not only are both schemas and resources actual, they are also not mutually exclusive: the boundary between them is not sharp but fuzzy. Consider Sewell's insistence that schemas do not include "formally stated prescriptions— the sorts of things spelled out in statutes, proverbs, liturgies, constitutions, or contracts," because "publicly fixed codifications of rules are actual rather than virtual and should be regarded as *resources* rather than as rules" (1992: 8; emphasis in original). I do not dispute that codified rules can be marshaled as resources. But it does not follow that codification should automatically strip schemas of their capacity as schemas. For instance, if a manager formalized her daily routines in an office manual, they would not suddenly cease operating as schemas. Likewise, the Catholic belief in apostolic succession, to use one of Sewell's examples of a schema, is no less a schema because it is a part of the church's Dogmatic Constitution (p. 13).[11]

The fuzziness is prevalent. With general approval, Sewell writes, "Giddens places a great deal of weight on the notion that actors are *knowledgeable*. It is, presumably, the knowledge of rules [or schemas] that makes people capable of action" (1992: 7; emphasis in original). Later, he notes, "*Knowledge* of a rule or a schema by definition means the ability to transpose or extend it" (p. 18; emphasis added). Summing up this line of argument, and once again underlining the coequality of schemas and resources, Sewell concludes, "Agents are empowered by structures, both by the *knowledge* of cultural schemas that enables them to mobilize resources and by the access to resources that enables them to enact schemas" (p. 27; emphasis added). Broadly encompassing not only conscious, discursive knowledge but also a whole range of tacit, habituated, and unconscious knowledge that agents embody and enact, "knowledge" in these statements is clearly aligned with the supposedly virtual, semiotic side of structures. But without comment, "knowledge" also appears on the other, ostensibly actual side, in Sewell's definition of human resources: "physical strength, dexterity, *knowledge*, and emotional commitments that can be used to enhance or maintain power, including *knowledge* of the means of gaining, retaining, controlling, and propagating either human or nonhuman resources" (p. 9; emphases added). This is not merely a rhetorical overlap but a substantive one, which could be made more obvious by replacing "means" with "schemas" in the participial phrase above. Like light in quantum physics, which evinces properties of both wave and particle, knowledge can be seen as exhibiting characteristics of both schema and resource. This argument could be extended as well to other human resources, which could be understood as various forms of knowledge in the broader sense of being embodied schemas. For example, to access the "emotional commitments" of friendship as a resource for international migration is to transpose the schemas of friendship: accessing the resource is enacting the schemas. Nonhuman resources are not immune to fuzziness. They are not objects per se but "objects . . . that can be used to enhance or maintain power" (p. 9). This implies that objects are not resources in the absence of schemas. Resources are contingent on, though not reducible to, schemas all the way down.[12] Conversely, even schemas of the least power-implicated structures require at least a dyad of knowledgeable agents, who themselves constitute human resources. Schemas, then, are contingent on, though not reducible to, resources all the way down.

None of this gainsays the useful idea that structures are composed of mutually sustaining schemas and resources. In any given analysis, the fuzziness of many schemas and resources can be—and, for practicability, needs to be—assumed and bracketed. For example, a study on social movements may invoke money as a resource without tangentially having to specify it as an effect of schemas, while the schema-dependency of money may be precisely the point of another study (Zelizer 1994). The usefulness of the idea, however, does not rest upon and is lessened by theoretically re-creating the divide between the semiotic and the material within the concept of structure and slotting schemas and resources into separate "virtual" and "actual" realities. This divide turns out to be yet another false opposition.

RACISM AS STRUCTURES OF RACIAL
INEQUALITY AND DOMINATION

In Bonilla-Silva's theory, *racism* refers to the dominant ideology of the racial structure of which it is a constituent part. Since the dominant practices at the other levels of the racial structure—economic, political, and social—do not warrant separate concepts, and since the historically accrued rhetorical power of the word *racism* confers import on what it designates, there is an implicit privileging of ideology, on the one hand. On the other, there seems to be a residual tinge of epiphenomenalism in his discussion of racial stereotypes that suggests the opposite: "crystallized at the ideological level," they "must relate—although not necessarily fit perfectly—to [a given] group's *true* social position," which is presumably determined at the nonideological levels (Bonilla-Silva 1997: 476; emphasis added). Neither hand is necessary or desirable. In fact, Bonilla-Silva is otherwise assiduous in his opposition both to the privileging of ideology and to epiphenomenalism that he finds to be rampant in other approaches.

Rather than restricting racism to the ideological level, I propose that *racism* denominate structures of inequality and domination based primarily or partly on *race*. Omi and Winant (1986: 68) define *race* as "an unstable and 'decentered' complex of social meanings constantly being transformed by political struggle." I concur with this exceptionally capacious, indeterminate, semiotic, contentious, and politically and historically contingent characterization, to which I would add the following: race is a modern mode of differentiating humans and forming identities; in contrast to kinship, for example, it is a categorical mode, unmediated by networks of interpersonal ties; though modern, it is almost always experienced as primordial, as natural; and relatedly and most distinctively, what gives race its recognizability and minimal coherence across different historical moments is the schema of "separat[ing] human populations by *some* notion of stock or collective heredity of traits" (Anthias and Yuval-Davis 1992: 2; emphasis added).[13] The emphasis on "some" underscores the idea that this schema itself is historically variable, for instance, with regard to how explicitly it is codified, whether and to what extent religion and contemporary science are brought to bear, how sexuality and reproduction are organized and policed, and so on.

In addition to not setting ideology apart, the proposed reconceptualization of racism also asserts its plurality. Racisms operate at various, articulated scales and depths. In this regard, let us first reconsider the nonideological levels of the racial structure posited by Bonilla-Silva: social, political, and economic. Intermittently, he hints at what these levels represent. In describing the nature of racial contestation, he writes, "Such a struggle may be social (Who can be here? Who belongs here?), political (Who can vote? How much power should they have? Should they be citizens?), economic (Who should work, and what should they do? They are taking our jobs!), or ideological (Black is beautiful! The term designating people of African descent in the United States has changed from Negro to Black to African American)." Later he states, "Changes are due to specific struggles at different levels among the races" (Bonilla-Silva 1997: 473, 475).

A straightforward reading could be that *levels* refers to more or less discrete—that is, relatively autonomous—spheres that make up a society or "social system." But if structures are many, and they intersect in numerous and often unpredictable ways, the discreteness of levels seems relatively minimal. They are thoroughly interpenetrated. Bonilla-Silva's parenthetical questions and statements imply as much. The political question "Should they be citizens?" can be the same as, and certainly cannot be divorced from, the social question "Who belongs here?" and is often driven by the economic sentiment "They are taking our jobs!," which could also be classified as an ideological statement.

Bonilla-Silva imports the concept of level from structural Marxism, the work of Nicos Poulantzas in particular. However, the insertion of the *social* level is new. Poulantzas speaks of economic, political, and ideological levels but not a social one. Aside from *social classes*, the adjective regularly turns up in *social formation*, the term for "a concrete society" as a whole (Poulantzas 1973: 33). The *social* characterizes each and every human relation, not a particular sphere, as evidenced by the phrases "economic social relations," "political social relations," and "ideological social relations" (Poulantzas 1975: 86). As Sewell (2005: 369) puts it, "the social is the [entire] complex and inescapable ontological ground of our common life as humans." As such, the social cannot be productively pared down to a level.

The notion of a delimited political level can pose a similar problem. To be sure, the political, or relations of power, does not match the all-encompassing scope of the social. While we may, following Foucault and others, conceive of power as pervasive, or "capillary," we still do not see it as comprehensive of social life. However, racism, which is intrinsically and wholly concerned with power, is as completely enclosed by the political as it is by the social.

Nevertheless, while it may be everywhere, power is not only capillary but also veinal and arterial. Bonilla-Silva's economic and political levels instructively highlight structures of immense power not to be overlooked in analyzing racism: capitalism and modern states. Still, these interpenetrated structures, along with ideology, hardly exhaust the social. Instead of three or four all-inclusive levels, there is a wide range of articulated structures in terms of scale, from an interaction between two people with negligible resources at stake to structures that ensnare nearly all of humanity and untold nonhuman resources. Overlapping, partially or wholly, with the far-flung structure that goes by the label "capitalism" are other structures of diverse power: states, racism, heteropatriarchy, industries, corporations, parties, financial markets, the World Trade Organization, labor markets, migration networks, professions, prostitution, universities, unions, factories, sweatshops, the drug trade, sports, and others. States are another unavoidable fact of modernity that intersect with capitalism, racism, heteropatriarchy, armies, courts, professions, parties, legislatures, migration networks, police, philanthropy, educational systems, public health, and so on. Structures of various sizes and with varying degrees of autonomy from capitalism and states include racism, heteropatriarchy, families, professions, religions, academia, nongovernmental organizations, arts, sports, riots, migration networks, friendships, etiquette, and social movements. The overlying lists intimate the intersections, imbrications, and embeddedness of structures.

Scales of Racism

I contend that no structure that involves relations of inequality and domination is a priori beyond the reach of racism, beyond being articulated with and becoming a part of it. The actual extent of this reach at a given historical moment is an empirical question, although the answer is likely to be vast. As an articulated ensemble—that is, the aggregate of racisms at all scales—racism is, and has been throughout its history, extremely powerful, employing and accumulating massive resources. This articulated whole is what Charles

Mills (1997: 20) aptly refers to as "global white supremacy."[14] Within the whole, racisms can vary greatly with regard to resources, human and nonhuman. For example, the postwar "urban crisis" in the United States—the impoverishment and segregation of Blacks in central cities—provides an example of racism involving millions of people and enormous nonhuman resources (Sugrue 1996). At the same time, through habits of gesture, comportment, posture, utterance, avoidance, and the like (e.g., clutching a handbag, crossing the street), ordinary everyday encounters of little resource consequence on city streets—as well as the perhaps even more ordinary lack of encounters—can help reproduce the larger racism of which they are a small part, reinforcing practical senses of fear, shame, guilt, disgust, discomfort, disdain, and indifference.[15] In between, there are myriad articulated structures of racial inequality and domination involving resources of different kinds and quantities, including employment discrimination, urban deindustrialization, relocation of capital and whites, housing policies and enforcement, homeowners' associations, organized terror and violence, and labor unions (Sugrue 1996).

The scale of racism that a research question addresses governs the appropriate unit of analysis, which suggests an amendment to Bonilla-Silva's theory. Throughout his article, he invokes the terms *social system, society,* and less frequently *social formation* and *social order* to indicate the scale of his analysis. Used interchangeably, they all appear to refer to what is usually called the "nation-state," an inference confirmed by his predominant use of the United States, in the usual nation-state sense, for his examples.[16] Though not discussed or explicitly advocated, analyses at more local scales are not precluded by his theory. They may even be implied, since the racial structure is the total sum of racialized relations in a society. But, analyses at scales beyond the national are more difficult to fit. Beginning with the "racialized social system" and the coextensive, but not synonymous, "racial structure," the theory implicitly sets the nation-state as the upper limit; even the concept of levels is coextensive with it. Much may go on within this bounded system, but not beyond it.[17] Here, the occasional references to "societies" other than the United States, like Brazil, Cuba, and Mexico, are instructive: they are additional examples of racialized social systems to be compared—similarly bounded and seemingly independent of one another and the United States.[18]

The alternative concept of structure advanced here is not tied to or limited by the nation-state. The national is just one scale at which structures exist and analyses can be carried out. This is not to say that nation-states, or states more generally, do not matter. Given the past and continuing salience of states, we could reasonably expect to find denser webs of structures within them than across them. But even the most isolated state is not hermetically sealed. Furthermore, among structures, racism has been so "transnational," or trans-statal, as to require little argument: its "transnationalism" is, if not axiomatic, historically incontrovertible. From its genesis to the present, even before the advent of "nations," racism has been part and parcel of globally momentous "transnational" structures, including slavery, colonialism, imperialism, and migration. For example, Paul Kramer's (2003, 2006) work on U.S. colonization of the Philippines demonstrates the entwined histories of racism under Spanish colonialism, extension of U.S. racism through colonial conquest and rule, interimperial flows and translations of racisms, transformation of racism in the Philippines and its extension back to metropolitan United States, and intraimperial migration of Filipinos and others. To take a historically resonant example from a century later, we could hardly understand the attenuation of rights of Arab and Muslim populations in the United States, including U.S. citizens, in isolation from the U.S. "war on terror" abroad (Cole 2003).

Deep Schemas of Racism

Racism is not only extraordinarily powerful, but also extremely deep, or durable. The continuous existence and spread of racism for a half-millennium attest to its depth and durability (e.g., Mills 1997; Winant 2001). Not as a complete inventory, I propose three schemas that may supply racism's exceptional depth. By depth, I mean that these schemas are subconsciously enacted in practice and cannot be simply "unthought." First and foremost, as discussed above, racism implies *race* or the mode of dividing humans "by some notion of stock or collective heredity of traits" (Anthias and Yuval-Davis 1992: 2).[19] A second schema is the presumption of suitability/unsuitability for civic inclusion on the basis of race, the negatively prototypical case in relation to U.S. immigration history being the presupposed inassimilability of the Chinese in the late nineteenth and early twentieth centuries. The last schema I propose is the presumption of superiority/inferiority on the basis of race, the negatively limiting case being the literal dehumanization, the "social death," of Blacks in the age of slavery—"a fate worse than [corporeal] death" (Patterson 1982: passim; Eltis 1993: 1409).[20]

These schemas have proven to be highly adaptable and have manifested in multifarious ways. To be clear, racisms *never* reduce to them and are *always* about much more, and the schemas themselves are historically specific, variant, and sundry. With regard to the first schema, a sine qua non for racism, how and how many racial categories come to be vary widely across space and time. The latter two schemas form major dimensions of social space along which racial categories are positioned in relation to one another. These deep schemas also provide conditions of possibility for the historically recurrent articulations of racism with other deep, durable structures. The race schema insistently combines with heteropatriarchy, producing and rationalizing racialized categorical boundaries through the regulation of sexuality, gender, reproduction, and kinship.[21] The suitability/unsuitability schema conjoins easily with nationalism, producing and rationalizing racialized inclusions and exclusions by the state and others.[22] The superiority/inferiority schema readily articulates with capitalism, producing and rationalizing racialized material inequalities.

In my own research on racism in prewar Hawai'i, *haole* (roughly, Euro-Americans), particularly the missionaries from New England and their descendants who came to dominate the sugar industry, brought and extended (i.e., transposed) their notion of race to categorize Hawaiians and migrant laborers from China, Portugal, Japan, the Philippines, and elsewhere. Articulated to the requisite resources, including those of the U.S. state, dominant haole practices concerning government (e.g., enactment of laws regarding the franchise, annexation), labor (e.g., placement in skilled positions, wage rates), and nearly all other spheres of life were inextricably shaped by race. To take the two largest segments of the plantation labor force from the 1910s onward as an example, haole defined, in contradistinction to themselves, the Japanese and Filipinos along the two principal dimensions of racism—presumed suitability/unsuitability for civic inclusion and presumed superiority/inferiority—but in markedly dissimilar ways. In this Pacific outpost of the U.S. empire, the Japanese, with their imputed loyalty to the rapidly emerging Japanese empire, were believed to be inherently anti-American, while Filipinos, who were U.S. colonial subjects, were merely regarded as unfit to be "American." Though deemed antithetical to the "American" nation, the Japanese in Hawai'i, racially indexed to the status of the Japanese state, were seen as superior to other nonhaole, including the Portuguese. Meanwhile, racially indexed to the U.S.-colonized Philippines, Filipinos were considered to be unequivocally inferior. Transposed to countless practices, these schemas helped to generate inequalities and exclusions in relation to the Japanese and Filipinos: what jobs they held, how much they were paid, where they lived, which schools they sent their children to, who were believed to be sexually dangerous, who were reputed to be manly, whom they could marry, how they interacted with each other, who would eventually be able to leave the plantation economy, who went off to fight and die in wars, who were deported and displaced, and even who were killed with relative impunity (see Jung 2006 and also chapter 5).

The social positions and meanings of racial categories, as well as the categories themselves, can and do change. But the deep schemas, though continually transformed through the practices they dispose, endure in recognizable forms. For example, ascribed to be hostile to the "American" nation, Arabs, Muslims, and others racialized as "terrorists" presently occupy a position analogous to prewar and wartime Japanese. And like the Filipino, and Mexican, migrant laborers of the past, Mexican-origin people in the United States today, particularly recent migrants, are considered to be less and other than, but usually not subversively antipathetic to, "Americans." To be sure, the concrete practices that the deep schemas help to generate are different in different historical moments, but those schemas are at the same time reinforced through the more "surface" transformations. In other words, there are many differences between Executive Order 9066 and the U.S.A. Patriot Act, but both embody and thereby reproduce and infix the core civic dimension of racism.

Transformations of Racism

On the flip side, the depth and durability of certain schemas of racism do not preclude significant changes, just as capitalism has undergone shifts in its mode of regulation while retaining what Sewell (1992: 25–26) identifies as its "core schema" of commodification. How does racism change? According to Bonilla-Silva (1997: 475), change happens through "racial contestation. . . . specific struggles at different levels among the races." I certainly agree, as discussed later. However, although racial contestation may be the primary mode of change, it is not the only one. Given the widespread epiphenomenalism that reduces racism to other structures, the exclusive stress on *racial* contestation by recent theorists is understandable, but it unnecessarily forecloses the possibilities of extra-racial sources of change, to which a theory of racism based on Sewell's concept of structure would be more open. There is a multiplicity of structures with different cultural logics and resources, and racism intersects with many of them. In such a context, schemas and resources of racism and other structures can be rearticulated, through the transposition of schemas and the remobilization of resources. And the resource consequences of such rearticulations are not altogether predictable, nor are, I would add, schema consequences.

In the late 1930s in Hawai'i, at the intersection of the Communist Party, multiple racisms, and a fledgling labor movement, leftist leaders transposed the party's notion of a "united front" to the movement, transforming the antisectarian schema against fascism into an antiracist schema that helped to mobilize workers against the haole capitalists. (Per my discussion of the fuzziness of schemas and resources, note that the knowledge of this "united front" schema could also be characterized as a resource.) In other words, an extra-racial schema of the Communist Party played an early role in building an interracial labor movement and transforming structures of racial and class inequalities and domination in Hawai'i (Jung 2006).[23] More recently, the terrorist attack of September 11, 2001, was an event at the conjunction of manifold structures, most proximately al Qaeda but also U.S. foreign policy in the Middle East during and after the Cold War, but it was not an act of *racial* contestation. Nonetheless, the event indelibly transformed racism against Arabs and Muslims in the United States and elsewhere, reinforcing the schema of presuming their utter and hostile otherness, which, combined with a host of other schemas and resources, later underwrote the war against Iraq that resulted in nearly half a million Iraqi deaths (Hagopian et al. 2013) and the preemptive or instant amnesia of them in the United States. I suggest that these types of transformations, albeit usually less remarkable, happen all the time, and they do not detract from the significance of racism. On the contrary, the sheer capacity of racism to proliferate and mutate through articulations and rearticulations with other structures—in *both* directions—is one of its signal qualities.[24]

IDEOLOGY AND CONTEMPORARY ANTI-BLACK RACISM IN THE UNITED STATES

Discursive and Nondiscursive, Reflective and Performative

Conceptualizing it as ideology, Bonilla-Silva (1997: 474) writes, racism "provides the rationalizations for social, political, and economic interactions between the races." At the same time, he continues, "This ideology is not simply a 'superstructural' phenomenon (a mere reflection of the racialized system), but becomes the organizational map that guides actions of racial actors in society"; "it provides the rules for perceiving and dealing with the 'other' in a racialized society." Elsewhere, he identifies "colorblind racism" as the prevailing racial ideology of the era since the Civil Rights Movement (Bonilla-Silva 2001, 2003). "Explain[ing] contemporary racial inequality as the outcome of nonracial dynamics," this ideology is "a formidable political tool for the maintenance of the racial order": "whites enunciate positions that safeguard their racial interests without sounding 'racist'" (Bonilla-Silva 2003: 2–4). In this later work, Bonilla-Silva defines racial ideology as "*the racially based frameworks used by actors to explain and justify* (dominant race) or *challenge* (subordinate race or races) *the racial status quo*" (2003: 9; emphasis in original).

I agree with Bonilla-Silva, and others (e.g., Eagleton 1991; Thompson 1984), that ideology is a matter of discourse and that it is discourse articulated to relations of inequality and domination. But there is some ambiguity in Bonilla-Silva's theory with regard to *how* the dominant racial ideology is articulated to relations of power. In both his earlier and later works, it rationalizes, explains, and justifies the existing racial order. In the 1997 article, however, he goes further, asserting that racial ideology also acts as "the organizational map" and "the rules for perceiving and dealing with the 'other'": it is not merely discursive representations but also schemas of perception and action. This more expansive conceptualization, however, is in tension with his later empirically based work on "colorblind racism," in which the dominant racial ideology no longer performs those additional functions.

As discussed earlier, the concept of structure on which Bonilla-Silva bases his theory does not allow for "culture" or meaning, but he appends ideology by way of structural Marxism. However, the concept of ideology cannot on its own deal with the theoretical bulk of all things semiotic. I propose that we first distinguish between discursive and nondiscursive practices that constitute racism. To be clear, this distinction should not be confused with the false opposition of culture and structure, much less the reductionist metaphor of superstructure and base. Though often taken to be, discourse is not the only province of meaning or schemas. Many practices, though meaningful, are not discursive.[25] The physical beating of Rodney King by the police, for example, was the enactment of a particular set of schemas, but most of it was not discursive but bodily. Likewise, the vigilant surveillance of Black shoppers is a meaningful but not necessarily a wordy practice.

Further, I would distinguish, though not definitely, between *constative* and *performative* discursive practices. Whereas the former describes or reports, the latter enacts what is uttered: it is the difference between the "performance of an act *of* saying something" and the "performance of an act *in* saying something" (Austin 1975: 99–100; emphases in original).[26] A performa-discursive practice refers to spoken or written utterance that carries out a practice beyond the practice of speech or writing itself.[27] A white supervisor's dismissal of a Black worker without due cause by saying some variation of "You're fired" would be an instance of a performative utterance, whereas her explanation of this action to her colleagues at lunch would be constative. As J.L. Austin (1975) shows, whether an utterance is performative does not inhere in the words themselves but also depends on the appositeness of the agent and the context. The supervisor's performative utterance presupposes her authority to terminate the employment of workers under her charge.

Whether enacted through nondiscursive and/or performa-discursive practices, I contend that most racist practices are enactments of tacit schemas: largely taken for granted, the operative schemas that are constitutive of utterances and other practices bypass, override, or influence, to varying degrees, conscious calculation and rationalization.[28] For example, in an audit study with Black and white testers who were chosen and trained to match in appearance and behavior, real estate agents were found to discriminate against Black potential renters and buyers. Blacks were told about and shown fewer homes (Yinger 1986; see also Turner et al. 2002, 2013). In a similarly designed study of car dealerships, salespeople quoted substantially higher prices to Black customers than to their white counterparts. There seemed to be little indication that the salespeople consciously set out to discriminate (Ayres and Siegelman 1995). If asked whether they practiced racial discrimination, most would probably have denied it and, if confronted with the findings, been genuinely surprised.

In contrast, ideology, for the most part, is not performative. It is constative or, more appropriate for our purposes, *reflective*.[29] By reflective, I do not mean in the reductionist sense of mirroring "reality" or "structure" but in the sense of being conscious and deliberative. In short, racial ideologies, both dominant and subaltern, are opinions about race. But, if the dominant ideology explains and justifies the racial status quo, as Bonilla-Silva argues and I agree, why are these discursive practices undertaken—likely, but not exclusively, by those of the dominant racial category for reasons of asymmetry discussed below? If racisms already couple tacit schemas and resources to the benefit of the dominant category of actors, why do they bother explaining?

For the most part, the dominant do not bother. What is continually underemphasized and misunderstood in the study of racism, and other forms of domination, is the dominant's massive *ignorance*. But ignorance is not an undifferentiated, homogeneous mass and needs to be theoretically secerned. Both in everyday life and in the social sciences, the most obvious and least consequential forms of ignorance are the naive absence of knowledge and the conscious refusal to acknowledge. One or the other is usually posited to underpin or causally link prejudice and discrimination and, underscoring the commonness of the sense, drives the narratives of most Hollywood fare on race.

The less obvious and more decisive and intractable forms of ignorance involve what Bourdieu refers to as *doxa*, the realm of the social unconscious. His *symbolic violence* designates the ordinary condition in which the dominated, as much as the dominant, find natural the order of things. Premised on the assumption of "the *unanimity* of doxa," it is the unconscious ignorance or acceptance of domination by all, save for a relatively narrow scope of conscious disagreement (Bourdieu 1977: 168; emphasis in original). In this book I identify two additional, complementary forms of doxic ignorance. Elaborated on in chapter 6, *symbolic perversity* refers to the paradoxical phenomenon in which the dominant implicitly ignore their own explicit knowledge of domination and inequality. It is an unconscious unknowing of knowledge they themselves consciously produce and consume, an ignorance rooted in depraved indifference.

Through the concept of *symbolic coercion*, which I explore in chapter 5, we can address the question of why the dominant take the trouble to rationalize. The answer begins with subaltern, or counterhegemonic, racial ideologies. Bourdieu's idea of the unanimity of doxa—that domination is unconsciously accepted by the dominant and the dominated alike—is problematic. Instead, I propose the notion of *asymmetry of doxa*. One effect of domination on the dominated is *double consciousness* (Du Bois [1903] 1965): forced to see the world from the viewpoint of the dominant as well as from their own, the dominated are conscious, albeit variably and far from fully, of much of what remains implicit or unconscious for the dominant. The dominated take less of the established order for granted than the dominant.[30] Put another way, on the short end of the stick, the dominated are more likely to question the justness of the stick and those on the other end sticking it to them. Subaltern ideologies are expressions of this consciousness, drawing on and reworking ideas from preexisting discourses of resistance as well as other sources, including discourses shared with the dominant.[31] These ideologies range in their coherence, and they may be asserted individually, collectively, or not at all.[32]

Most important, what subaltern ideologies do is critique and propose, more or less coherently, a transformation of existing structures of inequality and domination, a rearticulation of schemas and resources. As a corollary, struggles over resources are at once struggles over schemas—of who defines and controls resources and how. For example, socialism proposes to disarticulate the means of production, a set of resources, from the capitalist schema of private ownership and rearticulate them to the schema of collective ownership. Or, against Jim Crow segregation, civil rights activists asserted that resources such as public education and transportation should be coupled not with the schemas of racial segregation and presumption of Black inferiority that underlay it, but with those of equal treatment. Symbolic coercion occurs when the dominant implicitly ignore this explicit dissent (see chapter 5); but with sufficient pressure from below, the dominant are pushed into discourse.

The dominant ideology is foremost a rejoinder to subaltern ideologies, often incorporating and revaluing (i.e., co-opting) certain elements from them as well as drawing from other preexisting discourses.[33] It is a discursive *representation*—or reflective discourse—of the structure of inequality and domination by the dominant provoked by the dominated.[34] What it is not is a transparent discursive rendering of the structure of inequality and domination, and therefore we should not expect it to correspond homologously, much less identically, to the operative schemas of the structure. To find that the dominant ideology is, to varying degrees, inconsistent with the structure of domination that it represents is hardly noteworthy. It should be expected—not because the dominant ideology is an intentional pack of lies and obfuscations, although it can be, but because it is always a *partial* discourse, in both senses, in defense of the structure.[35] In this regard, to the extent that they fix solely on dominant *representations* and ignore the nonrepresentational, practical schemas at work, critical studies of culture may miss and underestimate their mark.[36]

There is no symmetry or equivalence between dominant and subaltern ideologies. Subaltern ideologies propose schemas alternative to the tacitly operative schemas of structures that are already in place. Dominant ideologies, above all, explain and justify these structures in response to subaltern ideologies. So, while subaltern ideologies may be in conflict with and are often forced to engage the dominant ideologies that they arouse, the more vital struggle they wage is against the operative schemas that are quietly, effectively, and most often subconsciously articulated to resources.[37] Subaltern ideologies ultimately aspire to be the unsaid, not the dominant sayings.[38]

Deflating "Colorblindness"

Bonilla-Silva (2003) and many others make a largely convincing case that "colorblindness" is the dominant racial ideology of the post–Civil Rights era in the United States. Whites tend to hold the opinion that "race does not matter that much today, so let's move on." According to this logic, everybody should be colorblind and is already for the most part, and race should not be the basis of efforts to lessen racial inequalities (Bonilla-Silva 2003: 178).[39] This discourse is corroborated by the general declivity in anti-Black attitudes among whites over the past half-century (e.g., Schuman et al. 1997).

Yet the social position of Blacks relative to whites has not improved evenly or greatly, and in some respects has worsened over the past several decades. Literally from birth to death, Blacks continue to face vast inequalities. At birth in 2007, Blacks could expect to live 4.8 fewer years than whites, a slight improvement over the gap of 5.3 years in 1957 (Arias 2011: 52). The age-adjusted death rate for Blacks was 1.20 times greater than for whites in 1960 and, after climbing and falling, was 1.21 times greater than for whites in 2010; the infant mortality rate for Blacks was 1.64 times that of whites in 1950 and peaked at 2.52 in 1999 before dropping slightly to 2.24 by 2005 (calculated from Murphy et al. 2013: 71, 147). Residential segregation of Blacks, far more extensive than for any other racial category, persisted at high rates, if declining slowly over time, while school segregation, after a brief period of decline, has rebounded to the levels of the late 1960s.[40] The unemployment rate for Blacks has been intractably around twice as high as that for whites regardless of the state of the economy (see chapter 6). The ratio of Black to white family incomes was 0.61 in 1970 and, after fluctuation, was back at 0.61 in 2010, while the Black median household wealth sank from an already preposterously low 6.7 percent to 5.0 percent of the white median between 1983 and 2010.[41] Even more alarming than the steep escalation in the overall rate of incarceration in recent decades, the racial composition of prisoners changed from 70 percent white in the mid-twentieth century to almost 70 percent Black and Latina/o by the century's end (Wacquant 2001: 96); the number of Blacks in prisons and jails rose from 98,000 in 1954, the year of the *Brown v. Board of Education* ruling, to 882,300 in 2007 (Mauer and King 2004; Sabol and Couture 2008). Other similarly dismal disparities could be inventoried seemingly without end.[42]

How do these racial inequalities coexist with the supposedly dominant ideology of "colorblindness"? The most unlikely answer is that, per the ideology, racism matters little and people and institutions act in a racially disinterested fashion. If "resources . . . are *read* like texts, to recover the cultural schemas they instantiate," and they validate and reproduce those schemas (Sewell 1992: 13; emphasis in original), the spatial and social separation of Blacks and all the relatively inferior housing, schools, access to jobs and health care, public accommodations, and so on that go with it do not make for a "colorblind" reading of the schemas at work.

In contemporary structures of racial inequality and domination, I propose that schemas of "colorblindness" operate at relatively "shallow" depths—as ideology but, even as ideology, principally in public discourse. In the wake of the Civil Rights Movement, political discourse, above all, takes "racial equality" to be an indisputably desirable principle, and most whites, across the political spectrum, espouse a rhetoric of "equal opportunity" and "colorblindness" (Omi and Winant 1994). Even David Duke, a one-time Republican member of the Louisiana legislature and a former Grand Wizard of the Ku Klux Klan, steered clear of explicit references to race, much less Black inferiority, in attacking welfare and affirmative action and proclaiming "equal rights for all Americans" during his bid for a U.S. Senate seat in the early 1990s (Bethell 1990: 21). Other public discourses, such as academic, journalistic, and legal, are similarly and carefully devoid of overt denigration of Blacks and other peoples of color. Most public opinion surveys, at least since the 1970s, confirm that the vast majority of whites do not view Blacks as *inherently* inferior (Hunt 2007; Schuman and Krysan 1999; Schuman et al. 1997; Sniderman and Piazza 1993).[43]

Digging below, or merely scratching, the surface, however, reveals the persistence of anti-Black schemas that belie the discourse of "colorblindness." Perhaps in the quest to identify a wholly new post-Civil Rights form of racism, many analysts tend to gloss over the glaring continuities.[44] Even public opinion surveys—frequently criticized for measuring only highly self-censored views— document the intransigence. Their otherwise optimistic interpretations notwithstanding, survey researchers Paul Sniderman and Thomas Piazza report that "what is striking is the sheer pervasiveness throughout contemporary American society of negative characterizations of blacks. . . . [I]mages of blacks as failing to make a genuine effort to work hard and to deal responsibly with their obligations [are] a standard belief throughout most of American society" (1993: 50–51).

Closer to practices on the ground and those who enact them, studies of urban labor markets by Devah Pager and colleagues reveal that employers consistently discriminate against Black male applicants for entry-level jobs. In an audit study of Milwaukee-area employers, Pager finds that Black applicants without a record of incarceration are 59 percent less likely to be called back for entry-level positions than their white counterparts (2003: 957–58). An audit study of New York City employers yields similar results: Black men without a criminal record are 51 percent less likely to receive a positive response—a call back or a job offer—than white men and 40 percent less likely than Latino men (Pager, Western, and Bonikowski 2009: 784). In both studies, white men *with* an imputed record of incarceration for a drug offense fare as well as or better than Black men *without* (Pager 2003: 957–58; Pager, Western, and Bonikowski 2009: 785–86).[45]

When asked by researchers, these employers can and do proffer opinions on race, some of which are consistent with the idea that "colorblindness" is the dominant racial ideology. They do not resort to explanations that Blacks are innately inferior, and in certain interview contexts, they indicate little racial bias. For example, a follow-up survey of the same Milwaukee employers produces a strikingly different result than the audit study, showing an "almost total lack of correlation" between the two. Presented over the telephone with hypothetical vignettes closely resembling the audit scenario, the employers evince not much difference in how they would treat Black and white job applicants: "the degree to which race is a factor in hiring decisions is virtually undetectable" (Pager and Quillian 2005: 369, 366).[46]

At the same time, just below this surface, if sincere, "colorblindness," the employers are forthcoming about their negative views of Black men. Asked generally about employment problems of Black men, most New York City employers, in in-depth interviews, blame Black men themselves for their "lack of work ethic, motivation, and personal responsibility," poor attitude and self-presentation, and "threatening and criminal demeanor" (Pager and Karafin 2009: 77–82).[47] Yet these general assessments soften when the employers speak of their own personal experiences with applicants and employees: more than half and two-thirds cite no racial differences in the quality of applicants and employees, respectively (Pager and Karafin 2009: 84–86).

Still, in real-life settings, employers make distinctions and disfavor Blacks in hiring, as the audit studies show. They do so tacitly, neither explaining nor revealing intentions. In the New York City study, the employers who discriminate against Black applicants make their decisions with "little or no personal contact" in "at least half" of the cases (Pager, Western, and Bonikowski 2009: 787). Even when there is such contact, the employers' interactions with Black auditors betray no outward signs of racist intent. Only by comparing their field notes to those of white and Latino auditors does the employers' anti-Blackness come to light: for example, Blacks are often subjected to higher "shifting standards" and, even when hired, are "channeled" to jobs inferior to those advertised (Pager, Western, and Bonikowski 2009: 788–92).[48]

What is clear from the studies is that employers' reflective discourses do not tell us much about their performative practices, discursive and nondiscursive.[49] The surveyed opinions of the employers, in response to hypothetical vignettes, approximate "colorblindness." Delved into in more depth, however, the vast majority of them ascribe negative judgments about Black men to explain their disadvantaged position in the labor market. Probed further to reflect on their own experiences with applicants and workers, they largely disavow the salience of race. Nonetheless, in the absence of curious researchers' provoking discursive reflection, employers tacitly go about evaluating and hiring. Without announcing themselves, these performative practices effectively produce starkly unequal outcomes, from which we can infer an underlying "deeper" logic of presuming Black inferiority. With the notion of depth and the related distinction between reflective and performative practices, we can reconcile the seemingly contradictory evidence of "colorblindness" ideology *and* racist practices, of declining *and* continuing significance of race.[50]

If my reading is correct, we can draw out a few interrelated implications. First, to argue against the idea that racism is irrational does not mean that racial practices are therefore always rational. We can discern and make sense of the cultural logics, or schemas, at work, but need not assume that they are logical or rational in any strict, utility-maximizing sense.[51] Only tautology or conceptual hyperinflation of rationality could construe all racial practices to be rational. Second, although not every study of present-day racism needs to be historical, it does not follow that we can fully account for it by focusing exclusively on contemporary interest-based struggles and disregarding the past. Racism, like all structures, cannot be reduced to material interests, or resources. Understanding the power dimension of racism does not necessarily lend much insight into its semiotic dimension, its schemas and their depth. For instance, I contend that the schema of presuming the inferiority of Blackness is extremely deep and transposable, with a long history and a global reach. Coherently, it is also highly adaptable: the countless particular practices which it has engendered, and through which it has existed and persisted, have varied over time, across space, and in scale.[52] An insistent, a priori presentism would miss the continuity and tenacity of the schema and thereby the historical durability, or depth, of anti-Black racism. I suggest that we cannot adequately answer many *contemporary* questions concerning anti-Black racism—such as why "Blacks," however variously categorized, continually fare worse than other dominated categories, let alone the dominant one, in the United States and elsewhere[53]—without acknowledging its *historical* origin in and evolution from the institution of chattel slavery.[54]

Finally, the significance of colorblind racism and its assumed, radical discontinuity with the past may need to be reevaluated, if not entirely overturned.

As I suggest above, "colorblindness" is a relatively surface phenomenon, largely confined to public discourse. People still recognize and employ racial categories, and they evaluate and act accordingly. On the whole, whites still blame Blacks themselves for the racial inequalities and domination to which they are subject. In this regard, rather than heralding a permanent shift, the Civil Rights Movement may have induced a relatively short and anomalous period during which whites conceded the importance of racism, soon after which they *reverted* to blaming Blacks (Schuman and Krysan 1999). Even the supposedly novel shift from presuming the *innate* inferiority of Blacks to presuming their *cultural* inferiority may be exaggerated.[55] For example, already in 1942, the "modal response" of whites was to attribute Blacks' lower life-chances to their "laziness"; by contrast, "'lack of native ability' was [cited] much less often" (Schuman and Krysan 1999: 853n7). And at least one national survey in 1990 could still find over 50 percent of whites judging Blacks to be "innately lazy and less intelligent" (Lipsitz 1998: 19). To be sure, there have been important changes in the past half-century that require careful analysis and critique. However, to see "colorblindness" as much more determinative than it is would be an error of analytical misrecognition, echoing the misrecognition that this ideology effects in public discourse.

CONCLUSION

Racism remains a key concept in the social sciences. As a consequence of its varied uses, it is also a deeply contested one. Critiquing, selectively incorporating, and expanding upon existing approaches, Bonilla-Silva's (1997) theory sets a benchmark for subsequent work. Above all, it advances a structural account of racism, avoiding, for instance, social psychology's tendency to decontextualize and individualize racial attitudes or Marxism's inclination to foreground class dynamics. Conceptualizing racism as grounded in and constitutive of a racial structure of a racialized social system, the theory undercuts the idea that racism is irrational or derivative of nonracial factors. Instead, it directs analytical attention to hierarchical relations with material inequalities and to the struggles, and thereby changes, that they produce.

The promise of this approach, however, is diluted by the choice to construct the theory on a watered-down concept of structure, a major drawback of which is the explicit exclusion of culture and, by extension, closely correlated categories such as ideology. At the same time, the theory posits racism as the dominant *ideology* of the racial structure. Racism is thus placed in an uneasy position in relation to the concept of structure that the theory is based on and, though ostensibly the principal concept under consideration, designates only one, and not the most consequential, level of the racial structure.

I redefine *racism* as the structures of inequality and domination based on race and consider the implications of incorporating and elaborating on Sewell's (1992) theory of structure. Just as capitalism denotes the capitalist structure itself, racism, in this view, refers to the structures of racial inequality and domination, not only the ideological component. Like other structures, racism is the reiterative articulation of schemas and resources through practice. It is plural, being composed of racisms of different scales, from fleeting everyday interactions to geopolitics. As an interconnected whole, racism has been and is enormously powerful, involving vast quantities and different kinds of human and nonhuman resources.

Through the notion of schemas, the cultural or semiotic dimension of social life is explicitly and fundamentally included in the concept of racism. I propose three "deep," or core, schemas that make racism exceedingly durable and transposable: *race* or the mode of categorizing people by some notion of "collective heredity"; the presumption of suitability/unsuitability for civic inclusion, or belonging, on the basis of race; and the presumption of superiority/inferiority on the basis of race. Schemas of racism also exist at shallower depths, as the core schemas are transposed to and articulate with more "surface" structures of inequality and domination. Governed by cultural schemas, the practices that compose racism, though not irrational, are not necessarily driven by rational interests in any narrow sense. As a corollary, the practices also cannot be reduced to contemporary material interests, as schemas are path-dependent historical formations.

Important implications also follow from Sewell's ideas that structures change through the rearticulation of schemas and resources, that there are countless structures of various kinds and sizes, that they intersect, and that the resource consequences and, I would add, schema consequences of structures are not entirely predictable. Given racism's range of scales and depths, and its intersection with other structures, I suggest that no structure of inequality and domination is a priori beyond being articulated to racism. Although most analyses tend to be bound by it, the "nation-state" provides no natural limit to this claim. Thoroughly articulated with other structures, racism also does not only change through racial contestation: extra-racial schemas and resources can be articulated with those of racism, and vice versa, resulting in transformations of racism and the other structures, many of them unforeseen.

I disaggregate and trim the concept of ideology, an unwieldy construct that cannot adequately deal with culture in toto. Agreeing with Bonilla-Silva and others that ideology is a matter of discourse, but conceiving of culture in terms of schemas, I distinguish between discursive and nondiscursive practices: many practices, though instantiations of meaningful schemas, are not discursive. I further distinguish between performative and reflective discourses. I contend that racism is composed largely of nondiscursive and performa-discursive practices that are enactments of tacit schemas. In contrast, racial ideologies are reflective discourses, opinions concerning race. Subaltern ideologies critique racism and propose its transformation, seeking to supplant the tacitly operative schemas that are currently articulated to resources. Provoked by subaltern ideologies, dominant ideologies are discursive representations of the structure of racial inequality and domination in defense of it. As such, they are always partial discourses and need not be homologous or identical to the tacit schemas at work.

Accordingly, the dominant racial ideology of "colorblindness" of the present era in the United States is relatively shallow, if widespread, and affects primarily public discourses. Although it warrants debunking and vigorous opposition—particularly when reflective and performative discourses overlap with weighty consequences, such as in court decisions and legislation—I caution against giving it undue analytical attention in other areas. It should come as no surprise that, for instance, what whites say and write *about* race fails to give much insight into structures of racial inequality and domination. I argue instead that the primary focus of social-scientific research on racism needs to be on the nondiscursive and performa-discursive practices that do their work without much comment.

Probably in part because there is so much skepticism about racism in public discourse, many social scientists may feel compelled to find the "smoking gun" in what people say to prove its enduring significance. And in the right hands, interviews, whether survey or in-depth, can yield valuable findings. For example, Bonilla-Silva's (2001, 2003) empirical work ably probes past its subjects' initial responses to unearth what lies below the rhetoric of "colorblindness." Nonetheless, interviews are intrinsically reflective discourses: even assuming that people answer in good faith, their conscious reflections may or may not correspond to their subconscious dispositions and, relatedly, to what they do, with words and deeds, in situ. As Amanda Lewis (2004: 637–40) points out, ethnographies, interviews of nonwhites, institutional analyses, and audits present alternative methodological strategies to get at them. Through close observations and interpretations of actual practices, ethnographers can notice and make sense of the practical logics that often operate outside the immediate conscious grasp of their practitioners. For reasons of asymmetry of doxa, nonwhite interviewees in the United States, and their counterparts elsewhere, are much more likely to be conscious of and perceptive about racist practices that whites tend to take for granted. Less concerned with stated motives than with organizational practices, studies of institutions, like the welfare state, can trace the mechanisms through which racial disparities are produced. Audit studies, with matched and trained testers of different racial categories, can be particularly effective in uncovering unconscious biases in real-life situations, such as employment or home and car sales.

To this list I would suggest three additional research approaches. First, though likewise decontextualized, experimental social psychology and neuroscience can ascertain unconscious and unintentional processes that interview-based studies rarely can.[56] Second, although the study of racism has been largely segregated from the growth of, and the cultural turn in, historical sociology, I think it holds much potential for shedding light on the tacit schemas of racism. With temporal distance, we can apprehend more easily the meanings of past practices that were taken for granted and thus unnoticed at the time. Historicizing *current* practices can likewise denaturalize them and help us to comprehend their differing depths. Finally, one activist strand of ethnography offers a variation on Marx's eleventh thesis on Feuerbach.[57] Combining direct political action with research, "observant participation" ruptures the smooth structural reproduction of racism and investigates the fractures to render explicit previously implicit practices.[58] For example, mimicking commonplace practices of middle- and upper-class neighborhoods, activists in Rio de Janeiro, including anthropologist João H. Costa Vargas, installed gates and cameras to protect a *favela* from the police and the drug trade. Though short-lived, this disruption of common sense caused a national furor and disclosed the usually unspoken assumptions about Blacks, criminality, and favelas underlying the dominant practices of racial and class oppression (Vargas 2006b). The point is that we may be able to interpret the world better by changing it.

PART II
DENATURALIZING
THE NATION-STATE

And this is called America, where Columbus got lost and thought he had found India. That is why the people—the Reds, the Native Americans—have been called Indian; they had to say something to Queen Isabella. All geography now is doubtful, and where we are now, on the medieval map there was a place where the world ended. On the map it said, "Here are dragons." But we are men.

James Baldwin, "Black English: A Dishonest Argument"

CHAPTER 3

THE RACIAL
CONSTITUTION OF THE
U.S. EMPIRE-STATE

"Today, for the first time in our Nation's history, the Court confers a constitutional right to habeas corpus on alien enemies detained abroad by our military forces in the course of an ongoing war. The Chief Justice's dissent, which I join, shows that the procedures prescribed by Congress in the Detainee Treatment Act provide the essential protections that habeas corpus guarantees; there has thus been no suspension of the writ, and no basis exists for judicial intervention beyond what the Act allows. My problem with today's opinion is more fundamental still: The writ of habeas corpus does not, and never has, run in favor of aliens abroad; the Suspension Clause thus has no application, and the Court's intervention in this military matter is entirely *ultra vires*."[1] Thus began Justice Antonin Scalia's dissent in *Boumediene v. Bush* (2008), in which Samuel A. Alito, John G. Roberts, and Clarence Thomas joined.

The lead plaintiff in the case, one of the "aliens" in question, Lakhdar Boumediene, had been imprisoned indefinitely at Guantanamo Bay Naval Base in Cuba since January 2002. A little over a month after September 11, 2001, the naturalized Bosnian citizen of Algerian birth had been picked up in Bosnia by local authorities, under U.S. pressure, for allegedly plotting an attack against the U.S. embassy there. Set to be released, after three months, for lack of evidence, he and the rest of the "Algerian Six" were instead handed over to the U.S. military and abducted to Guantánamo. Never convicted, he was eventually freed in 2009.[2]

For Scalia, the naval base at Guantánamo, which the United States occupies through an open-ended lease with Cuba that Cuba does not recognize, is a place "abroad"—definitely outside the United States: certainly for "aliens," if not U.S. citizens, constitutionally guaranteed rights, like the privilege of the writ of *habeas corpus*, do not reach, which was precisely why the U.S. military held "enemy combatants" there. But in the opinion of the court, written by Justice Anthony Kennedy, the majority do not agree that "the Constitution necessarily stops where *de jure* sovereignty ends," even for noncitizens: "In every practical sense Guantanamo is not abroad."[3] Yet, beneath the disagreement between the Kennedy and Scalia camps, as substantial and consequential as it is, lies a shared set of basic assumptions: that the U.S. state wields legitimate power in Guantánamo; that Guantánamo is, in a political and juridical sense, on an unequal footing in relation to the fifty states of the Union; and, although aliens in Guantánamo may now have the right to *habeas corpus* and possibly other due process rights, they compose a distinctly lesser category than citizens.

The ongoing, open-ended "war on terror"—or, as Scalia would have it, the "war with radical Islamists"[4]—has stirred much talk of an "American empire" in the past decade. Despite sharp disagreements, the general consensus has been that the United States is a relatively new and decidedly informal—that is, noncolonial or nonterritorial—empire, particularly in comparison with the European powers of the past.[5] The United States may assert its power over foreign lands and peoples, but it does not outright impose formal sovereignty; for instance, the *Boumediene* ruling "accept[s] the Government's position that Cuba, and not the United States, retains *de jure* sovereignty over Guantanamo Bay."[6] Even for most of those few who acknowledge a longer history of U.S. empire, the only true foray into formal, colonial empire-building by the United States was at the turn of the twentieth century, consequent to the Spanish-American War.[7] Otherwise, the United States has been distinctly a nation-state, even if an informally imperialist one.

Against this prevalent assumption, I concentrate on lands over which the United States has indisputably claimed formal sovereignty and make three arguments: the United States has never been a nation-state; the United States has always been an empire-state; the United States has always been a racial state, a state of white supremacy.

My strategy in this chapter is simple and straightforward: I discuss several concepts and apply them in, by turns, broad and fine strokes to the case of the United States. None of the concepts or applications are, or should be, controversial in and of themselves, but taken together, they may cohere into something original and useful, theoretically and politically.[8] I examine the early development of the U.S. empire-state, the long nineteenth century, drawing evidence from constitutional law.[9] The Constitution, its initial framing and subsequent interpretations and amendments, provides and represents the basic foundation or architecture of the evolving U.S. state. Although my aim is not to assert their primacy in relation to other state institutions or nonstate actors, constitutions are undeniably a crucial component of modern state formation (Arjomand 1992).[10]

The empire-state approach aims to bring together studies of race, the state, and empire, which is generally lacking with respect to the United States. It allows us to make unified sense of, and see connections between, the heterogeneous histories of peoples who have been racially subjected to and have struggled against the U.S. empire-state, without overlooking significant differences and particularities. I begin with a few words on a few concepts and introduce the argument that the United States has always been an empire-state, not a nation-state. I flesh out this idea in the subsequent sections, analytically separating the two defining dimensions of colonialism: the hierarchical differentiation of spaces and of peoples. Focusing on the acquisition and disposal of "territories" and on American Indian sovereignty, I show how U.S. state formation has always entailed the racial construction of colonial spaces. Given the racial subjection of various peoples of the U.S. empire-state, which has been copiously, but mostly group-specifically, documented, I ask whether and on what basis we should study the imperial subjection of colonized and noncolonized peoples within the same framework. I answer through an in-depth analysis of a counterintuitive Supreme Court case, *Dred Scott v. Sandford* (which makes a fleeting but relevant appearance in *Boumediene*).[11] The chapter concludes with several implications of the empire-state approach.

RECONCEPTUALIZING THE U.S. RACIAL STATE

In their widely and justly celebrated *Racial Formation in the United States*, Michael Omi and Howard Winant ([1986] 1994) place the state squarely at the center of their analysis. Three decades after its first publication, the book is still one of the rare exceptions to the ongoing mutual nonrecognition and disengagement between theories of racial formation and of state formation (Goldberg 2002: 2–4; James and Redding 2005: 193; King and Smith 2005: 79). In contrast to other theories of racial inequality and domination, many of which emphasize, for instance, economic interests and relations, Omi and Winant foreground the political. The U.S. state, they argue, "from its very inception has been concerned with the politics of race" (Omi and Winant 1994: 81). In their Gramscian perspective, the racial order at a given historical moment is "equilibrated by the state—encoded in law, organized through policy-making, and enforced by a repressive apparatus." Periodically, especially since World War II, social movements may successfully pressure the state and destabilize the racial order, with the state responding variously to establish a new "unstable equilibrium," a new racial order (p. 84). "Inherently racial," the state, for Omi and Winant, is "increasingly the preeminent site of racial conflict," and "race will always be at the center of the American experience" (pp. 5, 82).[12]

I agree that the U.S. state is inherently racial and, in all likelihood, will always be racial. As "inherently" and "always" signal, Omi and Winant are not proffering purely empirical statements about the U.S. state but theoretical claims about its intrinsic character. But on what basis can we make such assertions, and how has the U.S. state been racial? I suggest that the questions remain considerably unanswered and unanswerable because the U.S. state is almost universally assumed to be, and to have been, a nation-state.[13]

Let us first define the constituent, hyphenated terms. A *nation* is, as Benedict Anderson memorably put it, "an imagined political community—and imagined as both inherently limited and sovereign." A categorical identity, it entails direct membership and is "always conceived as a deep, *horizontal* comradeship" (1991: 6, 7; emphasis added).[14] *States* are "coercion wielding organizations that are distinct from households and kinship groups and exercise clear priority in some respects over all other organizations within substantial territories" (Tilly 1992: 1). Modifying Max Weber's classic definition, Charles Tilly concurs on the basic importance of coercion and territory but scales back on the idea that the state claims a monopoly of coercion or its legitimacy.[15]

My contention is that, for the United States, the political community to which the *state* has been coupled has never been the *nation*. I do not mean in the trivial sense that the *nation-state* is an ideal type no actual nation-state fits precisely, but that the United States has not been a nation-state in a fundamental, square-peg-in-a-round-hole sense. By virtue of the assumed internal horizontality of nations, nation-states imply politically homogeneous populations of *citizens*, or state members. As a corollary, territories over which nation-states claim sovereignty are politically homogeneous spaces, symbolized in atlases by evenly colored, neatly bounded blocks. The United States has never come close to achieving these political "ideals" and, in all probability, is constitutionally, both literally and figuratively, incapable of doing so.

The polity to which the U.S. state has always laid claim in fact, if not in rhetoric, is an empire. Unlike nation-states, *empire-states* (Cooper 2005) are not horizontally homogeneous but hierarchically differentiated.[16] Empire-states entail the usurpation of political sovereignty of foreign territories and corresponding populations. In terms of geography, an empire-state encompasses spaces of "different degrees of sovereignty" (Stoler 2006: 128), territories of unequal political status. In terms of belonging or membership, the peoples of an empire-state effectively, through *de jure* and *de facto* practices, have differential access to rights and privileges. These conditions are what George Steinmetz (2008a: 591) refers to as the "sovereignty" and, following Partha Chatterjee (1993), "rule of difference" criteria of *colonialism*, the formal supplanting and exercise of sovereignty over territories and peoples. Here I would attach an addendum to the rule-of-difference criterion. Steinmetz writes, "Where conquered subject populations are offered the same citizenship rights as conquerors in exchange for their assimilation into the ruling culture, we are better off speaking of modern state making rather than colonialism" (2005: 348; see also Cooper 2005: 27). But if we were to view the rule of difference from the vantage point of subject populations, like the indigenous peoples of North America and Hawai'i, we would find that the *imposition* of "equal" citizenship can be and, by many, is seen as a practice of colonial rule (Porter 1999; Bruyneel 2004).[17] In other words, without the consent of the colonized, unilaterally ridding the rule of difference through assimilation rather than decolonization may not eliminate, but instead reproduce and even deepen, colonial domination. After all, extermination and assimilation were both constitutive of the U.S. state's genocidal colonial policies toward American Indians in the nineteenth century and beyond, summed up respectively by the infamous quotes "The only good Indian is a dead Indian" and "Kill the Indian in him and save the man" (Wolfe 2006: 397).[18]

RACIALIZED SPACES OF THE U.S. EMPIRE-STATE

> The main battle in imperialism is over land, of course.
>
> Edward Said, *Culture and Imperialism*

> I am persuaded no constitution was ever before as well calculated as
> ours for extensive empire and self-government.
>
> Thomas Jefferson, letter to James Madison, April 28, 1809

The continual misrecognition of the United States as a nation-state, not least by the state itself, has been integral to U.S. nationalism, and its attendant sense of exceptionalism, and thereby to the formation, fortification, and imperception of the United States as an empire-state.[19] As Steinmetz (2006: 137) notes, "American power . . . seems continually to generate the mirage of its own disappearance." This is not, however, due to "the deceptively *informal* character of American empire since the early nineteenth century," that "American power . . . does not typically annex and permanently occupy foreign lands— with the important exceptions of the westward expansion of the continental state, Hawai'i, and the colonies created from the spoils of the Spanish-American War" (Steinmetz 2006: 136, 137; emphasis in original).[20] Although the informal, or nonterritorial, facet of the U.S. empire has been immense,[21] the "important exceptions" have been important but hardly exceptional, which is readily apparent when we take in their spatial expanse: the overland and overseas annexations of the long nineteenth century stretched from the original thirteen states westward to the Eastern Hemisphere, northward to above the Arctic Circle, and southward to below the equator and, with certain exceptions such as the Philippines and the Panama Canal Zone, are still under the *formal* jurisdiction of the United States.

Many may object that the vast majority of the lands under U.S. sovereignty are the fifty states, which are all of equal standing and in which the U.S. Constitution fully and evenly applies, and that genuine colonial empire-building by the United States was but a short-lived episode. Obsessed with comparisons to what they imagine to have been the prototypical (i.e., European) empires, the British above all, academic and nonacademic commentators alike eagerly point out how the United States has been and is exceptional. Of course, a careful examination would reveal an equal number of empires and exceptions (and ideologies of exceptionalism), as well as repertoires of ruling practices that greatly overlapped, and varied, between empires and changed over time within them.[22] No one, or one type of, empire-state epitomizes the category to the exclusion of others, and the United States is no exception.

Also troubling is how the U.S. state's own practical categories of colonial rule double as analytical categories. Foremost, in much of the literature on the U.S. empire, the legal distinction between *incorporated* and *unincorporated* territories, drawn by the Supreme Court in the *Insular Cases* in the early twentieth century, marks the analytical distinction between metropole and colony: states and incorporated territories on the one hand, and unincorporated territories on the other (see discussions below). Therefore Guam, the Philippines (up to 1946), and Puerto Rico are treated as bona fide colonies, whereas Hawai'i, Alaska, and all parts of what are now the forty-eight contiguous states are not.

The uncritical reproduction of U.S. exceptionalism and state categories has a couple of related consequences: the temporal depth and spatial breadth of the U.S. empire-state are routinely and often grossly underestimated, and its history oversimplified. As a countermeasure, I propose that we see less like the state and more like the ruled.[23] In the context of the U.S. empire-state, such an optical shift must begin with the indigenous peoples.[24] From the vantage point of the Native peoples of North America, the birth of the United States as a state was at once the birth of the United States as an empire-state. If we accept that England had established colonies in North America, usurping the political sovereignty of Native American peoples and territories, what changed after the colonies broke away and founded a state, or a federation of states, of their own? For the indigenous peoples, the United States immediately became one more empire-state with which they had to contend. After all, as Christopher Tomlins (2001: 365) reminds us, the colonists declared independence, "in large part, in order to free themselves from imperial constraints that restrained their own colonizing (or to use the preferred anodyne phrase, their own 'westward movement')."

As already indicated, the metropole/colony distinction is of limited utility in analyzing the U.S. empire-state.[25] In part, this may have to do with its principally overland character. But much more than that, the vulgar and deadly immodesty of the state's and its white citizens' colonial ambition rendered metropole and colony largely overlapping and, at times like the present, nearly coterminous. Taken as a whole, the abiding colonial logic was to wrest land away from indigenous sovereignty and control. In North America, it was to empty the land of Indians, through coerced cessions, broken treaties, extermination, and assimilation, and geographically confine the survivors on ever shrinking reservations with diminished Native sovereignty. In effect, doing away with the metropole/colony distinction itself has been part and parcel of the U.S. colonial project, a condition of possibility for assertions that the United States has been a nation-state, not an empire-state. Native survival and resistance, above all, have been what put the lie to such claims. Indigenous territories under colonial rule today consist minimally of the Indian reservation lands, maximally of the entire United States, and quite reasonably of all the lands that were never ceded.[26]

Colonial rule over Indian-held lands was one of the fundamental issues for the United States from the very beginning. Under the British, a royal proclamation in 1763 had drawn a line along the Appalachian Mountains to keep Indians and white settlers apart, prohibiting, if futilely, the latter from the western portion that extended to the Mississippi River and was designated Indian territory. The newly independent states had to decide what to do with the territory, a crucial issue since some states, as a carryover from the British era, had claims to it, and others none. As one of the latter, Maryland cited the former's relinquishment of their claims as a precondition for its ratification of the Articles of Confederation, which required unanimous assent. All states eventually ceded their trans-Appalachian claims.[27] In this way, the very formation of the U.S. state hinged on lands occupied by Indians but over which it asserted ultimate sovereignty (Meinig 1986; Nobles 1997). The issues originally raised by the trans-Appalachian territories would continue to shape, bedevil, and haunt the geography of U.S. empire-state formation: the acquisition and disposal of "territories," and Indian sovereignty.

The legitimating blueprint for the nascent state, the U.S. Constitution expressly acknowledged the reality of spaces under U.S. sovereignty that did not enjoy equal standing with the "several states"—in short, colonial spaces. In Article IV, section 3, it vested Congress with the "Power to dispose of and make all needful Rules and Regulations respecting the Territory or other Property belonging to the United States." The "United States" was therefore not literal: it comprised not only the states but also other political spaces, which were to be ruled ultimately as Congress saw fit and would not have voting representation in the federal government. The constitutionality of *further* acquisition of territories was initially and periodically uncertain. Nonetheless, by 1853, with the Gadsden Purchase from Mexico, the United States had assumed sovereignty over the entire area of today's forty-eight contiguous states, with that of sixteen future states still composed of territories.

The Constitution did not address how territories could be transformed into states, merely stating in the aforementioned article and section, "New States may be admitted by the Congress into this Union" (Article IV, section 3).[28] The widely held assumption during the nineteenth century was that the process followed the principle set out in the Northwest Ordinance of 1787 for the disposal of the northwestern portion of the trans-Appalachian territories (Sparrow 2006): temporary governments organized by Congress, followed by "establishment of States, and permanent government therein . . . on an equal footing with the original States, at as early periods as may be consistent with the general interest" (section 13).[29]

The acquisition of overseas territories in the late 1890s, particularly the former Spanish colonies of Guam, the Philippines, and Puerto Rico, profoundly upset the tacit assumption. Above all, racism toward their nonwhite, non-Anglo Saxon inhabitants incited the uproar and debate, both among imperialists and anti-imperialists, and centrally informed the construction of the categories of "incorporated" and "unincorporated" territories, distinguishing those slated to become states and others that could be kept and governed *indefinitely* as territories (Burnett and Marshall 2001b; Kramer 2006).[30] But this categorical bifurcation of territories did not suddenly inject racism into a hitherto nonracial practice of empire-state formation. Rather it laid bare the white supremacist underpinnings.[31]

Acquiring territories, even under the assumption that they would be turned into states, has always been a racist process. The politics around conquering and taking possession of Texas and what would become the U.S. Southwest from Mexico, for example, was patently structured by anti-Mexican racism, as numerous studies have shown.[32] The new territories of 1898, however, provoked a more radical doubt of whether white supremacy could be maintained through the usual colonial practices of the U.S. state, a doubt resolved through the *Insular Cases'* doctrine of territorial incorporation. The deviant case of Hawai'i was revealing. Like the island colonies obtained through the Spanish-American War, it was seized in 1898, located overseas, and inhabited predominantly by nonwhites—Native Hawaiians and migrant laborers from China, Japan, and elsewhere. However, unlike these other colonies, Hawai'i was slotted into the newly invented "incorporated" category, the same one to which all past and then present U.S. territories on the North American continent retroactively belonged. The decisive difference was that Hawaii's economy and politics had long been dominated by white settlers from the United States, namely descendants of missionaries from the Northeast.[33] It was precisely because U.S. white supremacy was already and sufficiently guaranteed that Hawai'i was incorporated while other overseas territories were not. Still, principally because of its concerns about the nonwhite-majority population, Congress would not grant Hawai'i admission into the Union as a state until 1959 (Bell 1984; Jung 2006; Merry 2000; Osorio 2002; Thompson 2002).[34] On the flip side, we can infer that the relatively short and smooth transition of most territories to statehood was also underwritten by white supremacy, that the taken-for-granted certainty of white dominance was a necessary condition of possibility.[35] And in the antebellum period, the transition always took into account the delicate sectional balance of power in the U.S. Senate between the North and the South, evening out the numbers of "free" and "slave" states admitted. Needless to say, the equilibration helped to preserve and prolong the white supremacist institution of slavery (Sparrow 2006).

In addition to acquiring and ruling territories, incorporated and unincorporated, U.S. empire-state formation has always entailed the construction of colonial spaces in relation to the indigenous peoples. But the Constitution was evasive. "Indian" appeared twice in the original Constitution, in the Three-Fifths and Commerce Clauses, but neither mention dealt directly with Indian lands.[36] Nonetheless, given the intrinsic coloniality of the U.S. state, built as it was on soil that was once exclusively the domain of Native Americans, constitutional questions about their political status were unavoidable. The initial answers were proffered in the early nineteenth century in three related Supreme Court cases, whose prevailing opinions were penned by Chief Justice John Marshall. In *Johnson v. M'Intosh* of 1823, the court formally invoked the extra-constitutional, and profoundly white supremacist, doctrine of discovery as the basis for U.S. sovereignty over Indian territories, adopting and adapting the centuries-old colonial logic and rationale of European rule over non-Europe: "This principle was, that discovery gave title to the [European] government by whose subjects, or by whose authority, it was made, against all other European governments, which title might be consummated by possession."[37] In other words, each European power acquired title to non-European lands that it "discovered" to the exclusion, and customarily with the tacit agreement, of other European powers. The court reasoned that the "original inhabitants" retained the "right of occupancy" and use of the land, but "their rights to complete sovereignty, as independent nations, were necessarily diminished," as the "ultimate dominion" lay with the European "discoverer."[38] As a corollary, the latter held the right of preemption, the "exclusive right to extinguish the Indian title of occupancy, either by purchase or by conquest." According to the decision, the United States, upon its independence, inherited this unmistakably colonial relationship from Britain and "unequivocally acceded to that great and broad rule by which its civilized inhabitants now hold this country."[39]

The remaining two cases further specified the relationship. Both concerned the Cherokee, whom the state of Georgia ultimately wished to expel. In *Cherokee Nation v. Georgia* of 1831, the plaintiff sought "an injunction to restrain the state of Georgia from the execution of certain laws of that state, which, as is alleged, go directly to annihilate the Cherokees as a political society, and to seize, for the use of Georgia, the lands of the nation."[40] Ruling against the Cherokee on jurisdictional grounds, the court considered whether they—and, by extension, other Native American nations—constituted a state and, if so, what kind of state.[41] On the first question, the court decided in the affirmative: "They have been uniformly treated as a state from the settlement of our country. The numerous treaties made with them by the United States recognize them. . . . The acts of our government plainly recognize the Cherokee nation as a state, and the courts are bound by those acts." However, indigenous peoples were not "*foreign* States." Rather, they were to "more correctly, perhaps, be denominated domestic dependent nations" in a "state of pupilage" with a relationship to the United States "resembl[ing] that of a ward to his guardian," striking a rhetorical echo for the unincorporated territories to come.[42]

A year after effectively undermining Native sovereignty in relation to U.S. states, the Supreme Court retracted and recalibrated its position in the second case involving the Cherokee and the state of Georgia, *Worcester v. Georgia* (1832). The ruling proclaimed the definiteness of Native sovereignty and its inviolability against interference by states: "The Cherokee nation, then, is a distinct community occupying its own territory, with boundaries accurately described, in which the laws of Georgia can have no force, and which the citizens of Georgia have no right to enter, but with the assent of the Cherokees themselves, or in conformity with treaties, and with the acts of congress."[43] At the same time, Marshall affirmed the inferiority of Native sovereignty in relation to the United States. While recognizing that "Indian nations had always been considered as distinct, independent political communities, retaining their original natural rights, as the undisputed possessors of the soil, from time immemorial," he pointed out, per the discovery doctrine, "the single exception of that imposed by irresistible power."[44] And the authority of that imposition by the United States lay entirely with the federal government.[45]

The scope of federal authority grew and turned out to be without limit. A half-century of white settler encroachment and violence, genocidal warfare, cession treaties, and removals onto reservations later, the Supreme Court weighed in on *United States v. Kagama* in 1886 to uphold a new federal law that intruded on the *internal* affairs of Indian reservations for the first time.[46] Extending the logic of the Marshall opinions, again on extra-constitutional grounds, the court further eroded Native sovereignty and conferred on Congress plenary, or complete, power over Indians (Wilkins 1997).[47] Having already passed a law in 1871 to no longer deal with Indians bilaterally through treaties, Congress was now constitutionally empowered to, and did, legislate unilaterally to reorder and seize Indian lands and otherwise regulate Indian lives.[48] In 1903, the Supreme Court outdid itself again. Asserting that the "plenary authority over the tribal relations of the Indians has been exercised by Congress from the beginning" and that, citing *Kagama*, "Indian tribes are the wards of the nation. . . . communities dependent on the United States," the court, in *Lone Wolf v. Hitchcock*, declared that Congress, but not Indians, could disregard *existing* treaties at its discretion: "When, therefore, treaties were entered into between the United States and a tribe of Indians it was never doubted that the power to abrogate existed in Congress."[49] Attesting to the ruling's manifest racism, a U.S. senator responded at the time, "It is the *Dred Scott* decision No. 2, except that in this case the victim is red instead of black. It practically inculcates the doctrine that the red man has no rights which the white man is bound to respect, and, that no treaty or contract made with him is binding" (Matthew Quey as quoted in Wilkins 1997: 116).[50] Lest we dismiss such cases as relics of the past, the ruling in *Lone Wolf,* like those in the *Insular Cases,* still obtains, as does, it should be clear, the U.S. empire-state (Aleinikoff 2002; Biolsi 2005; Sparrow 2006).

RACIALIZED PEOPLES OF THE U.S. EMPIRE-STATE

> But the principal meaning of colonization has come to involve
> people rather than land.
>
> Frederick Cooper, *Colonialism in Question*

> These Indian Governments were regarded and treated as foreign
> Governments as much so as if an ocean had separated the red man
> from the white.
>
> Roger Taney in *Dred Scott v. Sandford (1857)*

The hierarchical differentiation of space and the hierarchical differentiation of people, both immanent and foundational to empire-state formation, are plainly related.[51] Since the hierarchical differentiation of space is not about space in itself but about the *politics* of ordering space, it is inextricably, always already about the politics of ordering people. And, as argued above, the construction of U.S. colonial spaces—whether they be Indian lands, incorporated and unincorporated territories, the "several states," or the United States as a whole—centrally turned on the racialization of their inhabitants, on the production and reproduction of white supremacy. With little controversy, at least on the left and even among liberals, we could probably agree that certain peoples were colonized by the U.S. state: the indigenous peoples of North America and Hawai'i, Mexicans of northern Mexico/U.S. Southwest, and peoples of the so-called unincorporated territories. (With a little controversy, we could also acknowledge that most, if not all, of them continue to be colonized.)[52]

What about other peoples of color, others subjected to racial domination? In much of the literature on colonialism, the binary oppositions of colonizer/colonized, European/native, and citizen/subject are unproblematically assumed to refer to the same relationship.[53] How then should we conceive of *noncolonized, nonnative subjects*? For the United States, does it make sense, for example, to categorize Blacks, past or present, as *colonized*? This is exactly what theories of internal colonialism once contended (e.g., Blauner 1972), with which I disagree specifically but agree generally.[54] The racial domination of Blacks in the United States has not been one of *colonial* domination, which by definition would involve the formal usurpation of territorial sovereignty. The formation of the U.S. empire-state did not entail the expropriation of lands over which Blacks had prior claims. In other words, the "main battle" has not been "over land" (Said 1993: xii).

In a broad sense, however, theories of internal colonialism were right to frame the oppression of Blacks in terms of colonial empire. First, as a matter of historical fact, the state with which they have had to contend for the past two and a half centuries has been an empire-state, not a nation-state. Second, Blacks have always been treated, through *de jure* and *de facto* practices, as less than full citizens, as less than equal to white citizens. But even so, while it may be of undoubted relevance with respect to colonized peoples, like Native Americans, Puerto Ricans, or Samoans, does the imperial rather than national character of the U.S. state significantly impinge on how we understand the racial domination of Blacks, and other noncolonized peoples, who have been systematically treated as less than white citizens? Has the imperial state form been merely incidental to anti-Black or most anti-Asian racisms? Had the U.S. state been a nation-state, would the exclusion of Blacks and other noncolonized peoples from full citizenship have been significantly different? Put simply, what do we gain analytically by insisting on an empire-state theoretical approach?

In an empire-state, the racial domination of colonized peoples does not happen in isolation from that of noncolonized peoples, and vice versa. Though qualitatively different, they are intimately and intricately linked. Rather than a series of self-contained dyadic relations between whites and various racial others, white supremacy comprises a web of crisscrossing discursive and practical ties. It is a unified, though differentiated, field that calls for a unified, though differentiated, theoretical framework. For example, in the afterglow of the Louisiana Purchase of 1803, President Thomas Jefferson envisaged in the newly acquired territory an expanded "empire of liberty" in which his vaunted citizenry of white yeomen could grow and flourish. He also saw potential solutions to vexing racial problems supposedly posed by those beyond the pale pale of citizenship: "the means of tempting all our Indians on the East side of the Mississippi to remove to the West" (as quoted in Meinig 1993: 78) and of "diffusing" and thereby defusing Blacks, slavery, and the dreaded threat of insurrection, made all too real by the Haitian Revolution (Freehling 2005).[55] Such articulations of empire, white supremacy, racialized citizenship, and colonial and noncolonial imperial subjection were not rare or limited to the early nineteenth century and the ruling elite. At the turn of the twentieth century, the state and the public, military and civilian officials, legislators and judges, academic and popular commentators, officers and soldiers, business and labor

Figure 3.1. "School Begins" by Louis Dalrymple. Source: Puck 44 *(1142), January 25, 1899, pp. 8–9, http://hdl.loc.gov/loc.pnp/cph.3b48925 (retrieved August 14, 2012).*

leaders, editorialists and cartoonists, and many others apparently could not imagine, talk about, write on, wage war against, or govern the newly colonized peoples of the former Spanish colonies and Hawai'i without references to Blacks, Native Americans, and the Chinese (see Figure 3.1).[56] They compared, differentiated, analogized, contrasted, transposed, extended, ranked, and homogenized. As much as the imperialists, anti-imperialists—whether white former abolitionists, Black anti-lynching activists, or white trade unionists in the anti-Chinese and anti-Japanese movements—made the associations, though with obviously divergent intentions and effects (e.g., Jacobson 2000; Kramer 2006; Murphy 2009).

The U.S. state, itself a unified but differentiated field, is a principal agent, or set of agents, in the field of white supremacy. Like other agents, it too confronts and helps to reproduce the field that is a unified but differentiated whole: it makes certain distinctions between colonial and noncolonial imperial subjects as well as within those categories, but it also generates identities, parallels, and overlaps. Explicitly and implicitly, intentionally and unintentionally, the state thus divides *and* unites as it rules. (It thereby sets barriers against and, dialectically, possibilities for coalitions of resistance.) The Supreme Court, compared to many nonstate agents and even among state institutions, has relatively fewer degrees of freedom, constrained as it is, at least nominally, by *stare decisis* and the Constitution itself.[57] Nonetheless, it too continually affirms the interconnectedness of practices of racial rule, the overall "unity" of a "'complex structure' . . . in which things are related, as much through their differences as through their similarities" (Hall 1980: 325). To illustrate, I turn to a case that is identified hardly ever with empire and almost exclusively with African Americans: *Dred Scott v. Sandford* (1857).

Marking one of the most significant moments in the history of African Americans, the *Dred Scott* decision denied U.S. citizenship to Blacks, both "free" and enslaved, in no uncertain terms, drawing an unambiguous distinction between "the citizen and the subject—the free and the subjugated races." According to the odious opinion of the court, authored by Chief Justice Roger Brooke Taney, the Constitution was unequivocal in distinguishing between the "citizen race, who formed and held the Government, and the African race, which they held in subjection and slavery and governed at their own pleasure."[58]

Evincing the complex unity of white supremacy, this case quintessentially about Blacks could also be seen, in a nontrivial sense, as a part of Native American, Asian/Asian American, Pacific Islander, and Latina/o histories.[59] Toward the start of his opinion, right after summarizing the question before the court, Taney takes a seemingly gratuitous detour for a long paragraph. It is entirely devoted to contrasting the "situation . . . of the Indian race" to that of "descendants of Africans": since the "colonial" era, "although [Indians] were uncivilized, they were yet a free and independent people, associated together in nations or tribes and governed by their own laws. . . . These Indian governments were regarded and treated as foreign Governments as much so as if an ocean had separated the red man from the white, and their freedom has constantly been acknowledged." Therefore, although they were "brought . . . under subjection to the white race . . . in a state of pupilage," Indians could "without doubt, like the subjects of any other foreign Government, be naturalized by the authority of Congress . . . and if an individual should leave his nation or tribe and take up his abode among the white population, he would be entitled to all the rights and privileges which would belong to an emigrant from any other foreign people."[60]

A decade before, however, the Supreme Court, in another opinion written by Taney, had arrived at a contrary conclusion (Hoxie 2007). In *United States v. Rogers* (1846), lands held by Indians were judged to be "a part of the territory of the United States" that had been merely "assigned to them." Further, ever since European "discovery," "native tribes . . . have never been acknowledged or treated as independent nations."[61] How do we account for the inconsistency? In *Dred Scott*, Taney contradicted his earlier opinion regarding Indians to forestall a presumably more dire contradiction regarding Blacks. In 1790, Congress had passed a law restricting the right of naturalization to "aliens being free white persons."[62] Evidently not satisfied with this statutory proscription, Taney sought to *constitutionally* block even the future *possibility* of naturalized citizenship for Blacks. One of the two dissenters in the case, Benjamin Robbins Curtis conceded, needlessly, that Congress's constitutional power of naturalization was confined to "aliens."[63] But he went on to note that being "colored" itself did not pose a constitutional barrier and that, in fact, American Indians and Mexicans had already been made U.S. citizens through treaties.[64] The other dissenter, John McLean, likewise remarked, "Under the late treaty with Mexico, we have made citizens of all grades, combinations, and colors. The same was done in the admission of Louisiana and Florida."[65]

Presumably because they had uncontroversially been seen as "aliens" before U.S. annexation, Taney did not bother to address Mexicans of the Southwest or nonwhites of the Louisiana and Florida territories in his opinion. He also granted that "color" was not a constitutional hindrance to naturalization.[66] But, though not explicitly pushed by Curtis, the issue concerning Native Americans could not be so easily dispensed with: some Indians who had been born under U.S. sovereignty according to previous rulings, including his own, had been accorded U.S. citizenship. If they could be naturalized, why could Blacks not be? Taney resolved the apparent dilemma by insisting that the Constitution "gave to Congress the power to confer [citizenship] upon those *only* who were born *outside* of the dominions of the United States" and asserting that Indians, abruptly redefined as "aliens and foreigners," fit this description.[67] Thus lacking the capacity to "raise to the rank of a citizen anyone born *in* the United States who . . . belongs to an inferior and subordinate class," Congress could not naturalize Blacks even if it were so inclined.[68]

In *Dred Scott,* ruling on Blacks led to a reexamination into the rule of Indians (and Mexicans and others). The racial subjection of one was related to the racial subjection of the other, evidencing a common field of white supremacy. The articulation in this instance was one of difference. To refuse U.S. citizenship to all Blacks, the Supreme Court was provoked to state explicitly how Native Americans were dissimilar, modifying its previous view on Indian sovereignty. In this way, the court instantiated and justified the differential treatment of the two "subject" populations, one rooted in slavery and the other in colonization. At the same time, the decision alluded to the inevitable imbrications of imperial subjection. In support of the court's opinion, Taney cited a number of state laws that ostensibly formed a consensus against the idea of Black citizenship. Though not commented on by the court, three of the statutes—two forbidding intermarriage with whites and one prohibiting travel without a written pass—applied not only to "any negro" or "mulatto" but also "Indian."[69]

The decision in *Dred Scott* with regard to Black citizenship was overruled, at least formally, by the passage and ratification of the Thirteenth, Fourteenth, and Fifteenth Amendments to the Constitution during Reconstruction. But some of its reasoning survived to be debated anew decades later. One of the arguments put forth by the plaintiff Dred Scott was that his residence from 1836 to 1838 at Fort Snelling, where he was taken by his owner, had made him free. With the Missouri Compromise of 1820, which had simultaneously admitted Missouri as a slave state and Maine as a "free" state to maintain sectional balance, Congress had prohibited slavery in the remaining territories of the Louisiana Purchase lying north of 36 degrees and 30 minutes latitude; this area included the part of Wisconsin Territory in which the aforementioned army post stood.[70]

The Supreme Court rejected Scott's claim, concluding that Congress had overreached: the Missouri Compromise, already voided by the Kansas-Nebraska Act of 1854 by the time *Dred Scott* made its way to the court, was unconstitutional.[71] According to Taney, Congress's constitutional "Power to dispose of and make all needful Rules and Regulations respecting the Territory . . . belonging to the United States" (Article IV, section 3) was immaterial: the Territorial Clause pertained *only* to the territory claimed by the United States at the time of the Constitution's original adoption and could "have no influence upon a territory afterwards acquired from a foreign Government."[72] The lone means to acquire and, implicitly, govern additional territories was instead through the Admissions Clause: "New States may be admitted by the Congress into this Union" (Article IV, section 3). From acquisition to admission, temporary territorial governments organized by Congress were permissible, but it had no plenary power to "establish or maintain colonies . . . to be ruled and governed at its own pleasure." Just as in the several states, Congress had "powers over the citizen strictly defined, and limited by the Constitution," but "no power of any kind beyond it."[73] Thus, legislating as it did for the Louisiana Purchase territories in the Missouri Compromise, Congress had overstepped its definite powers and infringed on U.S. citizens' right of property, the "right of property in a slave."[74]

Having pronounced that Congress had "no power . . . to acquire a Territory to be held and governed permanently in that character," *Dred Scott* was bound to reemerge when various state and nonstate actors were clamoring to do just that in the overseas territories annexed at the turn of the century, and others were mobilizing in opposition. It appeared extensively in *Downes v. Bidwell* (1901), "generally considered the most important of the *Insular Cases*"; Justice Edward Douglass White's opinion in the case, immediately about tariffs on Puerto Rican goods, introduced and detailed what would eventually become the controlling doctrine of territorial incorporation (Burnett and Marshall 2001a: 7).

Somewhat dissonant with the amply deserved infamy of *Dred Scott*, Taney's opinion on territories perversely took on a kind of "premature anti-imperialist" quality (Levinson 2001: 130).[75] For the four dissenting judges in *Downes*, the Constitution included all territories when referring to the "United States" and was fully in effect there. As John Marshall Harlan averred in his dissent, "The Constitution is supreme over every foot of territory, wherever situated, under the jurisdiction of the United States, and its full operation cannot be stayed by any branch of the government."[76] In the opinion signed by all of the dissenters, Chief Justice Melville Weston Fuller drew on *Dred Scott*, noting that "the Court [had been] unanimous in holding that the power to legislate respecting a territory was limited by the restrictions of the Constitution."[77]

In the lead opinion in *Downes*, Henry Billings Brown took a diametrically opposing position. For him, the "United States" referred strictly to the constituent states: "In short, the Constitution deals with states, their people, and their representatives."[78] The Constitution applied to any given territory "only when and so far as Congress shall so direct."[79] Brown discussed *Dred Scott* at great length and concluded that Taney's thoughts on territories were irrelevant as legal precedent (Sparrow 2006: 88): the question in *Downes* was "readily distinguishable from the one" on slavery, and that *Dred Scott* had taken up the territory question at all had been unnecessary and "unfortunate."[80]

White's concurring opinion, joined by two others, split the difference between the maximalist and minimalist definitions of the "United States." Like Brown, he affirmed Congress's plenary power over territories, which had been disputed by *Dred Scott* but, both before and after it, had been sustained in other cases.[81] But he disagreed with Brown's criticism of *Dred Scott* and partly sided with Fuller: "the principle which that decision announced, that the applicable provisions of the Constitution were operative" in U.S. territories was still valid. The issue was not, per Brown, "whether the Constitution is operative, for that is self-evident, but whether the provision relied on is applicable" to a given territory, a question that hung on "its relations to the United States."[82] Some territories, such as the continental ones and Hawaiʻi, were "incorporated" into the United States. Others, such as Puerto Rico and by extension the other former Spanish colonies, were "foreign to the United States in a domestic sense, because the island[s] had not been incorporated into the United States, but [were] merely appurtenant thereto as . . . possession[s]." In other words, the "United States" included some territories but not others, although all were "subject to [U.S.] sovereignty."[83] The precise meaning and consequences of "incorporation" remained fuzzy, but this and subsequent cases seemed to suggest that the Constitution "fully" applied in the incorporated territories.[84] For the unincorporated territories, White's opinion, though theoretically different, had practical implications identical to Brown's: "only certain fundamental constitutional prohibitions"—underspecified but certainly fewer than in incorporated territories—"constrained governmental action there" (Burnett and Marshall 2001a: 9–10). In 1904, White's doctrine of territorial incorporation was adopted by a majority of the court for the first time, in *Dorr v. United States*, a libel case originating in the Philippines. Among other things, the opinion of the court quoted the same passage from Curtis's opinion in *Dred Scott* that White had cited in *Downes*.[85]

As in *Dred Scott*, and later *Insular Cases*, race and citizenship were pivotal in *Downes*. A major impetus for legally inventing the category of unincorporated territories was the prevention of incorporating their inhabitants on an equal footing with white Anglo-Saxon citizens and the empowerment of Con-

gress to calibrate how unequal the footing should be. In his lead opinion in
Downes, Brown gave voice to the animating fear: what would happen if Congress did not have the discretionary power to determine the citizenship "status"
of a territory's "inhabitants"?[86] After all, if territories "are inhabited by alien
races . . . the administration of government and justice according to Anglo-
Saxon principles may for a time be impossible."[87] But those "alien races" needed
not to worry, for "there are certain principles of natural justice inherent in the
Anglo-Saxon character which need no expression in constitutions or statutes
to give them effect or to secure dependencies against legislation manifestly
hostile to their real interests"—never mind how different their stated interests
may have been. To give credence to this paternalistic argument, Brown cited a
number of cases involving noncitizens who *already* lacked constitutional protection—one dealing with American Indians, *Johnson v. M'Intosh*, and several
dealing with Chinese "aliens [who were] not possessed of the political rights
of the citizens of the United States." The inhabitants of the new territories, or
any territory, would likewise not be "subject to an unrestrained power on the
part of Congress to deal with them upon the theory that they have no rights
which it is bound to respect"—the last phrase an obvious, if not obviously
negative, allusion to *Dred Scott*.[88]

White's concurring opinion sounded the same alarm about citizenship. He
illustrated his point with a hypothetical example, appealing to the discovery
doctrine espoused in *Johnson v. M'Intosh*, among other cases, and tacking on
a bit of concern about the potential tax burden on the colonized to his paramount apprehension about racial fitness for citizenship:

Take a case of discovery. Citizens of the United States discover an unknown island,
peopled with an uncivilized race, yet rich in soil, and valuable to the United States
for commercial and strategic reasons. Clearly, by the law of nations, the right to ratify
such acquisition and thus to acquire the territory would pertain to the government of
the United States. *Johnson v. M'Intosh*, 8 Wheat. 543, 595, 5 L. ed. 681, 694. . . . Can it
be denied that such right could not be practically exercised if the result would be to
endow the inhabitants with citizenship of the United States and to subject them, not
only to local, but also to an equal proportion of national, taxes, even although the
consequence would be to entail ruin on the discovered territory, and to inflict grave
detriment on the United States, to arise both from the dislocation of its fiscal system
and the immediate bestowal of citizenship on those absolutely unfit to receive it?[89]

Worse yet, as pointed out by Brown, even if immediate bestowal of citizenship were avoided, "children thereafter born, whether savages or civilized, [would be] . . . entitled to all the rights, privileges and immunities of citizens. If such be their status, the consequences will be extremely serious."[90] He closed his opinion with a warning, "A false step at this time might be fatal to the development of what Chief Justice Marshall called the American empire."[91]

Brown's reference to "children thereafter born" stated aloud what must have implicitly informed the other judges' discourse on citizenship. Though unmentioned in any of the opinions in *Downes*, he was alluding to *United States v. Wong Kim Ark* (1898), a case decided by the same court just three years earlier. To go a little further back, nine years before that case, the Supreme Court, in *Chae Chan Ping v. United States*, had *unanimously* upheld the racially based Chinese exclusion laws of the 1880s, specifically the Scott Act of 1888.[92] The broader effect of the decision was to establish Congress's plenary power over "aliens," which, like the plenary powers over American Indian sovereignty and over territories, still obtains to this day (Aleinikoff 2002).[93] (A corollary effect was that the constitutional sanction afforded to Congress to legislatively contravene international treaties, with China in this particular case, provided precedential support for the 1903 ruling in *Lone Wolf* that gave similar sanction to abrogate treaties with Native Americans—yet another example of the interconnectedness of racial rule, the imbrications of colonial and noncolonial imperial subjection.[94]) However, even the patent anti-Chinese racism of the court had its legal limits. Both Congress and the courts had consistently denied the right of naturalization to Chinese migrants and would continue to do so until 1943. But given the Fourteenth Amendment—"All persons born or naturalized in the United States, and subject to the jurisdiction thereof, are citizens of the United States" (section 1)—the Supreme Court could not but acknowledge, in *Wong Kim Ark*, the birthright citizenship of "all children here born of resident aliens," including the Chinese.[95] Consequently, as argued by Brook Thomas, "*Wong Kim Ark* forced any Justice[s] intent on denying citizenship to residents of the insular territories to restrict the definition of what comes within the territorial limits of the United States" (2001: 96; see also Levinson 2001: 132). And restrict they did.

On racial grounds, the court chose to define the "United States in a domestic sense" as being composed of states and incorporated territories and relegated the inhabitants of the unincorporated territories in Asia, the Pacific, and the Caribbean indefinitely to something always less than full citizenship—that is, colonial subjection. Uniformly denied initially, residents of today's unincorporated territories, except American Sāmoa, have been accorded U.S. citizenship over the years, with or without their consent.[96] Yet, in the context of the colonial relationship between the U.S. state and these territories, characterized by congressional plenary power, U.S. citizenship has never meant equality, not just informally but formally, and territorial inhabitants have been systematically withheld certain privileges and immunities.[97] (The same goes for American Indians, on whom U.S. citizenship was imposed, if not before through treaties, legislation, or other means, through the Indian Citizenship Act of 1924.[98])

With the exception of one justice, the same Supreme Court that heard *Wong Kim Ark* and *Downes* had also been on the bench for *Plessy v. Ferguson* (1896).[99] One of four dissenters in *Downes*, Harlan had been famously lone in that role in *Plessy*. Insisting that "there is no caste" and that the "Constitution is color-blind," he predicted, "In my opinion, the judgment this day rendered will, in time, prove to be quite as pernicious as the decision made by this tribunal in the *Dred Scott Case*" and "stimulate aggressions, more or less brutal and irritating, upon the admitted rights of colored citizens." Referring to Taney's opinion, he argued that the postbellum amendments to the Constitution were supposed to have "eradicated these principles" of excluding Blacks from the "rights and privileges which [the Constitution] provided for and secured to citizens of the United States."[100] Here, Harlan used *Dred Scott* to analogize the state-endorsed racial subjection of antebellum Blacks to what would follow from *Plessy*.

A former slave owner from a slave-owning family, Harlan has been hailed for his judicial antiracism (Chin 1996; Przybyszewky 1999; Sparrow 2006; Yang 2009). A product of its time, however, it had definite limits. Harlan's "antiracism" was one within the boundaries of white supremacy, one for *legal* equality that he was certain would not upset but safeguard white dominance: "The white race deems itself to be the dominant race in this country. And so it is in prestige, in achievements, in education, in wealth and in power. So, I doubt not, it will continue to be for all time if it remains true to its great heritage and holds fast to the principles of constitutional liberty."[101]

Harlan's opinion was firmly anchored to the notion of equal *citizenship*, and his temporal comparison of the plight of Blacks led to a second comparison. His discussion of Blacks' *Dred Scott* past and *Plessy* future segued to a timeless contempt for the Chinese:

There is a race so different from our own that we do not permit those belonging to it to become citizens of the United States. Persons belonging to it are, with few exceptions, absolutely excluded from our country. I allude to the Chinese race. But, by the statute in question, a Chinaman can ride in the same passenger coach with white citizens of the United States, while citizens of the black race in Louisiana, many of whom, perhaps, risked their lives for the preservation of the Union, who are entitled, by law, to participate in the political control of the State and nation, who are not excluded, by law or by reason of their race, from public stations of any kind, and who have all the legal rights that belong to white citizens, are yet declared to be criminals, liable to imprisonment, if they ride in a public coach occupied by citizens of the white race.[102]

The Louisiana law that the decision upheld, mandating racial segregation of railway trains, did not mention the Chinese; nor did it indicate to which of "the white, and colored races" they belonged; nor did it confine its purview to citizens (*Revised Laws of Louisiana* 1897: 762–63). Yet in discussing the subjection of Blacks, Harlan evidently felt compelled to do all three.[103]

Toward the beginning of his dissent, Harlan wrote, "While there may be in Louisiana persons of different races who are not citizens of the United States, the words in the act 'white and colored races' necessarily include all citizens of the United States of both races residing in that State. So that we have before us a state enactment that compels, under penalties, the separation of the two races."[104] The initial clause of the first sentence—and the statute itself, with its ambiguous conjunctions and punctuation—was unclear on how many "races" there were, but by the end of the sentence, Harlan definitively settled on two and equated "colored" with Black. He also narrowed the scope of the case to "citizens" and then further narrowed the scope to "citizens of . . . both races": constitutional protections were for U.S. state members only, and U.S. state membership included two and only two "races," Black and white. The tragedy, from his vantage point, was that the U.S. state would permit and abet the maintenance of racial distinction and inequality between these two categories of citizens. But he saw no contradiction between this "color-blind" jurisprudence and his acceptance and advocacy of other racial distinctions and inequalities, namely those concerning the Chinese (Yang 2009). That persons "belonging to [the Chinese race] are, with few exceptions, absolutely excluded from our country" was how it should be. Likewise for their inability to "become citizens." What rankled was that the "few" Chinese who were in the country would be able to "ride in the same passenger coach with white citizens," while Black citizens could not. For Harlan, the Chinese quintessentially constituted the *citizen*'s racial other—two mutually exclusive categories. In this light, Harlan's remarks on the Chinese in *Plessy* were hardly a throwaway digression at odds with his otherwise commendable antiracism, but spoke to a vital component of a coherent racism that prefigured his, and only one other justice's, unwillingness to recognize even the birthright citizenship of U.S.-born Chinese two years later in *Wong Kim Ark* (Levinson 2001; Yang 2009).[105] The difference between Harlan and the other justices was not that he was antiracist and they were racist, but that he and they drew, at the dawn of the twentieth century, the "color line,—the relation of the darker to the lighter races of men [sic] in Asia and Africa, in America and the islands of the sea"—differently in relation to U.S. citizenry and empire (Du Bois [1903] 1965: 221; Chin 1996; Thomas 2001).

CONCLUSION

Dred Scott v. Sandford was of a piece with the U.S. Constitution; naturalization laws; the Missouri Compromise; treaties with American Indians, France, Spain, and Mexico; *Johnson v. M'Intosh*; *United States v. Rogers*; Reconstruction Amendments; *Plessy v. Ferguson*; *United States v. Wong Kim Ark*; *Downes v. Bidwell*, *Dorr v. United States*, and other *Insular Cases*; *Boumediene v. Bush*; and more. The racial subjection, colonial and noncolonial, and fates of Blacks, American Indians, Mexicans, Chinese, Puerto Ricans, Filipinas/os, Samoans, Chamoru, and others were interlinked. So were the constructions of politically unequal spaces, including states, incorporated and unincorporated territories, and Indian reservations. Clear and stable demarcations between metropole and colony, domestic and foreign, citizen and subject, and colonized and other imperial subjects proved impossible, made impossible by the very efforts to clarify and stabilize them. Of course, this chapter only begins to touch on issues of race, geography, and citizenship in relation to one institution of the

U.S. empire-state; it does not broach the practices of other state actors, much less those beyond the state. But even with this simplified, myopic scope, we can glimpse the U.S. empire-state's complex structure of racial rule, a unified but differentiated field in which a tremor or quake in one area can set off intended and unintended aftershocks in others.

In a different context, Andreas Wimmer and Nina Glick Schiller warn of the pitfalls of "methodological nationalism," the pervasive, unquestioning "naturalization of the nation-state by the social sciences":

We have identified three variants of methodological nationalism: (1) ignoring or disregarding the fundamental importance of nationalism for modern societies; this is often combined with (2) naturalization—i.e., taking for granted that the boundaries of the nation-state delimit and define the unit of analysis; and (3) territorial limitation which confines the study of social processes to the political and geographic boundaries of a particular nation-state. (2003: 576–78)

In Pierre Bourdieu's terms, the variants are all a part of the dominant social-scientific *habitus*. When the object of analysis is the United States, we need to also recognize the unreflexive methodological meta-nationalism involved: a figment of U.S. nationalism, the nation-state has never been. The *illusion* of the nation-state, rather than the nation-state itself, is what is naturalized, and the *reality* of the U.S. empire-state is what is just as habitually denied.[106]

An empire-state approach has manifold theoretical and empirical implications. Frederick Cooper (2005) incisively explores many of them for the far-flung interdisciplinary field of colonial studies. I turn my attention to a relatively neglected tract of that field, the sociology of the United States. Overall, methodological nationalism simply can no longer operate as habitus, which, if taken seriously, has the potential to unsettle the entire discipline. In the sociology of race, a literature mostly segregated from colonial studies, an empire-state approach would expose the inadequacy of the standard practice of focusing on one particular white-nonwhite relation of domination at a time within the borders of a nonexistent nation-state, and questions of empire, absent since the demise of theories of internal colonialism, would rightly return to prominence. We would be more open and better positioned to discern connections between histories of racial subjection that have been treated as more or less discrete, especially between those of colonized and noncolonized peoples of color, *and* to make sense of the qualitative differences between them. Silence concerning the indigenous peoples of North America and the Pacific would be, one hopes, too deafening to persist. Heretofore all but ignored except in relation to racial categorization and the census, the racial state could no longer be overlooked and could be theorized on a firmer footing. And familiar topics could be seen from a fresh critical angle. For example, given the extraordinary rise, size, and racial character of the carceral state, prisons and the incarcerated (and the formerly incarcerated) could be seen for what they are: imperial spaces and subjects. What about "aliens," who, like territorial inhabitants and American Indians, are still subject to congressional plenary power? Are they citizens-in-waiting of this supposed nation of immigrants, or are many, especially the undocumented of color, subjects indefinitely without rights that the state and its citizens are bound to respect? How distinct is the line between citizen and subject, and how is it drawn?

For the sociology of the U.S. empire, an empire-state approach would open up this small but growing field. Temporally, the entire history of the United States awaits, not only the undeniably important turns of the twentieth and twenty-first centuries but also the turn of the nineteenth century and all other periods. Geographically, we need to correct for our hyperopia, obviously not to impair our improving capacity to see faraway overseas but to enhance our ability to see nearby overland. The constituent states of the Union and "incorporated" territories have not been politically homogeneous spaces to be classified unproblematically as the "metropole," coextensive with what has been misrecognized as the nation-state.[107] On a related note, U.S. colonialism and (nonterritorial) imperialism have not been serial moments but concurrent ones, which can go unnoticed if we look only overseas. The U.S. empire-state has always produced overlapping and competing temporalities and geographies, and we would be well advised not to accept the official ones, such as the notion that contemporary United States is a postcolonial nation-state. Finally, an empire-state approach to the United States would bridge the counterproductive divide between the sociologies of race and empire.[108] The imperial subjections of noncolonized peoples, usually the province of the former, and of colonized peoples, usually the province of the latter, form a unified but differentiated field of white supremacy that calls for critical and innovative research, and praxis, across existing boundaries.

People are always consoling me by pointing out that if one thinks of this country as an enormous hall, well, everybody got here, and they had to stand in line, and you know that by and by, standing in line, I'll get to the banquet table too. Well, of course, I got here first, and I helped to cook the food.

James Baldwin, "From *Nationalism, Colonialism, and the United States*"

CHAPTER 4

THE RACIAL UNCONSCIOUS OF ASSIMILATION THEORIES

If the problem of the twentieth century was the problem of the color line, the sociological answer of the twentieth century was assimilation. It was not the only answer, but it was the main, mainstream one. Ascendant in the early decades, assimilation theory thrived well into the postwar era. In a 1983 literature review of the preceding decades, Charles Hirschman observed that "the assimilation model has been the dominant perspective in sociological studies of ethnic relations." Even when the studies did "not draw formally upon assimilation theory," he found "almost always an implicit, if not always explicitly stated, hypothesis that trends will show a moderation of differences between ethnic populations" (Hirschman 1983: 399, 412).

By the time of Hirschman's assessment, however, assimilation theory as theory had been languishing. It might have still facilitated a steady accretion of empirical research but hardly shaped innovation. Then, rather quickly, U.S. social science experienced a robust "return of assimilation," according to Rogers Brubaker: "Since about 1985, . . . one can discern a renewed theoretical concern with assimilation in the scholarly literature" (2004: 125). The resurgence of international migration to the United States, especially following the Immigration and Nationality Act of 1965, spurred the theoretical reinvigoration of assimilation, as did periodic challenges from rivals (e.g., pluralism, transnationalism) and exaggerated reports of its demise, often anticipatory self-reports. Refocused more narrowly on immigration and immigrants and less broadly on the "color line," assimilation became, once again, the most important and dynamic theoretical approach for analyzing the lives of migrants and their offspring in the United States. As Mary Waters and Tomás Jiménez proclaimed, sounding the recurrent note of return, "The concept of assimilation, which played such a great role in understanding the experiences of European immigrants, is once again center stage" (2005: 826; see also Kivisto 2005).[1]

Assimilation theories of the past three decades are self-consciously and qualitatively different from their predecessors. Not only do they deal with new populations, notably recent migrants from Latin America, Asia, and the Caribbean and their descendants, but they also acknowledge earlier conceptual failings and propose significant modifications to overcome them. Most of all, the new theories no longer conceive of assimilation as necessarily destined or desirable. Though initially lagging, empirical research is now assessing and substantiating the theoretical developments; assimilation is, by all accounts, a multigenerational phenomenon, and only recently has the second generation of the new migrants begun to reach adulthood in large numbers.

There are currently two main strands of assimilation theory. What I refer to as neoclassical theory argues that, on the whole, assimilation continues to take place, with recent migrants and successive generations, like those at the turn of the last century, entering the "mainstream" of U.S. society. Segmented assimilation theory asserts that, unlike for European migrants of the past, there are now multiple possible paths of incorporation: upward mobility, not only through straightforward assimilation but also through selective retention of ethnicity, and downward mobility through assimilation into the "underclass."

My purpose is not to detail the empirical findings that address the debates within and between the two strands.[2] Nor do I assess the theories on their own terms and propose an alternative theory of assimilation. Instead, I examine some of the key taken-for-granted assumptions and habits of thought of this theoretical discourse. In particular, I analyze how race figures in the recent theories. I first summarize and underscore the innovations of neoclassical and segmented assimilation theories. I then undertake a detailed critique of their treatment of race. I conclude with a proposal for reorienting our theoretical approach to the politics of national belonging.

THE NEW WAVE OF ASSIMILATION THEORIES

Neoclassical Assimilation

Pioneering a revival, perhaps no scholars are as explicit, ambitious, or successful in their effort to restore the theoretical respectability and viability of assimilation as Richard Alba and Victor Nee, on whose work I focus here (1997, 2003; see also Alba 1995; Alba, Kasinitz, and Waters 2011; Bean and Stevens 2003; Brubaker 2004; Jacoby 2004; Kasinitz et al. 2008; Kazal 1995; Kivisto 2005; Morawska 1994; Pew Research Center 2013). They position their theory, though revisionist in many respects, squarely within the original assimilation tradition of the Chicago school: "Despite the accuracy of some of the criticisms of the canonical formulation of assimilation, we believe that there is still a vital core to the concept, which has not lost its utility for illuminating many of the experiences of contemporary immigrants and the new second generation" (Alba and Nee 2003: 9).

Alba and Nee (2003: 2–6, 15) identify several features that made previous versions of assimilation theory objectionable. There is a more or less strong current of ethnocentrism in the classical accounts, with middle-class Protestant whites as the normative reference category. Assimilation is assumed to be inexorable: it may take longer for some than others, but given enough time, it will happen. It is thought to be a unidirectional process of becoming assimilated *into* the dominant category. Not only inexorable and unidirectional, it is also seen as desirable. In other words, the old theories are not only descriptive but prescriptive. Finally, the potentially "positive" aspects of migrant ethnicity, like upward economic mobility through ethnic networks and niches, are not adequately considered.

To avoid these pitfalls, Alba and Nee redefine *assimilation* more neutrally as "the decline of an ethnic distinction and its corollary cultural and social differences."[3] Though not apparent in this catholic wording that could be about the lessening salience of *any* ethnic boundary, they are almost wholly concerned with the one between the "mainstream," more precisely the "American mainstream," and "minority individuals and groups" (2003: 11). What exactly do they mean by the *American mainstream?*

[It] encompasses a core set of interrelated institutional structures and organizations regulated by rules and practices that weaken, even undermine, the influence of ethnic origins per se. . . . A useful way of defining the mainstream is as that part of the society *within* which ethnic and racial origins have at most minor impacts on life chances or opportunities. (Alba and Nee 2003: 12; emphasis in original)

The authors explain that this definition does not require the equality of life chances within the mainstream in general but only with respect to ethnic and racial origins. For example, the mainstream comprises the entire range of social classes, from the poor to the wealthy, and the obvious inequality of life chances they imply. Assimilation therefore does not necessarily entail entry into the middle class, as many other theorists suppose. Further, race and ethnicity can still be "powerful determinants of opportunities in the society as a whole, particularly when those outside the mainstream are compared to those in it" (p. 12). Open to the possibility of the mainstream itself being transformed, Alba and Nee do not assert that assimilation is a one-way process; nor do they claim that assimilation is inevitable. They also consciously seek to suppress the normative impulses of the "canonical" literature—"assimilation without 'assimilationism,'" as Brubaker (2004: 125) puts it.

The most original theoretical contribution of Alba and Nee is that they specify the causal mechanisms that generate assimilation, something many past theorists, including the well-regarded Milton Gordon (1964), failed to do. At the individual level, they assume that everyone engages in *purposive action*, pursuing rational self-interest but, per the new institutionalism, as figured by "cultural beliefs." Moreover, the agents' rational choices are limited by "incomplete information," finite "cognitive capacity," and institutional opportunities and constraints. In this "context-bound" manner, migrants' and their descendants' practical quest for better jobs, education, places to live, and so on often leads to assimilation, mostly without their conscious intent and even against it (Alba and Nee 2003: 37–39). *Network mechanisms* refer to the ways in which "ethnic minorities," especially in hostile environments, "monitor and enforce norms of cooperation" toward collective "welfare maximization." For example, networks vitally facilitate labor migration and ethnic economies (p. 43). Besides network resources, or *social capital*, Alba and Nee point to other *forms of capital*, namely financial and human, that impinge upon the adaptation patterns of migrants and their progeny (p. 46). *Institutional mechanisms* provide the final piece in explaining assimilation. In relation to other theorists, Alba and Nee downplay, without discounting, the importance of economic growth. Above all, they emphasize the importance of "institutional changes," the two most significant of which are, in the wake of the Civil Rights Movement, the "monitoring and enforcing [of] federal rules [that] have increased the cost of discrimination in nontrivial ways" and racism's loss of "public legitimacy" resulting from "changes in values" (pp. 54, 57).

Before empirically testing this theory for the contemporary wave of migration to the United States, Alba and Nee reexamine the prewar migration from Europe and East Asia. Looking at various indicators, such as socioeconomic status and intermarriage patterns, they conclude that assimilation has indeed been the "master trend, and for the majority of whites and Asians descended from the earlier era of mass immigration, ethnicity does mean considerably less than it did a generation or two ago" (Alba and Nee 2003: 101). The precise mechanisms of this master trend are hard to nail down, they concede, because research interest dipped in the middle decades of the twentieth century, leaving us with relatively clear "before" and "after" pictures but only a few blurry ones in between. Nonetheless, the authors highlight three factors in relation to this hazy time period, when a majority of the early migrants' children came of age, that generally confirm their model: "social mobility" through expanding opportunities, and concomitant incentives for assimilation, in employment, education, and residence; "cultural change" in the mainstream toward accepting the previously excluded; and "institutional changes stemming partly from collective action by the ethnics themselves," for example, with regard to admission to elite colleges (p. 120).

Alba and Nee then turn their attention to the postwar migration, particularly since the 1965 Hart-Celler Act removed the national origins quotas that had been in place for four decades. They choose to "focus . . . on the non-European groups, for they are thought to represent the hard test for assimilation" (2003: 184). Marshaling an impressive array of data on "linguistic assimilation," "socioeconomic attainments," "spatial patterns," and "social relations," Alba and Nee conclude that "assimilation remains a potent force affecting immigrant groups in the United States" (pp. 217, 230, 248, 260, 267). There are potential exceptions to this pattern. Some "labor migrants"—as opposed to "human-capital migrants" with high levels of education and skills—stagnate socioeconomically by the third generation. And residential integration and intermarriage with whites are more open to Asians and "light-skinned Latinos" than others. Nevertheless, they argue that assimilation remains the dominant pattern.

Segmented Assimilation

Neoclassical assimilation theory is, in part, a rejoinder to the more pessimistic interpretations that arose in the late 1980s and the 1990s. Although not all of the latter identify explicitly with the segmented assimilation framework, they all share a certain apprehension about the future prospects of a sizable segment of contemporary migrants and especially their offspring. In the fittingly titled article "Second-Generation Decline," Herbert Gans (1992: 173) worries "that a significant number of the children of poor immigrants, especially dark-skinned ones, might not obtain jobs in the mainstream economy." Speculating "about the unknown future," he fears that "they—Vietnamese and other Asian-Americans, Salvadorans and other Central and Latin Americans, as well as Haitians and others from the Caribbean, Africa and elsewhere—may join blacks, and the Puerto Rican, Mexican and other 'Hispanics', who came to the cities at an earlier time, as well as 'Anglos' (in some places) as excluded from, or marginal to, the economy" (Gans 1992: 174, 176). The combination of an unfavorable economy, with no sustained growth and declining demand for unskilled labor, and intractable racial discrimination against nonwhites, particularly those with dark skin, may keep many of the second generation in poverty. Prefiguring a major tenet of the segmented assimilation theory, Gans (1992: 183) foresees the possibility of "an early convergence between the present American poor and some second-generation poor."

The segmented assimilation theory, as first put forth by Alejandro Portes and Min Zhou (1993: 82), outlines three main "distinct forms of adaptation" for today's second generation: "growing acculturation and parallel integration into the white middle-class"; "permanent poverty and assimilation into the underclass"; and "rapid economic advancement with deliberate preservation of the immigrant community's values and tight solidarity." To explain the early stage of this refraction of adaptation experiences, Portes and Rubén Rumbaut point to three sets of "background factors" that bear on migration and initial settlement: "individual features," "mode of incorporation," and "family structure." Migrants' "individual features," including financial resources and human capital (education, job skills and experience, and language proficiency), have an obvious impact on their socioeconomic prospects. "Mode of incorporation" refers to the "contextual factors" that enable and constrain the migrants' deployment of their individual characteristics and resources: governmental policies toward migrants that can range from "exclusion" to "passive acceptance" to "active encouragement"; receptiveness of the "native population," especially the level of racial prejudice; and support from coethnics, which is contingent largely on the size and class composition of the ethnic community. Finally, Portes and Rumbaut posit that "the composition of the immigrant family, in particular the extent to which it includes both biological parents," can have significant impact on how the second generation fares (2001b: 46–49, 63).

The next part of the adaptation experience concerns intergenerational patterns of acculturation, or cultural assimilation, that can affect parental authority. What Portes and Rumbaut see as critical is the relative pace of acculturation between the migrant and second generations. Most likely among those migrants with substantial human capital, *consonant acculturation* happens when both generations acquire the language and customs of the "host" society and lose those of the "home" society at a similarly rapid rate. In *dissonant acculturation*, the children substantially outpace their parents. When both generations are "embedded in a co-ethnic community of sufficient size and institutional diversity," *selective acculturation* may occur, as the speed of assimilation is slowed and the children retain some of the parents' "culture." Portes and Rumbaut contend that dissonant acculturation undermines parental authority, putting the second generation "at risk." Consonant acculturation, on the other hand, allows parents to maintain authority over their children and enables both generations to face obstacles, such as discrimination, together. Selective acculturation affords another layer of support, as families can draw on the coethnic community of which they are an integral part (Portes and Rumbaut 2001b: 53–54).

With the diverse resources and constraints brought to bear by background factors and intergenerational patterns of acculturation, the second generation negotiates three "contextual source[s]" of "vulnerability to downward assimilation," two of which coincide with those Gans mentions. First, unlike those of European migrants of the turn of the twentieth century who were "uniformly white," the children of contemporary Asian, Black, and "mestizo" migrants face a formidable racial barrier. Second, because of "national deindustrialization and global industrial restructuring," the working-class part of the second generation enjoys fewer opportunities for social mobility than they did a half-century ago, as better-paying manufacturing jobs have disappeared or moved overseas, leaving an increasingly bifurcated "hourglass economy" in their wake. Finally, because migrants tend to live in large cities, there is a third source of vulnerability: contact with the "adversarial subculture developed by marginalized native youths" (Portes and Zhou 1993: 76, 83).

Among the migrant populations considered by Portes and Rumbaut (2001a, 2001b), Filipinas/os represent a case of relatively swift assimilation into the middle class, enabled by high levels of human capital and families with two biological parents to avoid most, if not all, of the hazards faced by the second generation. On the other end of the spectrum, many migrants arrive with few personal, familial, or coethnic resources and encounter hostile policies and society. Children not only assimilate faster than their parents, but into the "culture" of the native-born poor. Mexicans, Nicaraguans, Haitians, and West Indians frequently serve as examples of this downward assimilation (Portes and Rumbaut 2001a). Facilitated by entrepreneurial skills, favorable policies, low levels of discrimination, and a large and cohesive coethnic community, Cubans, particularly those who arrived before 1980 and their children, exemplify upward assimilation through selective acculturation. Of unique importance is an "institutionally diversified ethnic community" that can aid families in shielding and fostering the second generation (Portes and Rumbaut 2001b: 275; see also Portes and Stepick 1993; Portes and Zhou 1993). Even among migrant populations with lower levels of human capital and/or less active assistance from the government, tight families and ethnic communities can clear similar paths of controlled assimilation that can steer the second generation away from the dangers of downward assimilation. The Vietnamese in New Orleans and Punjabi Sikhs in California are proffered as examples (Gibson 1989; Portes and Zhou 1993; Zhou and Bankston 1994, 1998).

THE RACIAL UNDERTOW OF
ASSIMILATION THEORIES

Both the neoclassical and segmented assimilation theories introduce significant innovations to make sense of the current wave of migration to the United

States that is dissimilar in important ways, such as place of origin and class composition, from the last great wave and to overcome the conceptual deficiencies of earlier theories of assimilation that it inspired. Specifically with regard to race, Alba and Nee stress the consequential institutional changes that the Civil Rights Movement wrought, and Portes and colleagues chart the different routes, in large part because of racial discrimination, that assimilation can take. For all of their advances, however, the new assimilation theories do not adequately account for race. As the inadequacies inhere in implicit assumptions as much as in explicit analyses, I suggest that they call for a thorough rethinking of research on migrant settlement.

The reclamation of *assimilation*, for Brubaker, starts with the term itself. He recognizes that "transitive" and "organic" everyday definitions of the word reflect some of the old flaws of assimilation theory (2004: 119). In the *Oxford English Dictionary*, the first definition given for *assimilate* is a transitive one: "To make like *to*, cause to resemble" (emphasis in original). Other transitive definitions additionally have a decidedly organic bent. For example, the one cited by Brubaker reads, "To convert into a substance of its own nature, as the bodily organs convert food into blood, and thence into animal tissue; to take in and appropriate as nourishment; to absorb into the system, incorporate."[4] Echoing past theories, practices, and policies of assimilation, these transitive and organic meanings connote normative prescriptions, advocating and even forcing assimilation, and ethnocentrism, evoking Anglo-conformist images of complete conversion. Therefore, Brubaker calls for retaining only the abstract, intransitive sense of the word: "to become similar" (2004: 119, 129). It is in this sense, purged of unwanted denotations and connotations, that most revivalists of assimilation now employ the concept.[5]

Compared to the "classical" notions of assimilation, the semantic contraction is undoubtedly an improvement. Nevertheless, I argue that it may not be much better suited to contend with questions of race. In part, the word itself continues to pose conceptual difficulties, because the problem lies not only with marginal, discardable meanings of assimilation but its very core. Even shed of its transitive, organic meanings, it remains, in etymology and usage, rooted in the idea of similarity. No theorist of assimilation would disagree, and there appears to be, at first glance, little that is disagreeable. What is objectionable about *similarity* becomes clearer, however, when approached from the reverse

angle. What constitutes the absence or opposite of similarity? *Difference*—
which is the premise for Brubaker's "return" thesis: the "massive *differential-
ist* turn in social thought, public discourse, and public policy" is what we are
ostensibly returning from (2004: 117; emphasis added). In fact, the similarity/
difference binary or continuum undergirds the entire assimilation literature: to
assimilate is to become less different.[6] For instance, as noted above, Alba and
Nee redefine assimilation as "the decline of ethnic distinction and its corollary social and cultural *differences*"; the differences give an ethnic distinction
its "concrete significance" (2003: 11; emphasis added). *Inequality*, however, is
neither an antonym for similarity nor a synonym for difference. The same goes
for *domination*. Inequality and domination do produce and may even presuppose difference, but to examine inequality and domination *as* difference risks
mischaracterization or, worse, trivialization. And if the sociological literature
on race agrees on anything, it is that race is fundamentally about inequality
and domination.[7] Assimilation, then, would seem to be a mismatched conceptual tool with which to dissect racial dynamics. To be clear, I am not arguing
that assimilation theories wholly ignore race or that they do not at all address
inequality and domination. Rather, the concept of assimilation instills analytical tendencies to approach racial inequality and domination from an oblique
angle that misses and distorts, as well as illuminates.

Though exceptional in its inclusion of non-European migrants and its
reconsideration of European migrants in light of recent historical studies on
whiteness, Alba and Nee's analysis of prewar migration nevertheless turns out
to be a case in point. As Waters and Jiménez (2005: 106) summarize, "A number of scholars have noted that both popular and scholarly notions of what
constitutes success for post-1965 immigrants to the United States are either
implicitly or explicitly comparative with the experiences of immigrants who
came in the last mass immigration between 1880 and 1920." For nearly all,
the comparison is specifically between the *European* migration of the earlier
wave and the *non-European* migration of the contemporary wave. For example,
segmented assimilation theorists make the comparison to argue that many
contemporary non-European migrants and their children face a much more
perilous situation than did their European predecessors: today's migrants and
second generation, being nonwhite, confront daunting racial barriers, and the
increasingly deindustrialized economy offers ever fewer opportunities for the

unskilled.[8] There is an obvious demographic reason for this methodological penchant: a large majority of the early migrants were from Europe, and a large majority of contemporary migrants are not.[9] But, in addition to the significant minority of non-European migrants in the past and the significant minority of European migrants in the present, there are good reasons to break the habit. The historical contexts of the two migration waves are radically different.[10] Then, overlaying the historical difference coterminously with the difference in origin, European versus non-European, renders the comparison dubious: what meaningful inferences could be derived from such a conflated research design?

Alba and Nee (2003: x) also "compare the experience of [the] two major waves of immigrants to the United States and their descendants." But they add a promising twist. In their examination of the earlier wave, they include two groups of non-European origin: the Chinese and the Japanese. The promise, however, is betrayed by three analytical choices that, through the application of the assimilation concept, obfuscate racial inequalities and domination. First, Alba and Nee's focus on *East* Asians is crucial for whom it omits. It leaves out the third major stream of prewar migration from Asia: Filipinas/os.[11] Although the history of Filipinas/os is relatively less well documented, what we do know indicates that its "master trend" was hardly assimilation. Racialized as more inferior than other Asians and indefinitely relegated to mostly unskilled labor, particularly in agriculture, prewar Filipina/o migrants did not enjoy the upward social mobility that their Chinese and Japanese counterparts did. For example, in 1959, Filipino men earned $3,649 on average, while the comparable figures for all, Japanese, Chinese, and Black men were $5,308, $4,761, $4,034, and $3,740, respectively (Ong and Azores 1994: 127). Only with the post-1965 migration of middle-class Filipinas/os did they begin to be touted as exemplars of assimilation.

Second, Alba and Nee incorporate the experiences of prewar Chinese and Japanese migrants and their descendants too seamlessly into the same assimilation narrative as their European contemporaries. They begin their analysis at the end of the story, presenting the largely affirmative data, from the close of the twentieth century, on acculturation, socioeconomic parity, residential integration, intermarriage and "mixed" offspring, and shifts in ethnic identity among third- and later-generation descendants of migrants from the late nineteenth and early twentieth centuries (Alba and Nee 2003: 71–98). Then, as noted earlier, they surmise, based on admittedly limited secondary sources, the mechanisms that begat this "master trend": institutional and cultural changes in the mid-twentieth century that opened up opportunities (Alba and Nee 2003: 101). But this explanation oversimplifies: it projects the "effect" backwards in time and transfigures earlier inequalities between Europeans and Asians differing in kind into ones differing in degree. If we were to begin at the beginning, the "master trend" of assimilation would be far from evident. A cursory glance at just the formal practices enacted or sanctioned by the state, for example, would quickly reveal the *qualitatively* harsher treatments of the Chinese and the Japanese based on race that affected each and every aspect of "assimilation" until as late as the 1960s: segregated schools, denial of naturalized citizenship, alien land laws, mass internment in concentration camps, restrictive covenants, antimiscegenation laws, and so on. While third- and fourth-generation Chinese and Japanese may now resemble their European-origin counterparts in many respects, retrofitting a common "assimilation" narrative necessarily minimizes the racial inequalities and oppression the Chinese and the Japanese endured and resisted and necessarily confounds what were racially disparate historical trajectories.[12] It is a subtle, unregistered form of teleology.

Finally, just as they blur the racial inequalities between European and non-European migrants from the turn of the last century, Alba and Nee also emphasize the continuity between the two major waves of migration. They remind us that assimilation was not as easy and assured for the earlier wave as it is commonly portrayed by students of the contemporary wave. Drawing on findings in the burgeoning historical literature on whiteness, they question the stark racial contrast made by segmented assimilation theorists between the mostly "white" migration of the past and the mostly nonwhite migration of the present.[13] Alba and Nee take note that the "whiteness" of many early European migrants was not a given but an attainment.[14] The historical formation of whiteness thus serves as an example of how racial boundaries can fall away, from which they derive a direct implication for today's nonwhite migrants: "We see no a priori reason why a shift in the perception of racial difference could not take place for some contemporary immigrant groups and some segments of others. . . . [namely] new Asian groups and light-skinned Latinos." In this way, white racial formation is smoothly folded into the narrative of assimilation: "as these [disparaged European] groups climbed the socioeconomic ladder and mixed residentially with other whites, their perceived distinctiveness from the majority faded" (Alba and Nee 2003: 132). But, precisely because they read the scholarship on whiteness through the concept of assimilation, they blunt one of its cardinal points: whiteness has been, above all, a racial formation that presupposed and reproduced relations of inequality and domination between "whites" and their racial others (e.g., Guglielmo 2003; Jacobson 1998; Roediger 1991, 2005; Saxton 1971). The point is not that European migrants and native-born whites became similar, which they did, but that becoming similar, including "climb[ing] the socioeconomic ladder and mix[ing] residentially with other whites" (Alba and Nee 2003: 132), entailed perpetuating racial inequality and domination in relation to Blacks, the Chinese, and others.[15] It is telling that the concept of assimilation hardly figures in studies of whiteness, despite the obvious shared research interest in European migrants (Kazal 1995).

The narrow reading of the historical research on whiteness, obscuring racial inequalities and domination, overlaps with a ubiquitous, unreflexive practice of assimilation research of the past three decades: the absence of explicit analysis of native-born, or nonmigrant, Blacks. The absence is partly interrelated with a fairly recent divergence within sociology. Up to the mid-1980s, the sociologies of immigration and of race were overlying fields of inquiry. For instance, Hirschman's (1983) review of the literature on assimilation took for granted that both native-born and migrant minorities were populations to be examined, and it discussed alternative theoretical approaches that were also prominent in the sociology of race (e.g., split labor market, internal colonialism). Conversely, one of the major theoretical frameworks that Michael Omi and Howard Winant (1986) addressed in their influential book on racial formation was the "ethnicity paradigm," which largely examined migrant experiences. Since then, however, the two fields have drifted apart. On the whole, assimilation theories, now ensconced in the sociology of immigration, no longer encompass native-born Blacks within their purview. Yet African Americans continue to shape and haunt assimilation theories.

According to neoclassical assimilation theory, native-born whites were and are implicitly a part of the "mainstream," and the indications are that most migrants and their progeny did and continue to become a part of it. Aside from a relatively small number of migrants and their descendants, who is then shut out of the mainstream? In short, Blacks. In the past, from the Chicago school of the early twentieth century to the mid-1980s, assimilation theory treated African Americans as a population to be studied and made sense of within its framework. But by the last two decades of the twentieth century, African Americans have been cast as the exception, largely conceded to be unassimilated.[16] Whether intentionally or not, neoclassical assimilation theory salvages *assimilation* by pushing out nonmigrant Blacks and focusing on "immigration," a notion capacious enough to accommodate many generations of native-born descendants of non-Black migrants.[17] In other words, whereas assimilation theory used to squeeze African Americans into the scope of analysis, it now squeezes them out. According to Alba and Nee (2003), though never stated straightforwardly, Blacks have been, are presently, and most likely will be the mainstream's archetypal "other." While they may lament the prospect of Blacks' continued exclusion from the mainstream and also speculate on a more optimistic scenario, Blacks are nonetheless not a part of their empirical analysis: befitting the metaphor of the mainstream from which they are excluded, native-born Blacks appear almost entirely in the conclusion, but not in the substantive chapters, of Alba and Nee's book.[18]

The exclusion of native-born Blacks from the analysis is symptomatic of neoclassical assimilation theory's inattention to the unequal *relations* between the mainstream and the nonmainstream. If the mainstream is "that part of the society *within* which ethnic and racial origins have at most minor impact on life chances or opportunities" (Alba and Nee 2003: 12; emphasis in original), we can infer that "ethnic and racial origins" do have major impacts elsewhere. There are two possibilities: between the mainstream and the nonmainstream, and among the nonmainstream. Alba and Nee rightly see the former as more significant in terms of life chances: "particularly when those outside the mainstream are *compared to* those within it" (2003: 12; emphasis added). I stress "compared to," because the wording is revealing: the concept of assimilation invites, perhaps requires, *comparisons* to measure the degree of similarity but does not necessarily encourage discerning asymmetric *relations*. Specifically, they do not seriously consider the possibility that what goes on within the mainstream bears a relation to what goes on between it and the nonmainstream, that why and how race and ethnicity do not matter on the inside may be related to—may, in fact, be dependent on—why and how they do matter between the inside and the outside. Neither do they seriously consider the possibility that outsiders' becoming a part of the mainstream may require them to participate in keeping out others, especially Blacks. These possibilities are precisely the aspect of the historical scholarship on whiteness that assimilation theories neglect.

There are three layers of irony in relation to Blacks, only the first of which neoclassical assimilation theory recognizes. The "institutional mechanisms" that ostensibly facilitate assimilation—state enforcement of antidiscrimination policies and a steep decline in racism's "public legitimacy"—were brought about by the Black-led Civil Rights Movement but have been least effective for Blacks (Alba and Nee 2003: 57). The second irony is a reproduction of the first at the analytical level: neoclassical assimilation theory is aware of the significance of Blacks in forcing the institutional changes and the cruel injustice of Blacks' not benefiting from those changes as fully as others but, instead of placing this inequality at the center of its inquiry, *excludes* Blacks from the analysis.[19] Finally, although it was a mass social movement of those outside the mainstream, Blacks above all, that compelled the pivotal institutional changes, neoclassical assimilation theory has no *conceptual* room within it for explaining such movements or transformations; they are, in effect, historically unique *dei ex machina*.

Like its neoclassical counterpart, segmented assimilation theory is concerned with the assimilation patterns of migrants and their descendants, not of native-born Blacks. Nonetheless, Blacks figure more conspicuously in it—not as an absent presence so much as a marginal, and marginalized, presence. The theory features Blacks most visibly in one of its trimodal outcomes: "downward assimilation" in which some contemporary migrants—mostly those with few personal, familial, and coethnic resources—are immured in "permanent poverty" (Portes and Zhou 1993: 82, 83). For the second and presumably later generations, exposure to the native-born "underclass," in addition to racial discrimination and a deindustrializing economy, purportedly sets and keeps them on this track. Segmented assimilation theory, as Roger Waldinger and Cynthia Feliciano (2004: 377) point out, is not always forthright about who exactly belongs to this "underclass," but "it is not difficult to infer." At its core, the native-born "underclass" refers to poor urban Blacks, sometimes expanding to include similarly positioned Puerto Ricans and Mexicans.

In their mildly critical assessment of segmented assimilation theory, Alba and Nee write,

Yet the segmented assimilation concept risks essentializing central-city black culture in the image of the underclass, which the American mainstream views as the undeserving poor. This image overlooks the variety of cultural models found among urban African Americans and inflates the magnitude of the underclass population. To be sure, the black underclass may exercise a greater influence in shaping the cultural practices of the inner city than its relative size warrants. But the great majority of adult urban African Americans and Latinos hold down jobs, have families, and aspire to a better future for their children. . . . Thus, segmented assimilation, which has value in calling attention to an emergent social problem facing Afro-Caribbeans and arguably Mexicans and other Latinos, may predict an excessively pessimistic future for central-city minority youths. (2003: 8)

From the outskirts and outside of segmented assimilation theory, others voice similar reservations (Neckerman, Carter, and Lee 1999; Smith 2014; Waldinger and Feliciano 2004; Waters 1994, 1999). I think this criticism heads in the right direction but does not go far enough. Segmented assimilation theory not only *risks* essentializing but, in fact, does essentialize poor urban Blacks in the image of the "underclass." Contrary evidence is scant. I quote Alba and Nee at length to show how deeply taken-for-granted the concept of the "underclass" is in the assimilation literature, not only among segmented assimilation theorists but also among their supposed critics: the existence of the "underclass" is not put in question, just its size and the extent of its baneful influence.

Segmented assimilation theorists seldom, if ever, provide a definition of the "underclass." They may assume that it is unnecessary given their seemingly unmodified acceptance of the "underclass" literature from the 1980s and 1990s. William Julius Wilson's *The Truly Disadvantaged* is probably the most cited, and his definition of the "underclass" appears to capture what they mean by the term: "a large subpopulation of low-income families and individuals whose behavior contrasted sharply with the behavior of the general population. . . . inner-city joblessness, teenage pregnancy, out-of-wedlock births, female-headed families, welfare dependency, and serious crime" (1987: 3). As many have noted, *underclass* lacks conceptual coherence (e.g., Wacquant 1997): it does not refer to a class in any meaningful sense. Rather, what the unemployed, pregnant teenagers, the unmarried, non-nuclear families, recipients of public assistance, and criminals of this heterogeneous category have in common are "social pathologies": "behavior contrast[ing] sharply with that of mainstream America" (Wilson 1987: 6, 7).[20]

The lineage from the "underclass" literature, Wilson's work in particular, to segmented assimilation theory is quite direct. For example, Portes and Rumbaut (2001b: 59–60) write, "The result [of economic dislocation] was the rise of what Wacquant and Wilson [(1989)] have called the 'hyperghetto'—veritable human warehouses where the disappearance of work and the everyday reality of marginalization led directly to a web of social pathologies. Proliferation of female teenage pregnancy, high involvement of youngsters in crime, and the disappearance of work habits and discipline are common traits in these areas." The correspondence between theories of the "underclass" and segmented assimilation is not surprising. Both underscore the importance of political-economic forces, such as deindustrialization and a bifurcated labor market.[21] At the same time, they conceive of the "culture" (i.e., values, norms, behavior) of the "underclass" to be both a response to those forces *and*, echoing the "culture of poverty" thesis, a relatively autonomous force in its own right in producing detrimental outcomes.

In the scenario of "downward assimilation," segmented assimilation theory argues that the children of poor migrants who live in close proximity to "underclass" Blacks and others are liable to adopt their "deviant lifestyles" and fail to rise out of poverty (Portes and Rumbaut 2001a: 310). Because the second generation is still generally young, most research, until recently, centers on academic performance that stands in as a proxy for later trajectories (Portes and MacLeod 1996); follow-up studies empirically track the life courses to young adulthood, but there is little theoretical change (Haller, Portes, and Lynch 2011; Portes, Fernández-Kelly, and Haller 2005, 2009; Zhou and Xiong 2005). Here, segmented assimilation theory aligns with and draws on the anthropology of education of John Ogbu and colleagues.[22] Owing to the original "involuntary incorporation of blacks into American society" through enslavement and their "subsequent subordination and discriminatory treatment" by whites, African Americans, characteristic of "involuntary minorities," are subjected to inferior education, housing, and employment.[23] Discrimination does not, however, fully explain the "low school performance" of Blacks, which also results from how they respond to their oppression. They develop an "oppositional identity and cultural frame of reference" that devalues academic achievement and consequently simply do not try hard enough (Ogbu 1991a: 249, 259, 267). Ogbu argues that, although this oppositional stance partly reflects Black students' realistic perception of limited future opportunities, it takes on a "life of [its] own" (1991b: 446; quoted in Gould 1999: 177).[24] Others report similar findings among native-born Mexicans (Gibson 1989; Matute-Bianchi 1991).

Segmented assimilation theory is concerned with the effects of this "oppositional culture" of the "underclass" on the academic performance of children of migrants, which are posited to be entirely harmful. Portes and Zhou write that, for poor second-generation Haitians who attend Miami's "inner-city schools," a "common message [from their African American peers] is the devaluation of education as a vehicle for advancement of all Black youths, a message that directly contradicts the immigrant parents' expectations." While some Haitian students may successfully resist, most succumb to the "adversarial stance toward the white mainstream [that] is common among inner-city minority youths" and assimilate "not into mainstream culture but into the values and norms of the inner city" (1993: 81).[25] Tomás Rodríguez (2002) argues similarly about the negative impact of African Americans on the academic performance of Nicaraguan and Cuban youths in Miami. Although Waters (1994, 1999) herself is more circumspect with regard to the sway of "underclass" African Americans over second-generation West Indians in New York City, her work is regularly recruited to support the segmented assimilation theory's idea of "rapid assimilation into ghetto youth subcultures" (Zhou 1997: 79). In Zhou and Carl Bankston's (1994, 1998) study of poor second-generation Vietnamese in New Orleans, poor Blacks, who live nearby and attend the same schools, likewise appear as a potential source of peril. However, "intact families" and a tight-knit "ethnic community" enable the Vietnamese children "to receive high grades, to have definite college plans, and to score high on academic orientation," while only a minority of them fall prey to introjecting the "oppositional culture" of the Black "underclass" (Zhou and Bankston 1998: 81, 134; 1994: 821). For children of Mexican migrants, native-born Chicanas/os are ostensibly the primary source of the debilitating cultural influence (Gibson 1989; Matute-Bianchi 1991).

As critics note, second-generation "oppositional culture," past and present, does not require the influence of a native-born "underclass" to develop (Perlmann and Waldinger 1997), and native-born "whites as well as minorities engage in oppositional behaviors" (Kasinitz, Mollenkopf, and Waters 2002: 1031). In any case, with partial exceptions, advocates of segmented assimilation theory do not actually study African American and other native-born "underclass," the imputed source of cultural contamination (cf. Kasinitz, Mollenkopf, and Waters 2002; Kasinitz et al. 2008). It is more of a given than an object of their inquiry. They implicitly draw on and redraw the commonsensical, ominous image of the "underclass" that pervades not only U.S. society at large but social-scientific discourse, which marginalizes and racializes the very population whose marginalization and racialization it claims to analyze and even ameliorate through policy recommendations. Theoretical incoherence and empirical scarcity do not discourage but rather provide the conditions of possibility for unsubstantiated assertions about the "underclass."[26] In other words, not only do migrant parents see the native-born "underclass" as "a fait accompli conditioning their own and their children's chances for success" (Portes and Rumbaut 2001b: 61), so do many sociologists who study them. Consistently, normative, value-laden terms crop up in the rhetoric of segmented assimilation theory without comment or controversy. Aside from "underclass" itself, which is ubiquitous, words and phrases such as "pathologies" (Gans 1992: 174, 183; Portes, Fernández-Kelly, and Haller 2005: 1008; Portes and Rumbaut 2001b: 59; Zhou 1997: 80), "deviant lifestyles" (Portes and Rumbaut 2001b: 59; Portes, Fernández-Kelly, and Haller 2005: 1008, 1013 and 2009: 1080; Portes and Fernández-Kelly 2008: 14), "constructive forms of behavior," "traditional family values" (Zhou and Bankston 1994: 821), "maladaptation," "problem kids" (Zhou and Bankston 1998: 196), and "intact families" (Portes and Rumbaut 2001a: 313; Zhou 1997: 69; Zhou and Bankston 1994: 830) are summoned, all to the disadvantage of the Black, and sometimes other nonmigrant minority, urban poor.

Given the condemnation of "deviant lifestyles" and the exaltation of "intact families," "both biological parents," and "traditional family values," heteropatriarchal assumptions, not benign neglect, appear to underlie segmented assimilation theory's general silence on sexuality and gender (Donato et al. 2006; Manalansan 2006). A telling exception that demonstrates the rule, an opinion piece by Portes in the *Miami Herald*, published just a couple of years before his and Zhou's agenda-setting 1993 article on segmented assimilation, lays bare the assumptions. It is concerned with and about the "exaggerated estimates of social deviance, including homosexuality, imputed" to Cuban refugees from Mariel, stemming from, Portes surmises, "media images of the [refugee] camps [that] included the spectacle of blatant male homosexuality." He aims to disabuse the public of the notion that the then recent wave of refugees is "a uniformly deviant group," that "the common path followed by many members of this group [is] a homosexual career that ends with AIDS and death." Portes urges the reader to "remember that the majority of the new refugees . . . were just ordinary persons seeking a new life in the United States" and cites their high marriage rate as a reassuring "indicator of family ties that could facilitate social integration."[27]

If the Black "underclass" serves as a cauldron of contagious social ills, the "cultures" of migrants, largely regardless of whence they hail, are depicted explicitly and implicitly as the means to vaccinate them and their children. Just as the ways of the "underclass" are written about only in negative terms, those of migrants are held up in almost exclusively positive ones. Migrants bring with them or develop an array of virtues: hardworking, familially and coethnically cohesive, academically motivated, and so on. It is the protection and nurturance of these qualities that hold the most promise for migrants and their children, especially those with little financial or human capital. Segmented assimilation theory often emphasizes *social* capital—specifically "intact families" and coethnic networks—as much as or more than *cultural* values or norms, in an effort not to be confused with culture-of-poverty or cultural deprivation schools of thought. But when Zhou and Bankston (1994: 830) in their study of the Vietnamese in New Orleans, for example, extol "social capital, provided by their intact families," "the normative integration of families," and their community's "consensus over value and behavior standards" as enabling them to elude the pathologies of their unstudied Black neighbors, how different are the assumptions? Findings that underscore the importance of "strong adherence to traditional family values, strong commitment to a work ethic, and a high degree of personal involvement in the ethnic community" only further muddies the distinction segmented assimilation theory seeks to draw between the social and the cultural (Zhou and Bankston 1994: 821).[28]

Like assimilation theories of the past, segmented assimilation theory has a clear normative thrust. According to Portes and Rumbaut, "Despite the presence of large numbers of professionals and entrepreneurs in today's first generation, the majority of immigrants are still poor workers. The best chance for educational achievement and economic ascent among their children lies in selective acculturation": the path of measured assimilation through the retention of "a clear sense of their roots, the value of fluency in a second language, and the self-esteem grounded on strong family and community bonds" (2001a: 315–16; see also Portes and Fernández-Kelly 2008). The path to be avoided is downward assimilation into the "underclass" that results, in part, from insufficient defense against its cultural influences. In this theory, poor urban African Americans are both the cautionary tale and the ones who can drag poor migrants and their children into its plot, if they do not band together as families and ethnic communities.

Despite its explicit disavowals, neoclassical assimilation theory also harbors a normative desire, one for assimilation into the mainstream. After all, given their concept of the mainstream—"that part of society *within* which ethnic and racial origins have at most minor impacts on life chances or opportunities"—we should take with more than a grain of salt the claim that, in contrast to earlier assimilation theorists, Alba and Nee do not see assimilation (i.e., becoming a part of the mainstream) as "not only a 'normal' outcome . . . but also a beneficial one" (2003: 12, 15; emphasis in original).[29] Here, African Americans represent the outer limit of assimilation, in theory and practice: they are the unanalyzed quintessence of those shut out of the mainstream, past and present, if not necessarily in the future (Alba and Nee 2003: 290–91).

Both neoclassical and segmented assimilation theories are politically conservative in their assumptions and implications. What Zhou and Bankston admit of their segmented assimilation approach is equally applicable to neoclassical assimilation theory:

All theoretical approaches to social issues make value judgments and reflect built-in assumptions. Our approach is no exception. . . . The fundamental value judgment of this book lies in our choice of "adaptation" as a research question. To some extent, this question involves taking mainstream American society, with all its injustices and inequalities, as given, and focusing on the factors that enable the children of Vietnamese refugees to advance in that society. In this respect, then, our research may seem to have an inherently conservative strand. (Zhou and Bankston 1998: 19)

Taking "mainstream American society" for granted, both neoclassical and segmented assimilation theories are concerned with how migrants and their descendants navigate it, but the possibility of significant changes to it, including structures of racial inequality and domination, remain beyond consideration. Thus, as prominent as the Black-led Civil Rights Movement is in its explanation of contemporary assimilation, and as much as it expresses sympathy for Blacks, neoclassical assimilation theory cannot account for such movements or envisage anything but incremental changes. And, for all of their discussion of "oppositional culture," proponents of segmented assimilation theory conceptualize and discuss it in unwaveringly disapproving terms and fail to contemplate how it could offer a valuable critique of the status quo and how interactions between working-class and poor migrants and Blacks could be bidirectional and politically productive and transformative.[30] This type of productive interracial coalition and transformation is precisely what we find among Vietnamese and Black residents as they struggle, after Hurricane Katrina, to return to and rebuild the very New Orleans neighborhood studied by Zhou and Bankston (Tang 2011).[31] Even in the "mainstream" realm of electoral politics, do we have any doubt that the United States, as a polity, would be much more progressive and egalitarian if the voting preferences of the Black poor and working class were *more* influential, not less, including among migrants and their children?[32]

CONCLUSION

Specifying an alternative to assimilation theories lies beyond the scope of this chapter, the purpose of which is evaluative. I would like, however, to propose a fundamental reorientation for approaching such a task. Because assimilation theories are founded on "taking mainstream American society, with all its injustices and inequalities, as given" (Zhou and Bankston 1998: 19), they often miss and misrepresent how race structures what they refer to as "assimilation." For their "built-in assumptions" about race, their racial unconscious, they variously engage in suspect comparisons to the earlier wave of migration to the United States that had originally given rise to theories and practices of assimilation; read out or misread the qualitatively different historical trajectories of European and non-European migrants; exclude native-born Blacks from the analysis; fail to conceptually account for the key institutional changes that are purported to facilitate "assimilation"; import the dubious concept of the "underclass" to characterize poor urban Blacks and others; laud uncritically the "culture" of migrants; explicitly or implicitly advocate the "assimilation" of migrants; and discount the political potential of "oppositional culture." A critical approach would cut a sharper angle to the prevailing assimilationist current in mainstream theory and society to channel analytical attention to the racial inequalities and domination that flow by unnoticed.

The viability of assimilation theories has entailed exclusions. As I have emphasized in this chapter, assimilation theories could not and so now do not account for the history of African Americans. They ceased attempting to wedge the Great Migration of Southern Blacks into the grand assimilation narrative of European immigration. Nonetheless, native-born Blacks could not be wholly whited out from the story. From the banks of the mainstream, they reminded neoclassical assimilation theory of how their freedom struggles performed the necessary dredging that made others' "assimilation" possible, while the urban poor among them loomed menacingly in the anxious vision of segmented assimilation theory.

The viability of assimilation theories has also involved another exclusion. Robert E. Park's much cited 1926 article "Our Racial Frontier on the Pacific" has been famous and infamous for its proposition that the "race relations cycle which takes the form, to state it abstractly, of contacts, competition, accommodation and eventual assimilation, is apparently progressive and irreversible."[33] But the essay should be remembered as much for the expansive scale of its claim: "The melting pot is the world" (Park 1926: 196).[34] Like Du Bois's color line, Park's race relations cycle was planetary. In five dense pages, Park circumnavigated the globe, provincializing the then "racial conflict on the Pacific Coast of America" as but one instance of a perpetual, worldwide process.[35] In relation to the United States, immigration from Europe, for Park, was of a piece not only with the then contentious "Asiatic migrations [that] are, on the whole, not different" but also earlier Europeans' "displace[ment] with their populations and cultures [of] the native peoples," "the intimate and personal relations which grew up between the Negro slave and his white master," "the Philippines want[ing] independence," and "the Hawaiian Islands, where all the races of the Pacific meet and mingle on more liberal terms than they do elsewhere, [and] the native races are disappearing and new peoples are coming into existence" (1926: 193, 194, 196). The wide lens through which he observed the United States encompassed what I discussed in the last chapter.

The whole of the U.S. empire-state, in its broader global context, was within Park's field of vision, albeit not of critique.

Park was not alone among assimilation scholars and advocates. Putting into words the outlook pictorialized in Figure 3.1, Katherine Cook, chief of the Division of Special Problems in the Department of Interior's Office of Education (Wesling 2011: 18), described the task before the United States with respect to the "education of backward and underprivileged groups":

In terms of area, our outlying parts would together make almost half another continental United States. Alaska alone has nearly one-third as much territory. We are rich in islands. The Philippines, our second largest outlying territory, includes more than seven thousand, the Virgin group about fifty, beside the several which make up Hawaii, Puerto Rico, Samoa, and Guam. Together they total nearly 105,000 square miles in area.

But it is with the peoples in these far-flung territories, who through education must reach a homogeneous culture so essential to our common welfare, that we are most concerned. In continental United States minority groups include 11,891,143 Negroes, with a school age group of 3,870,451, about two-thirds of whom are in school; 236,000 Indians with a school population of 94,600 of whom 81 per cent are in school. In non-continental United States our largest population group is in the Philippines. Puerto Rico and Hawaii follow in the order named. Over 14 million people in 1930 lived in our several outlying parts. (Cook 1934: 20–21)

At once descriptive and prescriptive, Cook's article in the *Journal of Negro Education* was titled "Education among Native and Minority Groups in Alaska, Puerto Rico, Virgin Islands, and Hawaii." Signaling the colonial nature of the enterprise—"the schoolhouse has followed the flag"[36]—Cook stated the objective in these "outlying parts": "The ideal has been that of assimilation into a new civilization through education as a basic means" (1934: 22). Among other things, what surprises from the vantage point of today's sociology was Cook's matter-of-fact geography. Like Park's, her United States extended over all lands and peoples of the state, which is to say the empire-state.

As the twentieth century wore on, sociology unthinkingly scaled back, casting off colonized spaces and peoples. Repressing the past and present fact of colonial empire, methodological nationalism stifled sociological imagination. Assimilation theory did its part. In the postwar age of decolonization—as colonialism lost its legitimacy, if far from completely its actuality—the coupling of assimilation theory and policies, on the one hand, and the continuing reality and empirical scale of the U.S. empire-state, on the other, could not be sustained. At this juncture, sociology did precisely the obverse of what it ought to have done: it held on to assimilation theory and abandoned the empire-state scale. Sociology withdrew to what it imagined to be the "American nation-state," geographically retreating to the fifty, frequently just the contiguous forty-eight, states and treating them as a politically even, noncolonial space and demographically paring down to "Americans," current (i.e., the mainstream) and prospective (i.e., immigrants and their descendants). In effect, sociology discarded and disregarded theoretically and politically incommensurable lands and peoples of the empire-state and conjured a nation-state of immigrants into being for it to analyze. It fitted a square peg in a round hole and proceeded to spin theories of roundation.

Migrant settlement is a valid topic of study. It requires, however, vigilance against theoretical and methodological nationalism, hypervigilance in the case of the United States, an empire-state that presents itself, quite successfully and with social-scientific consent, as a nation-state. Though not framed as such, the phenomenon that assimilation theories are concerned with is "really the political process of nation-building" (Waldinger 2007c: 147; see also Wimmer and Schiller 2003). In other words, the continual making and remaking of the nation—who belongs to the "imagined political community" and how (Anderson 1991: 6). And if nation-making is a *political* process, it is, at root, about relations of power (i.e., domination) and the inequalities of and struggles over resources and cultural schemas that power relations ordinarily entail. Questions of similarity and difference—the explicit focus of *assimilation* as a term, concept, and theory—are not wholly unrelated, but they distract and distort: *claims* of similarity and difference figure centrally in mainstream political discourse, but we should be careful not to take them at face value. Claims of inassimilable difference in relation to Muslims or Mexicans, for instance, should not lead social scientists to unreflexively corroborate, or dispute, them. Rather, our critical task is to examine the relations of inequality and domination represented by, and partly exercised through, such claims.

In other words, the *politics of national belonging*, and not the degree of ethnic similarity and difference, is the critically useful object of study. The politics of *national* belonging is a particular scale of the *politics of belonging*, which can be more local, as in neighborhood or city, or more comprehensive, as in region or humanity.[37] I spotlight the national for it is today, and has been at least for decades, the dominant level and form of struggles over belonging.

If the politics of national belonging is our concern, states are naturally implicated. Modern states monopolize the legitimate regulation of physical movement across their territorial borders (Torpey 1998, 2000) and the conferral of state membership or citizenship. Particularly for an empire-state, such drawing of boundaries is not only between it and other states but also within, not only between citizens and various categories of migrant aliens but also in relation to other denizens of inferior standing than citizens. For instance, that travel to and from American Sāmoa to other parts of the United States requires a passport and that those born there are not U.S. citizens imply these capacities. Such examples should not be dismissed as negligible glitches but should be seen as expressions of immanent sovereign powers that also impinge upon migrants in related ways, as the previous chapter indicated.[38]

Through the formal mechanisms of marking and calibrating boundaries of state belonging, geographical and juridical, states influence, to varying degrees, the always more informal, less clear-cut drawing of boundaries of national belonging. The state helps to define the (dominant) nation by authorizing who has the right to be within its external and internal borders and under what legal conditions.[39] Such definitions are inflected by gender and sexuality, as they are established through kinship rules embodied in laws on marriage, immigration, citizenship, and so forth (Stevens 1999; Somerville 2005). Access to formal citizenship may not be sufficient for full acceptance as *nationals*, as the experiences of migrants from Asia and their offspring in the United States have continually shown, but may be vital and necessary, as the experiences of their counterparts of European origin have continually shown.[40] The normative assumption and ideal in this postwar age of nation-states are the identity of national and state belonging—that the state boundaries of territory and citizenry should enclose nationals and only nationals. Deviations in practice, as inevitable and commonplace as they are, particularly for non-nation-state states, give rise to various ideologies, policies, and practices of exclusion and subordination, which often have the effect of exacerbating the deviations. Those who are excluded and subordinated may attempt to fit in and seek out paths of acceptance and social mobility. They may also tacitly or overtly engage in resistance—from everyday ideological and practical struggles in schools, workplaces, churches, and so on to organized mass movements—and, at times, significantly alter existing structures of inequality and domination.

Capitalism is also squarely implicated in the politics of national belonging. With few exceptions, those who are physically within the territorial boundaries of a state but are excluded from exercising citizenship rights or being fully considered nationals (e.g., migrants, subordinated native-born minorities, colonized peoples) require gainful employment of some sort; for most migrants, it may be the overriding motive for migration. This is all the truer for those without access to the welfare state, most notably but not only unauthorized migrants. At the same time, different classes and class fractions of the (dominant) nation likely disagree on the desirability of non-nationals, usually pitting a set of employers who seek to increase the supply of labor against various others, often but not only working-class nationals. Conflicts between employers and non-national workers, between national and non-national workers, and between subordinated native-born and migrant workers are also likely and frequent. States juggle and vacillate between the competing national demands for labor, traditionally unskilled but more recently both unskilled and highly skilled, and for restrictions and exclusions, from territories and citizenship rights. One favored compromise in relation to interstate migrants is for states to grant them entry for their labor power, or turn a blind eye to it, but deny them access to rights and privileges accorded to citizens. All of these dynamics are shaped by gender, reflecting and reproducing an unequally differentiated labor market and relations of production.

The approach advocated here generally corresponds with those of Waldinger (2007a, 2007c, 2011) and Wimmer and Schiller (2003; see also Wimmer 2008). Unlike the literature on assimilation, the nation, the state, and the congruence of the two are not taken for granted but problematized, and politics, not ethnic similarity or difference, becomes the focal point. Further, unlike the literature on assimilation, subordinated native-born minorities, who are excluded variously from the nation, are not excluded from the analysis. However, following from the analyses of the previous and present chapters, I would add and stress two things. First, in relation to the United States and other misrecognized empire-states, the assumed congruence between the nation—that is, the dominant nation—and the state requires a more thoroughgoing destabilization. Second, race needs to be accounted for more fully. If *ethnicity* were to stand in as the umbrella category for all types of peoplehood, I have no objections to "'race' [being] treated as a subtype of ethnicity, as is nationhood." But if race were to be thought of in this way as a "special case of ethnicity" (Wimmer 2008: 973–74), its *specialness* calls for, though rarely receives, explication and theorization.

The prominence and importance of race in the politics of national belonging, in relation to the United States and many other states, are hard to miss but are nonetheless routinely dismissed or diminished. Given the overwhelming historical evidence, the question, though empirical in character, is usually less about *whether* race matters than it is about *how* and *how much*. As argued elsewhere, affinities between race and nation as modes of inventing and dividing peoples—conceptually largely empty, historically specific and contingent, greatly variable in practice, objectively modern but subjectively primordial—form the condition of possibility and probability for their recurrent articulations in history (Jung 2006). Nations define themselves not only positively but also negatively, against those who putatively do not and shall not belong. For nations born of colonial empires and/or settler colonies, including "Americans" of the United States, these self-definitions have been shot through and through by race. States have reflected and shaped those definitions through the differential distribution of rights and privileges of citizenship and, increasingly from the latter half of the nineteenth century, the differentially restrictive control of movement across, and within, their borders. Likewise, in conjunction with nation and state, as well as gender, race has been, to paraphrase Stuart Hall (1980), the modality in which class has been continually lived, determining those who are allowed to participate in the "national" economy, to which sectors and jobs they have access, with and against whom to identify and struggle, and so on. The particular ways in which the politics of national belonging articulate with race, gender, the state, and class, as well as other categories, are up for theoretical elaboration and empirical investigation. But the general approach of centering politics, including racial politics, to reveal the relations of power involved in the making, remaking, and even unmaking of the nation seems preferable to assimilation theories that take the "nation-state" and other structures of inequality and domination for granted.[41] Barriers to equality and freedom, not similarity, should agitate our theoretical hackles.

PART III
DENATURALIZING
IGNORANCE

Well, the first difficulty is really so simple that it's usually overlooked: to be a Negro in this country and to be relatively conscious, is to be in a rage almost all the time. So that the first problem is how to control that rage so that it won't destroy you. Part of the rage is this: it isn't only what is happening to you, but it's what's happening all around you all of the time, in the face of the most extraordinary and criminal indifference, the indifference and ignorance of most white people in this country.

James Baldwin, "The Negro in American Culture"

CHAPTER 5

SYMBOLIC COERCION
AND A MASSACRE
OF FILIPINOS

On September 9, 1924, toward the end of a long, drawn-out strike of Filipino sugar workers in Hawai'i, the police shot dead sixteen strikers in what came to be known later as the "Hanapēpē Massacre," losing four from its own ranks by the end of the violent confrontation.[1] Edward Beechert (1985: 222) writes,

Who or what precipitated the violence is not known. The special deputies, armed with hunting rifles and positioned above the exit road on a bluff, fired repeatedly into the massed strikers, killing sixteen and wounding others. Four policemen were killed in the melee.

One hundred and sixty-one strikers were rounded up and jailed. Subsequently, seventy-six Filipinos were indicted for rioting; fifty-seven others pled guilty to charges of assault and battery. A single counsel was provided for the seventy-two men tried and convicted. The county attorney was assisted by two special deputy attorney generals hired and paid for by the HSPA [Hawaiian Sugar Planters' Association].[2]

One of the bloodiest episodes in the blood-soaked history of U.S. labor, this incident in Hanapēpē, on the island of Kaua'i, accounts for nearly 1 in 15 of all strike-related deaths of the 1920s and 1930s.[3]

As reproachful as it may appear in retrospect, the incident did not arouse contemporary public censure nor bring into question the legitimacy of the coercive agents and their actions. While scores of the strikers were arrested, tried, and convicted, no charges were ever brought against the police. In fact, there is no evidence that doing so was seriously considered. This chapter inves-

tigates how the state can perpetrate such physical coercion "legitimately," in
the case of the Hanapēpē Massacre and in general.[4] To do so, I develop a new
concept to discern a dominant form of ignorance that is immanent to racism,
and to other structures of domination. First, I think with and beyond Pierre
Bourdieu's counterintuitive concept of *symbolic violence*.[5] The concept and
Bourdieu's theory of social order and domination in which it is situated provide a powerful vocabulary and a productive starting point. In particular, his
writings on the state bring together and provide suggestive linkages between
symbolic domination, physical coercion, and legitimacy. At the same time, they
raise a number of questions that call for an amendment. Incorporating W. E.
B. Du Bois's notion of *double consciousness*, I propose the concept of *symbolic
coercion* to better explain the possibility of "legitimate" physical coercion in
support of domination. Second, examining the Hanapēpē Massacre, I analyze
how racial symbolic coercion made possible and legitimate the deadly use of
physical coercion against Filipino working-class men.

SYMBOLIC VIOLENCE AND SYMBOLIC COERCION

Bourdieu defines the state as that organization "which successfully claims the
monopoly of the legitimate use of physical and *symbolic* violence over a definite territory and over the totality of the corresponding population," stressing,
in italics, his point of departure from Max Weber's classic formulation (1994:
3; emphasis in original).[6] The definition establishes a link between symbolic
violence—his innovative and widely cited concept—and physical violence. It
also raises a number of questions. How does symbolic violence relate to the
notion of legitimacy? What exactly is the theoretical link between symbolic
violence and physical violence, aside from their supposedly common claim-
ant? How does the state successfully claim a monopoly on the legitimate use
of symbolic violence?

"A gentle violence, imperceptible and invisible even to its victims," symbolic
violence, according to Bourdieu (2001: 1), operates in the realm of *doxa*, the
typical condition of correspondence between a social order and agents' *habitus*
or system of internalized dispositions of perception, appreciation, and action
structured by and thus adapted to that very social order. The correspondence
makes the social world appear natural, even to those who fare badly in it. Sym-

bolic violence refers to this tacit acceptance of oppression by the oppressed: "doxic submission of the dominated to the structures of a social order of which their mental structures are the product" (1994: 14). It is the unconscious consent that the dominated give, or cannot but give, to the relation of domination because they, as well as the dominant, take the established social order for granted (Bourdieu 2000: 170). For example, as Bourdieu (2001: 35) points out with respect to gender domination in contemporary France, most women profess to want a husband who is older and taller than themselves.

Although Bourdieu retains the word "legitimate" from Weber's definition of the state, it is somewhat redundant, because symbolic violence is meant to address the issue of legitimacy.[7] Again, Bourdieu contrasts his own position to that of Weber: "The recognition of legitimacy is not, as Weber believed, a free act of clear conscience. It is rooted in the immediate, prereflexive, agreement between objective structures and embodied structures, now turned unconscious" (1994 :14; see also 2000: 177). That is, our mental structures internalize, or embody, objective social structures, through gradual inculcation, thereby rendering them homologous, mutually reinforcing, and unconscious. In modern, differentiated societies, the state effects this prereflexive agreement by "incarnat[ing] itself simultaneously in objectivity, in the form of specific organizational structures and mechanisms, and in subjectivity in the form of mental structures and categories of perception and thought" (Bourdieu 1994: 4; see also 2000). For example, prototypical among state institutions, the educational system legitimates class domination, among dominant and dominated classes alike, by transforming the inherited economic and cultural advantages of the children of the dominant classes—through ostensibly disinterested, meritocratic practices that align with and favor those advantages—into universally recognized academic advantages and credentials that reproduce their dominant class positions (Bourdieu 1996; Bourdieu and Passeron 1977).[8]

No doubt Bourdieu is right to attenuate the realm of consciousness in the reproduction of relations of domination. The "paradox of doxa" is that so little of the established order is questioned (Bourdieu 2001: 1). Shifting the point of contention between Marxism and its critics, he writes, "In the notion of false consciousness that [Marxism] invokes to account for effects of symbolic domination, that superfluous term is 'consciousness'" (1994: 14). How (un)consciously the dominated's "active consent" (Gramsci 1971: 244) to the established order is produced is also, according to Bourdieu and Wacquant (1992: 168), the point of contrast between symbolic violence and *hegemony*. Although the distinction is probably overdrawn—since one of the signal merits of Antonio Gramsci's concept, particularly in relation to antecedent Marxist theories of ideology, is that it does not refer only to a "conscious system of ideas and beliefs" (Williams 1977: 109; see also Bourdieu and Eagleton 1994; Eagleton 1991)—Bourdieu undoubtedly places much more emphasis on the tacit in legitimating relations of domination, quite radically "reducing that of . . . consciousness" (Bourdieu and Wacquant 1992: 25). While he allows for a narrow realm of conscious conflicts and disagreements, much of what constitutes relations of domination "belongs to the order of *belief*" and thus goes unquestioned (Bourdieu 1994: 14; emphasis in original).[9]

The term itself derives its rhetorical force, in part, from its jarringly oxymoronic pairing of "symbolic" and "violence," disturbing commonsensical boundaries of what violence is and bridging the often, if falsely, counterposed spheres in the social sciences of meaning and materiality. Bourdieu's symbolic violence is also ironic: conceived as "tacit agreement," it excludes a sense of coercion, unless coercion itself were understood ironically, or at least obliquely (1994: 14).[10] In this way, the usual semantic association between "violence" and adjectives like "gentle" and "imperceptible" is inverted. As a corollary, rather than an analogous concept to physical violence, symbolic violence is rendered its negative complement: the need for physical violence to maintain the established order arises from insufficient symbolic violence.[11] If translated, albeit incongruously, into Gramscian terms, winning consent, as well as exercising coercion, would be considered violence—symbolic and physical, respectively. Thus, Bourdieu's concept inflates the notion of violence to encompass not only physical force but also the condition of its absence.

While it identifies something real and important, *symbolic violence* needs to be complicated with complementary concepts that draw analytical distinctions among different forms of symbolic domination. Most relevant for this chapter, Bourdieu's theory of symbolic violence misses what I refer to as *doxic asymmetry*, the analysis of which has the potential to help elucidate the legitimate use of physical force against the dominated.

Bourdieu's theory of order and domination rests, I argue, on a problematic assumption. He posits the "*unanimity* of doxa," that is, the unanimity of what is taken for granted. Not meant as an ideal type or a limiting case, this unanimity is intended to be quite literal: "nothing is further from the correlative notion of the *majority* than the *unanimity* of doxa" (1977: 168; emphases in original). Though stated in absolute terms here, there is some ambiguity in his other writings. For example, his illustration of women's doxic submission was based on surveys that found "a large *majority* of French women say[ing] they want a husband who is older and also (quite coherently) taller than themselves" (Bourdieu 2001: 35; emphasis added).

Whatever the ambiguities, I do not dispute that there is a large realm of the established order that goes unquestioned by the dominant and the dominated alike, for the study of which Bourdieu's social theory and research are vital. What I dispute is that there exist only two realms: the "universe of the undiscussed (undisputed)" and the "universe of discourse (or argument)" (Bourdieu 1977: 168). In Figure 5.1, the solid, oval boundary represents this mutually exclusive division between the unconscious doxa on the one hand, in which symbolic violence takes place, and the consciously orthodox (i.e., dominant) and heterodox (i.e., dominated or subaltern) opinions on the other. Partitioned neatly into what is implicitly agreed and what is explicitly disagreed, this theoretical model leaves no room for disagreement over what is implicit.

In one sense, the foregoing omission is puzzling, for all of Bourdieu's analyses presuppose and demonstrate the ubiquity and durability of hierarchical social divisions, foremost class ones. But these social divisions do not divide the "universe of doxa." Instead, Bourdieu assumes, as John Thompson notes, "a certain kind of *consensus* with regard to the values or norms which are dominant in the society concerned" (1984: 61; emphasis in original).[12] As much as the dominant, the dominated find natural the order of things.

It is hard to accept, even ideal-typically, that there is no systematic disagreement over what is taken for granted, for example, between capital and labor, men and women, whites and people of color, citizens and subjects, teachers and students, and so on. I suggest that there is a certain *asymmetry of doxa* that accords with, if imperfectly, the asymmetry of relations of domination. The dominated are conscious of, albeit variably and far from fully, much of what remains unconscious for the dominant. This asymmetry is, for instance, precisely what feminist and antiracist research has consistently shown. Occupying unmarked, normative categories, men and whites remain oblivious to the

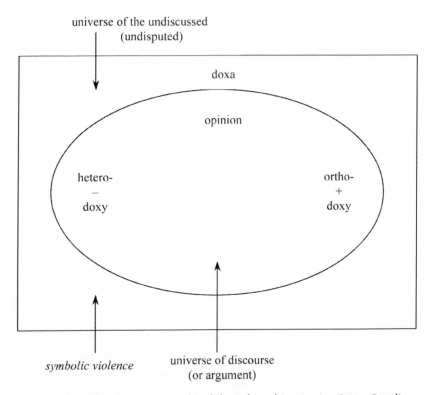

universe of the undiscussed
(undisputed)

doxa

opinion

hetero-
−
doxy

ortho-
+
doxy

symbolic violence   universe of discourse
                              (or argument)

Figure 5.1. Pierre Bourdieu's Diagram of Symbolic Order and Domination. Source: Bourdieu (1977: 168). Otherwise identical to the original, this figure includes the conceptual location of symbolic violence in accordance with Bourdieu's theory. Copyright © 1977 In the English language edition Cambridge University Press. Reprinted with the permission of Cambridge University Press.

breadth and depth of gender and racial domination, while women and people of color are forced to be much more aware of not only the relations of domination but also the obliviousness to which they are subject.[13]

Doxic asymmetry corresponds to Du Bois's *double consciousness,* an undervalued concept in mainstream social theory. Intrinsic to the idea is an asymmetric slippage in what is and is not taken for granted, because those who are oppressed are, owing to their oppression, "gifted with second-sight," able, and indeed compelled, to see the world through the eyes of the dominant as well as through their own ([1903] 1965: 214–15). Put in Bourdieu's idiom, the dominated recognize, if only partly, the cultural arbitrary of the relation of domination that the dominant misrecognize as natural. For example, doxic asymmetry may account for why the best past writings on race by people of color, like Du Bois's, tend to read less dated today than those written by their white counterparts, because they recognized contemporarily the cultural arbitrary of a racial formation that whites could recognize only retrospectively.[14]

Ironically, Bourdieu provides an apt example of "second-sight" from his personal biography, characterized interestingly as an effect of "racism." Of his provincial social origin, he states,

It gives you a sort of objective and subjective externality and puts you in a particular relation to the central institutions of French society and therefore to the intellectual institution. There are subtle (and not so subtle) forms of social racism that cannot but make you perceptive; being constantly reminded of your otherness stimulates a sort of permanent sociological vigilance. It helps you perceive things that others cannot see or feel. (Bourdieu and Wacquant 1992: 209)

This account echoes what Du Bois ([1903] 1965: 215) had long ago described: "always looking at one's self through the eyes of others, of measuring one's soul by the tape of a world that looks on in amused contempt and pity." As his autobiographical example shows, Bourdieu does not posit that mental structures are always, implicitly attuned to social structures. They can fall out of sync for a number of reasons (Bourdieu 2000: 159–63). In Bourdieu's personal case, his highly improbable trajectory into the rarefied ranks of the French academic elite induces the misalignment, allowing for critical, conscious reflection. What his theory overlooks, however, is the intrinsic misalignment, never total but never absent, that relations of domination generate among the dominated.

If we were to modify Bourdieu's theory by incorporating Du Bois's insight, there would be a third realm in the symbolic order in which subaltern consciousness, or heterodox discourse, is not consciously recognized, or even recognizable, by the dominant. I propose the concept of *symbolic coercion* to refer to this *tacit nonrecognition* (see Figure 5.2). It shares with Bourdieu the idea that symbolic domination is a matter of course for the dominant, requiring no conscious formulation of intention, but differs in that the dominated consciously recognize and question aspects of the established order that the dominant take for granted. To be clear, I do not mean that the dominated are conscious of all or, ordinarily, most aspects of domination; the degree of doxic asymmetry would be empirically variable, as would the degree of doxic submission. But, symbolic *coercion* occurs

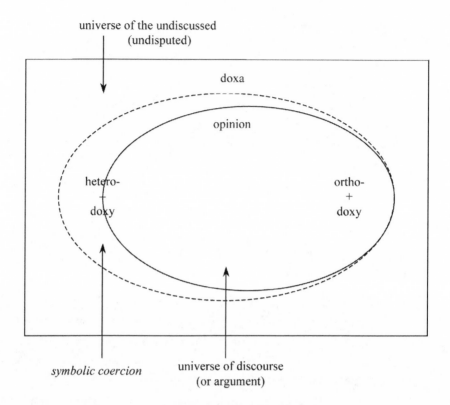

Figure 5.2. Modified Diagram of Symbolic Order and Domination

when certain subaltern discourses are not recognized because deeply held dominant beliefs (i.e., doxa), and dominant discourses structured by them, preclude it.

The latter point concerning dominant discourses needs some clarification, as the present case illustrates below. According to Bourdieu, once provoked to discourse by the "competing possibles" posited and implied by subaltern discourses, the dominant attempt, "without ever entirely succeeding," to "restor[e] the primal state of innocence of doxa" through orthodoxy, "straight, or rather *straightened*, opinion" (1977: 169; emphasis in original). Though mostly in agreement, I suggest that doxa can sometimes remain unfazed even when awakened into discourse. Some dominant discourses, even if they refer to subaltern discourses, may not be consciously straightened opinions. Rather, they may be doxa sleeptalking, as it were. There may be no conscious engagement or "argument," in Bourdieu's sense, because the dominant do not hear that there is anything to be argued, even as they argue. In other words, the restoration of the "innocence of doxa" may not always be necessary, because the dominant may not recognize that it is threatened. They remain oblivious.[15]

Whereas symbolic violence, for Bourdieu, designates the unconscious agreement of the dominated, symbolic coercion denotes the conscious disagreement of the dominated that goes unconsciously unrecognized by the dominant. Symbolic coercion recovers an unironic sense of force, akin to what Judith Butler identifies as the "force of exclusion [that] is set outside of the domain of contest," which has "not yet been thought through in the explicit discourse of legitimacy," and that entails an "unknowingness"—an unrecognizability or illegibility (2002: 17, 19).[16] Most relevant in relation to the Hanapēpē Massacre, this conceptualization supplies pivotal leverage in understanding the *legitimate* use of physical force in support of domination. The effect of symbolic coercion is to render its sufferers—whose discourses are so *illegitimate* as to be below conscious recognition and engagement by the dominant—susceptible to various forms of subordination and exclusion, including physical coercion.

Symbolic coercion accords with what we mean, in ordinary speech, when we speak of the "voiceless" or the "vulnerable." By "voiceless," we mean that certain opinions contrary to the established order are unrecognized, not that those opinions do not or even cannot exist, save for during exceptional moments of "crisis."[17] For example, it is not that poor Black communities are unaware of or do not speak against—in other words, are tacitly complicitous with—the police brutality they regularly face which makes them vulnerable to it. Rather, it is the tacit nonrecognition of the Black poor's discourse against police brutality by whites and the state, structured by doxic beliefs to the contrary, that makes police brutality legitimate police practice (Nelson 2000; Ogletree et al. 1995). In contrast, conscious recognition and engagement of subaltern discourses by the dominant, however antithetical the engagement may be, would more likely bring under scrutiny the legitimacy of any conservative acts of physical coercion.[18] Here, note once-legitimate forms of physical coercion that no longer command widespread legitimacy (e.g., lynching).

As for Bourdieu's symmetric assertion that the state successfully claims a monopoly of the legitimate use of both symbolic and physical violence, many studies could and do show that the state, though uniquely powerful, holds no such exclusive claim over the former.[19] In fact, Bourdieu's (1984, 2001) analyses of cultural consumption and gender domination, among others—in which symbolic violence is prevalent, but the state, though not absent, does not assume centrality—illustrate this point. The same goes for symbolic coercion. The link between symbolic coercion and the legitimate use of physical coercion, or violence, is not the monopolization of both by the state. Instead, a singular power of the state may be its routine capability to articulate symbolic coercion, much of which occurs beyond the state, to physical coercion, of which the state does claim, if not necessarily successfully, a monopoly.

HANAPĒPĒ MASSACRE

With certain exceptions, such as the much discussed death of Captain James Cook in 1779, violence has not been a major focus of historical research on Hawai'i.[20] The paucity can be attributed largely to the long-standing assumption, both without and within academe, of Hawaii's exceptionalism: that Hawai'i, the so-called "Paradise of the Pacific," has enjoyed social equanimity unimaginable on the "mainland."[21] Implicating an economic and political core of prewar Hawai'i, its quintessential sugar industry, this chapter seeks to establish that the Hanapēpē Massacre was not an inexplicable anomaly, as is commonly thought.[22]

The most fundamental empirical question for this chapter is twofold: how was the massacre of Filipino strikers possible, and how did it not provoke a crisis, or the merest doubt, of legitimacy? In line with the conceptualization of symbolic coercion outlined above, I propose that Filipino men in Hawai'i had been subject to a particular racial, and gendered, form of symbolic coercion that made possible and legitimate the lethal use of physical coercion against them.

Although dating back to the early nineteenth century, Hawaii's sugar industry remained relatively undeveloped until the Reciprocity Treaty of 1876.[23] The treaty between the Kingdom of Hawaii (and, from 1894 to 1898, the Republic of Hawaii) and the United States permitted the duty-free entry of unrefined sugar from Hawai'i into the U.S. market; the Republic of Hawaii was established by an elite group, led by U.S. Americans, in a forcible overthrow of the Hawaiian monarchy. The U.S. annexation of Hawai'i in 1898 and its political status as an incorporated territory continued the tariff protection.[24]

The access to the protected U.S. market led to a tremendous growth of the sugar industry.[25] It also touched off an intense concentration of capital, as the large investments needed to finance the growth drove out small, independent producers. Consequently, a handful of agencies or factors, commonly referred to as the "Big Five," came to dominate the industry.[26] Moreover, the Big Five were, in turn, controlled and owned by a small number of *haole* families descended from the Christian missionaries of the nineteenth century; the category "haole" referred to non-Iberian people of European ancestry, mostly of U.S., British, and German origins. The concentration of capital, as well as interlocking directorates among the Big Five and intermarriages among the "missionary" families, impelled industrial cohesion and the formation of the HSPA (Dean 1950; MacLennan 1979).

Leveraging their commanding position in sugar, the Big Five assumed a similar dominance in the maritime industry. Later, the Big Five also made considerable inroads in pineapple, obtaining a majority market share of what would fast become Hawaii's second largest industry by the early 1930s (Brooks 1952). Nonetheless, sugar remained the backbone of the Big Five and of Hawaii's economy, accounting for about $75 million of the territory's $109 million in exports in 1924.[27]

Until the New Deal, the Big Five's stranglehold on Hawaii's economy was cozily tied to an amenable territorial government. It intervened consistently on behalf of powerful employers and against workers, most of whom were either disenfranchised or—in cases of the Portuguese and the Hawai'i-born Japanese *nisei*—pressured by haole into Republican consent (USBLS 1940; USHR 1940).[28]

With the rapid development of the sugar industry, labor supply was a continual concern for employers. From the mid-nineteenth century, Hawaiians and migrants—actively recruited in overlapping succession, primarily from China, Portugal, Japan, and the Philippines—labored on sugar plantations. Following their initial contractual stints in sugar, they moved on, to varying degrees, and worked in other industries. When the Gentlemen's Agreement of 1907–08 between the United States and Japan halted the migration of Japanese laborers, the Philippines became the planters' only major source of additional labor.[29] From 1912 onward, Japanese and Filipino workers were the most numerous in the sugar industry, with the latter becoming the largest by 1922. In 1920, there were 19,474 Japanese and 13,061 Filipino workers, combining for 73.4 percent of the sugar labor force. In 1924, the respective numbers were 12,781 and 19,475, accounting for 81.5 percent (*Hawaiian Annual* 1913: 35; 1921: 17; 1923: 14; 1925: 12).[30]

The 1924 strike of Filipino sugar workers had its origin in a strike four years earlier. The five-month strike in 1920 involved around 8,300 Japanese and Filipino workers on Oʻahu, representing 77 percent of the island's work force. It was conducted by Oʻahu members of two separate unions, the Federation of Japanese Labor and the Filipino Labor Union (FLU), with members on the outer islands continuing to work and contributing their wages to the strikers. The unions struck for higher wages, eight-hour workdays, overtime pay, maternity leave, and better health and recreational facilities (Reinecke 1979: 95). The strike ended in defeat with the planters officially making "no concessions whatsoever, either direct or implied," although they quietly adopted changes afterward.[31]

At the center of the strikers' concerns in 1920 was the plantations' bonus system. Receiving much of their wages through bonuses that were pegged to the price of sugar, workers anticipated a drop in the World War I–inflated price and demanded a higher basic wage and a restructured bonus system. As feared and predicted, the wholesale price of sugar plunged precipitously, from a record high of 12.33 cents per pound in 1920 to 4.63 cents per pound in 1922 (Taylor 1935: 168). The turnout bonus was consequently worth only about a penny an hour (Beechert 1985: 217). The daily wage of an unskilled laborer was, for all intents and purposes, the industry's minimum wage of one dollar, the sugar industry's repeated protestations about the "average" wage being much higher notwithstanding. Filipinos were the most acutely affected, being largely confined to minimum-wage unskilled jobs.

In the fall of 1922 and again in 1923, Filipino workers, many of whom were veterans of the FLU, held a series of meetings on various plantations.[32] In the meetings—helmed by Pablo Manlapit, a former sugar and dock worker turned lawyer and labor leader who had led the FLU in the 1920 strike, and George Wright, the haole head of an AFL local who had led a short-lived drive for an interracial labor movement—the workers drafted a petition with a list of their "requests," for which over six thousand signatures were collected (Manlapit 1933: 34).[33] As indicated by the name they adopted for the union, the High Wages Movement (HWM), the primary requests or demands of the workers were the raising of the minimum wage to two dollars and the elimination of the bonus system. The other demands were reduction of the workday to eight hours, time-and-a-half for overtime and double-time for work on Sundays and legal holidays, equal pay for men and women, pay increases for skilled and semiskilled workers, and recognition of the right to unionize.[34]

The petition, along with a letter, was sent to the HSPA on April 10, 1923. Holding to its past practice of dealing with labor unions, the HSPA ignored the petition. The HWM sent another letter and a second copy of the petition in early November 1923, which the HSPA again ignored. A third attempt was made on December 20, 1923 with the same result.[35] Reasoning that the HSPA was not an incorporated body but a "purely voluntary clique" with no legal standing, the HWM then made a last ditch effort at presenting the petition to the "individual plantation companies, which [were] incorporated and legally responsible."[36] Predictably, neither the HSPA nor the individual member plantations responded (Manlapit 1933: 61).

As outlined in the HWM manifesto of January 1924, the HSPA's refusals led the union to proceed with its intention to strike. In March 1924, the Executive Committee of the HWM drafted a "Strike Proclamation," calling for the strike to commence on April 1, 1924. The proclamation stated that workers on some plantations would engage in a "direct strike," while those on the other plantations would "go on a silent strike," essentially a slowdown.[37] Whether non-striking Filipino workers actually went on a "silent strike" is unclear, but the "direct strike" did begin its erratic career on the island of Oʻahu on April 1, though with minimal organizational structure, strike fund, or means of communication (Beechert 1985: 219). It then meandered haltingly through the island of Hawaiʻi, beginning in June, and the islands of Maui and Kauaʻi, beginning in July (Manlapit 1933: 65; Reinecke 1996: 32–34). Illustrative of the indeterminate character of the strike, it ended sometime in 1925, but an exact date cannot be pinpointed, although it was effectively over with the Hanapēpē Massacre. Over its course, the strike directly involved thirty-four of the islands' forty-nine plantations and up to three-fifths of the Filipino work force (Reinecke 1996: 30–33).

The HWM's lack of organization, like that of its predecessor FLU, was not surprising, given Filipino workers' limited institutional support and itinerancy. The latest to be recruited, Filipino sugar workers were almost exclusively young

men without families (Lind 1980: 41–43; Nordyke 1977: table 4b.7). Severely cir-
cumscribed in their opportunities, owing not only to their late arrival but also to
unremitting subordination, Filipinos were and would remain overwhelmingly
tied to the plantation economy as unskilled labor (Jung 2006). In 1928, over two
decades after their first arrival, more than three-fourths of all Filipinos in Hawai'i
lived on sugar plantations.[38] Also far outpacing all others, over 90 percent of gain-
fully employed Filipino men were classified as "laborers" in the 1930 census (Lind
1980: 84–85).

Socially isolated in plantation communities, Filipinos worked in the worst
jobs and lived in the worst housing. With few resources to spare, they did
not establish much in the way of durable institutions: "Unlike the plantation
Japanese with their temples, language schools, young men's associations, and
neighborhood stores, the Filipinos had no community roots." Filipinos also
had no stable press of their own, and the mainstream newspapers provided
no viable alternative, as scarce references in them to Filipinos were typically
of arrests and industrial accidents. Adding to the lack of community stability
was the high turnover rate among Filipinos, who moved from one plantation
to another in search of higher wages. In 1923, the rate of turnover for Filipino
workers was 80 percent (Reinecke 1996: 2–3).

As much as the strike's lack of organization proved to be a liability, its
improvisational, tortuous tour of the islands proved to be an unpredicted
asset as well. To its frustration, the sugar industry never knew when, where,
or for how long the workers were going to strike. Nevertheless, the sugar
industry coalesced in the face of the amorphous strike and did not hesitate
to apply all due force. As in the past, compromise was not entertained. Ten
days prior to the strike, the HSPA set up a strike claims committee to deal
with strike losses, diffusing the costs to the entire industry. The struck plantations evicted the strikers, forcibly if necessary (Beechert 1985: 220). Acts
of espionage and frame-ups of labor leaders through informants and *agents
provocateur* were also standard practice by 1924 (Manlapit 1933: 66–67;
Reinecke 1996: 40, 43). Conducted at a time of labor scarcity, the industry's
main source of strikebreakers was newly arriving Filipino workers, a thousand of whom, according to Manlapit (1933: 67–68), joined the strike. Per
usual for prewar strikes, it ended with the workers officially obtaining none
of their material demands.

Although a few historical accounts have well described the Hanapēpē Massacre over the years, most comprehensively by John E. Reinecke (1996: ch. 10), they have not put forth a theoretical explanation for its possibility and for the prevailing unconcern for the dead and wounded Filipinos and the large number of Filipinos promptly accused and convicted of causing the bloodshed. I argue that the deeply held, doxic beliefs of the haole elite and the broader public about Filipino men, specifically their imputed natural predisposition toward violence, precluded the recognition of contrary Filipino discourse and practice. This symbolic coercion—tacit nonrecognition of Filipino workers' discourse and practice of nonviolence—rendered them vulnerable to physical coercion, the legitimacy of which would not be questioned.

In Hawai'i, migrant workers of different origins faced qualitatively different racisms. In contrast to the supposedly anti-American but racially advanced Japanese, for example, Filipinos were believed to be unequivocally inferior to, and by, haole and nearly all non-Filipinos in prewar Hawai'i. That they hailed from a U.S. colony figured centrally, just as the ascendant Japanese empire, rival to Western "great powers," served as an emblem and measure of the Japanese "race." In the Philippines, as elsewhere, colonial rule required and produced a presumption of inferiority of the colonized. Although there was disagreement among colonial officials about whether and which Filipinos could be taught to govern themselves, their racial inferiority and immediate incapacity for self-government were assumed. In Hawai'i, anti-Filipino racism, directed as it was to a population composed almost wholly of poor migrant laborers, was even more taken for granted (Jung 2006).

As they had been earlier in the Philippines, Filipinos were racialized in Hawai'i as childlike and unmanly (Hoganson 1998). "They are so like children," a sugar agency executive opined.[39] This judgment was widely shared among the haole elite of the 1920s, as a study by a pair of University of Hawaii psychologists unintentionally corroborated. For their study, the authors obtained "social ratings" of Hawaii's major "races" from twenty-five "objective" evaluators. All twenty-five were likely haole, and most were plantation managers (Porteus and Babcock 1926: 90).[40] They ranked Filipinos at the very bottom, giving them a mark of 33 on the study's 100-point composite scale. Filipinos scored last or second to last on seven of the eight traits: they were perceived as extremely short-sighted, suggestible, impulsive, irresolute, overemotional, unstable in their interests, and undependable (Porteus and Babcock 1926: 92–97, 109). The study concluded, "Summing up these characteristics we may say that the Filipinos represent a fine example of a race in an adolescent stage of development" (Porteus and Babcock 1926: 67).

Indicative of the link between colonization and presumption of inferiority, all of the U.S. colonial subjects included in the psychologists' study—Native Hawaiians, Puerto Ricans, and Filipinos, in descending order—rated the lowest on the composite scale. Among the colonized, there was a notable internal difference, one that placed Filipinos in a more inferior and menacing position in the racial imagination of haole. Unlike the supposedly gentle Hawaiians, for example, Filipinos were deemed volatile and violent by nature. As with the presumption of Filipino inferiority in general, the belief that Filipinos were violent was widely shared by most non-Filipinos in Hawai'i. An astute contemporary observer as well as historian of prewar Hawai'i, Reinecke (1996: 3) wrote, "Between the Filipinos and other ethnic groups there was a wide social distance. . . . A great part of the population stereotyped them as hotheaded, knife-wielding, overdressed, sex-hungry young men." Symptomatically, they were commonly subjected to slurs like "poke poke" and "poke knife" for their putative propensity to engage in violence, especially with knives.[41]

The perception that Filipinos were singularly violent related to their mode of colonial incorporation. U.S. colonization of Hawai'i or even Puerto Rico did not involve violence on the order of the Philippine-American War, during which an estimated 16,000–20,000 Filipinos were killed in battle and perhaps another 200,000 died of war-related causes (Hoganson 1998: 7; Welch 1979: 42). The United States waged a brutal "race war" and projected the brutality onto the Filipinos (Jacobson 2000; Kramer 2006). Characterization of Filipinos as "savages" survived the war and migrated to Hawai'i, along with Filipino labor. For example, plantation supervisors and others in Hawai'i took up the racist epithet *goo goo*, predecessor to the more notorious *gook*, that U.S. soldiers likely coined during the war.[42] Similarly, Porteus and Babcock (1926: 66) imported the term and notion of "running amuck" to cast Filipinos as susceptible to irrational bouts of violent rampages, tapping into U.S. colonial discourse in the Philippines, as well as its British and other European antecedents in Southeast Asia (Okamura 2010; Ugarte 1992; Worcester 1898).

In Bourdieu's terms, impressions of Filipinos' violent nature and racial inferiority were dominant *beliefs*, not empirically controvertible propositions open to argument, and their sway extended beyond the haole elite. For example, of the nisei subjects in her study, who overwhelmingly had negative views of Filipinos, Jitsuichi

Masuoka (1931: 162) wrote, "Evidently some of the second generation Japanese are so conditioned that mere perception [sight] of a Filipino man calls forth [a] conditioned response." One of the presumably typical respondents quoted in Masuoka's study, a nisei woman recalled an early childhood incident—her "first experience with the Filipinos" and "a very frightful one"—to explain her racial enmity:

While picking [guavas] I saw three Filipinos approaching us. I thought I saw them carrying knives, so I told my friends about it. We threw our guavas away and started to run toward my parents. One of my friends was so frightened that she yelled for help.

Whenever, I pass this place now I always smile, because I know that the Filipinos did not carry knives with them but it was only an illusion. Since we were told so often that the Filipinos carried knives with them and carried away girls that app[a]rently those three innocent Filipinos appeared to us dreadful people on earth.

I am very much afraid of the Filipinos. It is because of my early experience with some of the Filipino men.

After telling another similar story, she concluded, "Even now I do not feel at ease in the presence of the Filipinos" (Masuoka 1931: 162–63). In other words, the stories—although she consciously recognized them as empirically unfounded and as conditioned by having been "told so often" about Filipinos—served to *confirm* her belief, unconsciously incorporated as "experience," about Filipino men's violent predisposition, especially toward "girls."[43]

An assumption of inevitable violence suffused the 1924 strike: "Everyone," according to Reinecke (1996: 35), "expected a Filipino strike to be a violent one." A Japanese newspaper that *supported* the Filipino workers editorialized, "If the strike is once commenced, violent deeds would be perpetrated everywhere. We may witness nearly every day . . . arson and murder."[44] Even Wright, who would be fired from his job at the Pearl Harbor Navy Yard in 1925 for his part in the strike, betrayed a similar belief in his reaction to the dismissal:

I accepted the responsibility [of advising the High Wages Movement] because I believed my influence among the Filipinos would be effective in restraining them and directing them along recognized legitimate lines, avoiding all violent and destructive tactics. . . . Anyone who has followed my work from the beginning must agree that I have been frank and sincere, exerting a conservative influence and teaching these primitive people the American principles and ideals. (As quoted in Reinecke 1996: 158n49)

Recounting the strike much later, a working-class resident on Kaua'i stated, "[At] that time, Filipinos, they go for broke, they no scared. Not like now; kind of civilized."[45]

Contrary to the notion of the unanimity of doxa, Filipino workers themselves consciously recognized and resisted the dominant beliefs of their predisposition toward violence and, more generally, of their inferiority.[46] Aware of the widespread fears, Filipino workers explicitly and repeatedly called for nonviolence. For example, their "Strike Proclamation" declared typically, "Let us stand together, avoid violence, use every lawful means to gain our ends, and we will WIN THE FIGHT."[47] In an addendum titled "WARNING," it went on to state,

The Executive Committee of the High Wages Movement hereby warns all strikers against committing acts of violence and breaking the laws. The planters have their laws against vagrancy, picketing, they use some wrong and put you in jail, or frame up cases against your leaders. . . . Strikers who deliberately violate the law must expect punishment and need not look to this committee for defense or protection. . . . Watch out for traps set for you by stool pigeons and traitors. In every strike there are always some of the skunks who mix with the strikers and try to stir up trouble. When you catch any of these fellows, don't be rough or cruel to them, that would be against the law. Be orderly, cheerful, quiet and patient. You are fighting for justice and a square deal, and for American ideals. Get the sympathy of the public by your good behavior.[48]

The wife of one of the strikers in Hanapēpē vividly recalled hearing Manlapit emphasize nonviolence in a speech.[49] Another remembered the discourse of the workers in similar terms: "That was really the understanding, that the strike would be won and would be pursued by the strikers not through a troublesome kind of way, but it would be done through a peaceful way. They really didn't want to use arms."[50] This discourse of nonviolence also circulated through the union newspaper, *Ang Batay* (Beechert 1985: 219).

Up until the Hanapēpē Massacre, the strike was indeed notably free of violence.[51] A striker in Kāpa'a, on Kaua'i, remembered, "So, we continued living down there on the beach [in the strike camp], and we lived in a very peaceable kind of way. We didn't make any trouble and we didn't want any trouble."[52] Similarly, Hilo saw no rise in crime as it took in a huge influx of strikers from the Big Island's plantations; the island was where the strike grew to be the largest. Even the decidedly antistrike newspapers, *Hilo Tribune-Herald* (June 28, 1924) and *Honolulu Advertiser* (August 15, 1924), made note of the unexpected calm in Hilo (Reinecke 1996: 52, 56). Admitting grudgingly that, before the massacre, the strikers "never made trouble," one Kaua'i couple who regarded Filipinos as uncivilized and violent reconciled their beliefs with this inconvenient fact by suspecting that the Filipinos "were scheming what to do."[53]

Exemplifying what I refer to as symbolic coercion, the dominant haole elite could not go against, or even put into question, their belief of Filipinos' violent nature to recognize the workers' discourse and practice of nonviolence. What J. K. Butler, the HSPA's secretary, heard in their pacific discourse was precisely its opposite: "sabotage . . . preached by indirection" (as quoted in Reinecke 1996: 25). The sugar industry and the territorial government prepared, quite literally, for battle, as the former funded the latter to hire "special police" and as both stockpiled weapons. A week after the HWM's "Strike Proclamation" and ten days before the start of the strike, the HSPA, as a part of its establishing a strike claims committee, set up funds for "hiring special policemen." With these funds, the HSPA paid the government to hire more police for the express purpose of quelling the strike, all but erasing the line between interests of capital and the state.[54] On O'ahu, over a hundred special police officers were hired. On Kaua'i, 20 at the start of April grew to 200 by September. On the Big Island, the number on active duty reached over 300. At its peak in Lāhainā, Maui, 107 police officers patrolled 600 strikers; at one particularly absurd point, 95 kept watch over 230 strikers (Reinecke 1996: 36, 83).

Two uneventful weeks into the strike on O'ahu, the HSPA sent out a directive to the plantations on the outer islands, ordering that "arms, ammunition, belts, badges, etc. which are able to be recovered and salvaged will be brought out to Honolulu, put in condition for use and ready for immediate distribution, if necessity should arise."[55] Two days before the directive, the HSPA had assessed each plantation 40 cents for each ton of the average produced for the years 1921–23 to pay the premiums for insurance against arson and violence (Beechert 1985: 220). In June, an HSPA bulletin instructed plantation managers, "If there are any violent speeches made, or any threats, or actions violative of the anti-picketing statute, it is hoped that the plantation managers will be able to cause the civil authorities to arrest Manlapit at once and prosecute him or any of his gang."[56] Unfazed by evidence at odds with his belief, the HSPA's Butler lamented, "It is unfortunately true that despite our surveillance we have not been able to get a good case against him. This would be highly desirable because there is no question of his many violations of law."[57] Targeting the leadership may have been seen as especially urgent, since Butler deemed the "majority of the Filipinos [to] have the mentality of 13-year-old children."[58]

A self-fulfilling prophecy, the arms build-up in anticipation of violence set the stage for its realization. On September 9, 1924, Kaua'i county's deputy sheriff and forty police officers, most of whom were special police, went to Hanapēpē to retrieve two Filipino men of Ilocano origin who had been detained forcibly by a group of Filipino strikers of Visayan origin the day before (Reinecke 1996: 75).[59] As the police took custody of the two men and were taking them away, the deadly violence broke out. After the armed conflict, the police arrested well over a hundred, rounding up all surviving Filipino men in Hanapēpē. Filipino labor leaders from the other side of Kaua'i, who had no connection to the violent conflict, were also arrested. Over ninety National Guards were dispatched to Kaua'i the next day. During their nineteen-day deployment, a unit of thirty "sharpshooters," organized by Kauai's sheriff from among the special deputies, trained under them (Reinecke 1976: 83).

There was little uncertainty in the dominant discourse that the Filipino strikers were to blame. According to a police captain at the scene,

The Filipinos were right up against us when they started firing. They had flourished guns and brandished knives. . . . When they began to shoot we returned the fire, but they kept coming until as one after another fell they scattered and fled into a banana grove besides the road. From their shelter in the grove the rioters continued to snipe [at] us with a scattering fire for a quarter of an hour.[60]

The National Guard's report to the governor closely followed the police account: "The strikers kept pressing closer and closer on the officers as they neared their cars, when finally a shot was fired at the police by the strikers which was returned by the police."[61] An assistant manager of a nearby plantation echoed these accounts as an eyewitness (Reinecke 1996: 77). The mainstream newspapers—Kauai's *Garden Island*, the *Honolulu Advertiser*, and the *Honolulu Star-Bulletin*—likewise placed the blame on the strikers, taking their cue and quotes from the police involved (Chapin 1996; Taniguchi et al. 1979). The *Star-Bulletin* referred to it as "mob-murder" and "strike murders," condemning not only the strikers in Hanapēpē but also the "criminal labor agitators and all their ilk."[62] The *Advertiser* immediately concluded that the "strikers fired first" and opined that the "riot was premeditated."[63] Predictably, the HSPA's position was that the "Kauai tragedy [was the] result of strikers' efforts to terrorize":

The Filipino strikers fired, killing one police officer and generally attacking the police with firearms, knives, clubs and other weapons, killing four officers and wounding several others, including the Deputy Sheriff, who suffered knife wounds.

Not until attacked murderously did the police use force.[64]

The president of the HSPA also cited the prevalence of guns among the strikers: "It seems very unfortunate that such a large number of these people have firearms in their possession, many of which were obtained through mail order houses on the mainland."[65] Officials of the Philippine colonial state denounced the strike leadership.[66]

In the general public, the police came under criticism not for their deadly use of force but for not having taken away the Filipino strikers' firearms beforehand. Not to be dissuaded by want of evidence, when a subsequent search of the strike camp in Kāpaʻa by the police and the National Guard, armed with a machine gun and fixed bayonets, turned up only two pistols, the explanation became that the strikers had already thrown their weapons into the ocean.[67] Asked much later if the bloodshed at Hanapēpē could have been avoided, the Kauaʻi couple from above responded, "Nah, at that time, Filipinos was just like cannibal, eh. . . . Filipinos, ho shit; they think kill[ing] people nothing."[68]

As before the killings, Filipino strikers' dissonant discourse continued to be ignored as a matter of course, not as a conscious strategy to silence. For example, that the Filipino strikers were not wholly responsible for the violent outbreak did not seem to be within the realm of possibilities in the dominant accounts, requiring no mention, even to dismiss. The killing of the sixteen strikers by the police failed to elicit scrutiny, much less reproof, in the dominant discourse. Accordingly, the families of the dead police officers received prompt compensation from the HSPA, while the dead Filipinos were unceremoniously buried in a mass grave.[69]

Though not recognized at the time, the Filipino strikers' interpretation of events did indeed differ markedly from the dominant discourse and the doxic beliefs about Filipinos that shaped it. No firsthand accounts were taken from the strikers' point of view (Reinecke 1996), but some would eventually get to tell their stories, if only long after the fact (ESOHP 1979).[70] To begin with, there was a general mistrust of the police. According to a striker on Kauaʻi,

And we were hoping that the police could see that our intention was not to hurt any-body or to cause any kind of trouble. You know, but as a matter of fact, the kind of police that they had during that time, they were the first ones to make some kind of trouble. The police themselves were against the strikers. And you know, that's really at base, what happened there at Hanapepe. That's why a lot of people died.[71]

More specifically, the strikers disputed the dominant assumptions that they had possessed many guns, that they had taken the first shot, and that the kill-ing of strikers by the police had been only in self-defense. These contentions turned out to confirm the lone newspaper account that, in Reinecke's (1996: 167) judgment, had come "the closest to giving the strikers' version": a paper with a fleeting existence of less than a half-year, the *Honolulu Times* reported the first shot being fired by the special police, only two Filipinos having pistols and only one firing, and eleven Filipinos being shot from behind.

According to the strikers at the Hanapēpē strike camp, there had been very few guns and perhaps even fewer bullets.[72] A newcomer to Kauaʻi from the Philippines, who did not strike, corroborated the strikers, "And you could hear the shooting all at once. And the strikers only had a weapon or two, if any, and almost no bullets. And so, that much shooting, it would have to come from the police. Pieces of wood don't shoot bullets."[73] On the question of who proximately touched off the violence, one recalled that "everybody was saying among the strikers, 'It was the police who started it.'"[74] Others were less sure: "I really don't know who started it."[75] As to the accepted nar-rative that the police had reacted only in self-defense, the strikers were clear in their disagreement. According to them, right after the initial outburst, the strikers ran away from the gunfire: "Really wrong, because if he [strikers] run like that, he protecting body, he no like die, that's why he run. But what? He [police] shoot."[76] The police, some of them positioned on a bank, continued to fire their rifles: "They just kept shooting and shooting and of course, a lot of strikers died. . . . The police were up there on a small hill and they had the advantage. They were just picking off the strikers."[77] In line with the strikers' account, a Filipino minister who saw the dead Filipino bodies remembered that most had been shot in the back.[78]

With regard to the dominant, I agree with Bourdieu (1977: 168) that they can recognize what they took for granted and misrecognized as natural "only retrospectively, when they come to be suspended practically." Indeed, this idea is borne out in the case of the Hanapēpē Massacre, evincing further that the dominant's nonrecognition of the Filipinos' discourse in 1924 had been tacit. Over a half-century after the massacre, during which Hawai'i underwent vast transformations, some of the dominant voices of the 1920s, from plantation management and mainstream press, came to hold opinions quite contrary to what had been the dominant discourse. According to Lindsay Faye, the manager of an unstruck Kaua'i sugar plantation in 1924, who arrived at the scene of the violence in Hanapēpē shortly after it began, "Nobody knows who fired the [first] shot." He remembered, "[B]y the time I got there, the strikers weren't shooting back. They were just the police themselves." "Last[ing] half an hour or so," up to a dozen police officers shot at "anybody that was running from behind the bushes there, they'd take a potshot. . . . It wasn't a real battle, it was a slaughter, really."[79] In 1924, Faye and his fellow plantation managers likely would have found it beyond belief that he would end up basically agreeing with Manlapit's (1933: 67) interpretation: "The Hanapepe Massacre, in which four police officers were killed and 16 Filipinos lost their lives. An unnecessary slaughter by sharp-shooters placed in ambush, using soft-nosed bullets on men who were trying to escape."

The reporter for the *Garden Island*, who had witnessed and covered the massacre, recalled similarly, "When they began dropping, everybody began taking off. And some of the goat hunters [police] were still taking potshots at 'em as they ran. . . . This is my opinion—I think a lot of unnecessary shooting happened after it was over, on those that were running."[80] Neither the *Garden Island* nor the Honolulu dailies carried such stories in 1924. It would be easy but mistaken to conclude that this journalist, and others, had consciously misrepresented the event in 1924; he gave no indication for such a conclusion. Rather, the unthinkable, doxa, became thinkable: "It's odd. I can look back on it, I wasn't shocked or anything [at the time]. It was just one of those things."[81]

The legal proceedings reproduced the symbolic coercion against Filipino strikers, once again legitimating the massacre. As the *Garden Island* reporter characterized the process much later, "It was an open-and-shut case, of course."[82] In other words, there was no other outcome that was possible or thinkable: it was a matter "of course." The arrested were kept in jail without being charged. As was common for the time, they were also not provided with lawyers or interpreters.[83] Fifty-seven of the indicted pled guilty to assault and battery. The only evidence against them, in most cases, was their mere presence in the strike camp in Hanapēpē—"hence," Reinecke (1996: 84) wryly notes, "their moral complicity in the riot." In fact, according to an arrested striker, the procedure for processing all of the arrested Filipino men was that they were paraded, one by one, in front of police officers who determined whether "they were there at the strike camp or not."[84]

A grand jury indicted seventy-six others on charges of rioting.[85] At the insistence of an arrested leader, one public defense attorney was then appointed to represent all of the accused. In contrast, directed by the territorial governor, Hawaii's attorney general appointed special deputy prosecutors in consultation with the HSPA, which also paid for them (Reinecke 1996). The dominant discourse in the courts and among the public was that the violent "rioters" had been led astray by their own leaders and, evoking the dominant discourse during the 1920 strike, possibly even the Japanese (Kerkvliet 2002: 52).[86] Unfortunately, "court records and documents which may have provided insights from the perspective of the strikers have been routinely destroyed along with other records of the same era" (Taniguchi et al. 1979: x–xi).[87] This loss was particularly unfortunate, for "each and every one of the defendants [had] insist[ed] on being placed on the stand to testify in his own behalf."[88]

In the end, fifty-eight received four years in prison, while two received four years and eleven months; sixteen were acquitted. Many of the convicted, likely those identified as the leaders in Hanapēpē, were later deported to the Philippines.[89] At the sentence hearing, the presiding judge, William C. Achi, scolded the convicted strikers:

> Your principal trouble lies and your greatest danger is in the radicalism of some of your most prominent leaders. You must not be misled by any queer notion that in order to be successful in your strike you must take law into your own hands and commit acts of violence. (As quoted in Reinecke 1996: 86)

As the strike's foremost historian Reinecke (1996: 85) observes, the judge's statement "enunciated clearly the prevalent view of the strike, which included throwing the blame for Hanapepe upon the top union leaders, whose public utterances (and their private ones, too, so far as is known) had been consistently against violence." The incarceration and deportation of convicted Filipinos added but another layer of physical coercion that was made legitimate by the symbolic coercion to which they were subject.

CONCLUSION

Since the world is not in a state of permanent revolution, much of the social order, though pervaded by inequality and domination, goes unquestioned, not only by the dominant but also by the dominated—"or else the world is a madhouse" (Sahlins 1985: 153). Bourdieu's social theory and research forcefully and convincingly argue this point. Shrinking the importance and purview of consciousness and discourse, he emphasizes the role of symbolic violence—tacit consent or doxic submission—in reproducing and legitimating relations of domination.

Although the concept of symbolic violence gets at an important aspect of symbolic domination, Bourdieu's concomitant assumption of the "unanimity of doxa" exaggerates the consensus with regard to what "goes without saying because it comes without saying" (1977: 167–68). Patricia Hill Collins (1991: 8) writes, "On some level, people who are oppressed usually know it." For Bourdieu, barring moments of exogenously generated crisis, the level of this knowledge is confined to what he refers to as the universe of discourse, the restricted realm of consciously conflicting opinions between the dominant and the dominated that is mutually exclusive of the realm of unconscious unanimity, the universe of doxa. Du Bois's concept of double consciousness, I argue, offers a valuable critique, inserting a third realm that contravenes the assumption of doxic unanimity. Relations of domination induce the dominated to perceive the world doubly, from the vantage point of the dominant as well as that of the dominated, making them conscious of much of what remains unconscious for the dominant. Put simply, the dominated take less of the established order for granted than the dominant. Relations of domination entail asymmetry, not unanimity, of doxa.

The asymmetry of doxa implies that some subaltern discourse is disregarded by the dominant as a matter of course. I propose that this *tacit nonrecognition* constitutes symbolic coercion. It is the explicit disagreement of the dominated that is implicitly ignored by the dominant. The dominant are ignorant in a deep and true sense. Most relevant for this chapter, the proposed reconceptualization helps to explain the legitimate use of physical coercion against the dominated. Symbolic coercion renders its sufferers—whose contrary discourse is tacitly unrecognized and unengaged by the dominant—vulnerable to conservative acts of physical violence, among other forms of subordination and exclusion. It is through the *delegitimation* of the dominated's knowledge that acts of physical coercion against them are made *legitimate*.

How did the police kill sixteen Filipino strikers on the island of Kauaʻi in 1924 with unquestioned and uninterrupted legitimacy? To this day, the killings are more likely to be remembered, if at all, as a riot, a battle, an incident, or a tragedy than as a massacre. How was the nakedness of the deadly brute force not seen? After all, the sugar industry had paid the government for the hiring of hundreds of special police, many of whom took part in the massacre, specifically in anticipation of and response to the strike.

Constituting the dominant common sense, Filipinos in prewar Hawaiʻi were believed to be inferior to and by others, especially haole. One inferior characteristic ascribed to Filipino men, in particular, was a natural predisposition toward violence. Filipino workers, however, did not internalize this dominant belief as common sense: there was no unanimity of doxa, no tacit agreement between the dominated and the dominant. Rather, leading up to and during the 1924 strike, Filipino workers were conscious of the dominant belief of their violent nature and explicitly advocated nonviolence. There was asymmetry of doxa, as the dominant took for granted what the dominated did not. Tacitly not recognizing the Filipino men's discourse and practice of nonviolence, the sugar industry and the territorial government together took extreme measures, including the stockpiling of weapons and the hiring of special police, to counter the violence that they could not fathom would not materialize, even as it did not materialize in the initial months of the strike. Believing was not seeing, or hearing.

The foregoing tacit nonrecognition, or symbolic coercion, secured the immediate legitimacy of the police violence in Hanapēpē that took the lives of sixteen Filipino strikers. The legitimacy of the physical violence against them rested upon the "prereflexive" illegitimacy of their contrary discourse. For the haole elite and, as far as is known, the public at large, the massacre only confirmed their preexisting beliefs about Filipinos. No justification for the sixteen Filipino deaths was needed, because no justification was ever called for. It was self-evident. Reproducing the symbolic coercion, the Filipino strikers' discourse on what had happened in Hanapēpē was also ignored as a matter of course in the aftermath, ensuring the "open-and-shut" criminal cases against dozens of Filipinos and legitimating, once again, the state's use of physical coercion—their incarceration and, in many cases, deportation.

The fact that the Hanapēpē Massacre was the deadliest conflict in Hawaii's labor history has led to the assumption that it was anomalous. But this instance of the "legitimate" use of physical coercion was predicated on symbolic coercion against Filipino working-class men that "normal" unequal social relations produced. Many other instances and forms of "legitimate" physical violence would no doubt yield similar analyses and conclusions. One obvious candidate, in line with the Hanapēpē Massacre, would be death-penalty executions in Hawai'i. Between 1911, when the first Filipino was hanged, and 1944, when the last person, also a Filipino, was hanged, twenty-four, or 77 percent, of thirty-one total executions were of Filipinos, whose proportion of the population peaked at 17 percent in 1930 (Lind 1980: 34; Theroux 1991: Appendix I).[90]

In fact, it is not hard to identify, either historically or contemporarily, cases of symbolic coercion that lead to the use of physical coercion whose legitimacy does not come into serious question. At the present historical moment, like other moments of ruthless inequalities, sufferers of symbolic and physical coercion, foreign and domestic, are not in short supply. Whether they be the Black poor, the incarcerated, Muslims, or unauthorized migrants, their "voicelessness"—or, more accurately, their unsilent but unheard voices[91]—routinely legitimates the physical coercion, and other forms of subordination and exclusion, they face regularly.

How is symbolic coercion, and the legitimate use of physical coercion that it makes possible, to be resisted? I suggest that, despite all the potential pitfalls, one possible answer lies with coalition politics. Symbolic coercion works, in part, through isolation. For example, in 1924, Filipino workers' discourse of nonviolence was tacitly unrecognized not only by the haole elite and the territorial government, their direct adversaries, but also by many others of the non-Filipino public, even those who supported the strike. It is through coalitions among sufferers of different forms and instances of symbolic coercion, who may be more able to hear one another and therefore to articulate a coherent politics, that their respective realms of symbolic coercion may be collectively pushed back.[92] In the late 1930s and 1940s, Hawaii's workers formed such a coalition across hierarchical racial divisions to struggle efficaciously against haole capitalists. One effect of the interracial labor movement was that acts of physical coercion against Filipino workers, like the Hanapēpē Massacre, could no longer take place with unquestioned legitimacy.[93] From Hawaii's workers, we should also take heed that the arduous building of their movement required consciously recognizing and actively subverting structures of inequality and domination within it, including anti-Filipino racism (Jung 2006).

Would America's white people stand for that—unemployment figures like those in the ghetto?

James Baldwin, as quoted in Robert Coles,
"James Baldwin Back Home"

CHAPTER 6

SYMBOLIC PERVERSITY
AND THE MASS
SUFFERING OF BLACKS

On October 21, 2000, Vice President and presidential candidate Al Gore gave a speech at Martin Luther King High School in Philadelphia. With jaunty awkwardness, he began: "What a crowd in Philadelphia! Whooooo! . . . Mayor John Street. You told me you'd throw a good party. . . . Live from Philadelphia! It's Saturday night! . . . It's great to be in a school named after one of my heroes. Tomorrow morning I will fly out of Philadelphia to Dallas, Tex., where I will speak to a large gathering with Coretta Scott King. And I'll be speaking about justice and values." Clearly in an upbeat mood, he boasted, "Let me tell you, we've got a lot of work left to do, but we have made some progress in the last eight years because we've turned the biggest deficits that they left us into the biggest surpluses. . . . Instead of high unemployment, we have the lowest African-American unemployment ever measured."[1] Indeed, the unemployment rate for Blacks had reached an all-time low of 7.0 percent earlier in the year, in April, although it crept up to 7.9 percent in August before settling back down to 7.3 percent by speech time.[2]

Across the state in Pittsburgh and eight years earlier, on October 30, 1992, another Democratic presidential hopeful had dispensed a more somber assessment. In the final days of a campaign whose pithy, resonant catchphrase was "It's the economy, stupid," Bill Clinton latched onto a remark made by his incumbent rival, "Mr. Bush also said we were crazy yesterday. Now, let me tell you something. I tell you what. . . . I'll tell you what I think is crazy. I think crazy is unemployment going up and incomes going down. It's 100,000 Americans a month losing their health insurance. It's one in 10 Americans on food stamps."[3] Unlike Gore, Clinton did not make specific references to Blacks or drop names of revered civil rights figures, no doubt reflecting the mostly white audience in attendance.[4] The overall unemployment rate at the time was 7.3 percent, 6.5 percent for whites.

This chapter questions how 7.3 percent, or even 6.5 percent, unemployment can be an index of intolerable human suffering to be alleviated through new policies by a new administration in one moment and a point of pride to be touted by that very administration in another. In recent decades, the notion that racism is fundamentally different since the Civil Rights Movement and is difficult to discern and analyze has become conventional wisdom, an assumption upon which a whole new set of theories are built.[5] What is often underappreciated are the deeper enduring schemas of racism that persist far and wide with mundanely devastating consequences. Moreover, much of this ostensibly new racism remains baldly visible.

In relation to unemployment, bald visibility is furnished to the public by dominant state and nonstate institutions in a monthly ritual revolving around the release of official statistics. This chapter begins with a brief discussion of the concept of *symbolic perversity*, a paradoxical tool designed to make visible what is already visible. I explain why I choose to focus on *unemployment* as the measure of economic inequality and on the *New York Times* as the dominant nonstate institution through which official state-produced information on unemployment is processed and circulated. The subsequent section consists of statistical analyses of unemployment and its coverage in the *Times* over a 460-month period, beginning in January 1972 when the U.S. Department of Labor started collecting data on Black unemployment. To further illustrate *symbolic perversity* at work, I then compare in depth the two most comparable months in Black and white unemployment. The chapter concludes with thoughts on the pervasiveness of symbolic perversity and what it means for how we understand contemporary racism.

TACIT NONRECOGNITION REVISITED

In the last chapter, I assayed and trimmed Pierre Bourdieu's notion of *symbolic violence* and proposed the concept of *symbolic coercion* to account for *doxic asymmetry* immanent to relations of inequality and domination and the dominant's *tacit nonrecognition* of critical subaltern discourses. Here, I would like to extend this line of inquiry, but in a different direction. In addition to symbolic coercion, there is a second sense in which the dominant are deeply ignorant. Like symbolic coercion, this ignorance straddles the universes of doxa and discourse. It, too, involves the dominant's (mostly) tacit nonrecognition of explicit discourse concerning inequality and domination. But it differs in that the discourse being disregarded as a matter of course is not that of the dominated but of the dominant; by dominant discourse, I mean discourse that is produced and consumed by and readily available to those in relatively dominant social positions.

Put in terms of race, the dominant, whether they be institutions or individuals, are typically well aware of many persistent racial inequalities, beyond those politicized and brought to their attention by subaltern discourses. The dominant possess discursive knowledge of the reality that certain racial category, or categories, of actors systematically fare worse than themselves and others. Much of this knowledge is produced by dominant institutions, like state agencies, research universities, and news media. Yet the dominant's consumption and circulation of this knowledge are censored and structured by an underlying racial logic that implicitly assumes radical difference between categories of people and renders the suffering of some incommensurable with and less worthy than the suffering of others. They can and do know about the suffering of their racial others, but this knowledge fails to register or matter—at least not to the same degree as the suffering of the dominant racial category. The effect of this knowing-unknowing is depraved indifference to racial inequalities—depraved for its knowingness but indifferent in usually unknowing, unreflexive ways. A quietly ubiquitous combination of conscious knowing and unconscious unknowing, it is this tacit nonrecognition that I refer to as *symbolic perversity*. Along with complementary concepts like *white ignorance* (Mills 2007), *culpable ignorance* (Bartky 2002), and *racial apathy* (Forman and Lewis 2006), *symbolic perversity*, as well as *symbolic violence* and *symbolic coercion*, belongs to an emerging sociology and epistemology of ignorance (Mills 1997, 2007).

On a different but not unrelated subject, Sven Lindqvist (1992: 2) states, "You already know enough. So do I. It is not knowledge we lack. What is missing is the courage to understand what we know and draw conclusions." True, but what is also lacking and precedes courage is recognition of the conditions that warrant courage. For the dominant, the moment of choice between bravery and cowardice often never comes: they know not what they know, for they care not what they know.

As a case study of symbolic perversity, I examine statistically the coverage of unemployment in the *New York Times* from 1972 to 2010 and then compare

selected months in depth. The *Times* is one of just several U.S. newspapers that
is "national" in scope, one that is self-consciously so (George and Waldfogel
2006). It ranks third, behind the *Wall Street Journal* and *USA Today*, in print
circulation and first in on-line readership (Alliance for Audited Media 2013;
Audit Bureau of Circulation 2010; Seward 2009). As the paper likes to market
itself, its audience is not only large but affluent and influential—affluential, as
it were.[6] Within mainstream journalism, it sits imperiously at the pinnacle. For
example, it far surpasses all other newspapers in the number of Pulitzer Prizes
won, having collected more of them than its two closest competitors, the *Washington Post* and the *Los Angeles Times*, combined (Shaw 2006). By any measure,
the *New York Times* is a dominant institution in the United States, indeed the
world.[7] Further, it is politically liberal, not only in its editorials but also its news
content (Groseclose and Milyo 2005). One could therefore expect that the coverage of unemployment in the *Times* would pose a harder test for demonstrat-
ing racial symbolic perversity than that in its more conservative counterparts.
The paper would not likely set out to be intentionally discriminatory toward
Blacks and would be more mindful than the norm on matters of race; though
not investigated here, this statement probably also holds for periods before the
Civil Rights Movement, though obviously within a different set of parameters.

I choose *unemployment* for several reasons. It has an official definition that
is nearly universally accepted. The U.S. Bureau of Labors Statistics (BLS)
defines the unemployed as "people who are jobless, looking for jobs, and available for work." The unemployment rate is the percentage of the unemployed
in the labor force, which is the "civilian noninstitutional population 16 years
old and over" that is either employed or unemployed (USBLS 2009: 4, 7).
The BLS and the Census Bureau have together gathered, analyzed, and made
available nationally representative data on unemployment on a monthly basis
since 1940. Racial information was added in 1948, and a separate category for
Blacks, rather than the catchall "nonwhite" category, has existed since 1972
(Fairlie and Sundstrom 1997; USBLS 2009).

For large segments of the public, unemployment is something of grave and
immediate concern and consequence. Needing, seeking, but not having a job in
a capitalist society, particularly one with a relatively miserly welfare state, can
set off a whole host of negative, often dire, ramifications, including the loss of
housing, education, food security, health care, physical and mental well-being,
and so on. As the economist Joan Robinson ([1962] 2006: 45) once quipped,

"the misery of being exploited by capitalists is nothing compared to the misery of not being exploited at all." For related, though scarcely identical, reasons, political and economic elites also closely monitor the rate of unemployment. It is, for all concerned, an economic indicator of intensive and extensive interest. Hence, as the BLS notes, "[employment] figures, particularly the unemployment rate . . . receive wide coverage in the media" (USBLS 2009: 1), not least among them the *New York Times*.

In relation to skeptical readers, unemployment offers a couple of additional advantages for critical studies of racial inequality. It neutralizes the conservative assumption, suspicion, and argument that some people, particularly poor Blacks, do not work because they do not want to work—put bluntly, because they are lazy. By definition, the unemployed are those who "have actively looked for work in the prior 4 weeks" (USBLS 2009: 5): they want to work but cannot. Moreover, racial inequality in unemployment, if anything, underestimates the overall level of economic racial inequality, even if we focus narrowly on the labor market and do not deal with more imbalanced aspects, like wealth (e.g., Kochhar, Fry, and Taylor 2011). For example, Blacks are overrepresented among the underemployed (i.e., workers who are underutilized in terms of hours or qualifications) and the discouraged (i.e., the jobless who have ceased looking for work), whose inclusion would accentuate the racial gap (Jensen and Slack 2003; Johnson and Herring 1993; Lichter 1988; Zhou 1993). Incorporating Blacks' disproportionately high numbers among the incarcerated and the military would further underscore their unequal standing relative to the civilian labor market (Mare and Winship 1984; Western and Pettit 1999, 2005).

THE NUMBERS

Black unemployment and its coverage, in comparison with those of whites and the general population, constitute this chapter's focus. Along with American Indians, Blacks have consistently suffered the highest rates of unemployment (Austin 2009; Freeman and Fox 2005). And as noted above, the BLS and the Census Bureau have collected and made public disaggregated Black unemployment data since 1972. Given the time period, the study enables one particular appraisal of the state of anti-Black racism in the post–Civil Rights era.

From the BLS, I obtained unemployment data for the period from January 1972 to April 2010. The monthly data were seasonally adjusted and included rates for Blacks, whites, and the population as a whole.[8] In the thirty-eight-year span, the mean rate of unemployment for the country was 6.3 percent; it rose to a high of 10.8 percent in November and December of 1982 and sank to a low of 3.8 percent in April 2000 (see Table 6.1 for annual averages). We witnessed seven episodes of expansion and six of recession. The longest were, respectively, between March 1991 and February 2001 and between December 2007 and June 2009 (NBER 2010a, 2010b).

The rate of white unemployment has closely tracked the overall rate, though *always* trailing it. With an average of 5.5 percent, the white unemployment rate was 3.4 percent at its lowest, in January, April, June, and October of 2000, and 9.7 percent at its highest, in December 1982. Albeit more loosely, the Black unemployment rate also paralleled the overall rate, but it was much higher (see Figure 6.1). The *average* was 12.1 percent. As noted above, it never sank below 7.0 percent, reached in April 2000, and rose as high as 21.2 percent, in January 1983.

One irony of the postwar period of the Civil Rights Movement and its aftermath is that racial inequality in unemployment has been greater since the middle of the twentieth century than it had been earlier. Furthermore, from about 1950 onward, Blacks have been roughly twice as likely to be unemployed as whites (Fairlie and Sundstrom 1997; Vedder and Gallaway 1992). Since 1972, the ratio of Black and white unemployment rates has been 2.21 on average, never falling below the October 2009 mark of 1.67 and peaking at an astounding 2.77, in February 1989 (see Table 6.1 and Figure 6.2). In fact, the unemployment figures for Blacks and whites are so far apart that they barely overlap. The white *maximum* is 2.4 percentage points *lower* than the Black *average*. Black unemployment is higher than the white *maximum* in 357 of the total 460 months examined, while white unemployment matches or exceeds the Black *minimum* in only 61 of the months (see Figure 6.1). Perhaps we should institute a ban on the all-too-frequently bandied-about metaphor of rising tides and acknowledge that those in row boats and dinghies are much more vulnerable to unruly waves, including those agitated by corporate freight ships and posh cruise liners, and that far too many Blacks are *always* drowning.

As a measure of the *New York Times*'s coverage of unemployment over the past four decades, I performed a keyword search for "unemployment" in its online archive for each month from February 1972 to May 2010; in the following analysis, because the BLS releases at the beginning of each month

TABLE 6.1. ANNUAL AVERAGES OF MONTHLY UNEMPLOYMENT RATES AND RATIOS OF BLACK TO WHITE UNEMPLOYMENT RATES, 1972 TO 2010

Year	Overall	White	Black	B/W Ratio
1972	5.6	5.1	10.4	2.06
1973	4.9	4.3	9.4	2.17
1974	5.6	5.1	10.5	2.08
1975	8.5	7.8	14.8	1.91
1976	7.7	7.0	14.0	2.00
1977	7.1	6.2	14.0	2.25
1978	6.1	5.2	12.7	2.44
1979	5.9	5.1	12.3	2.43
1980	7.2	6.3	14.3	2.26
1981	7.6	6.7	15.6	2.34
1982	9.7	8.6	18.9	2.20
1983	9.6	8.4	19.5	2.33
1984	7.5	6.5	15.9	2.46
1985	7.2	6.2	15.1	2.43
1986	7.0	6.0	14.6	2.41
1987	6.2	5.3	13.0	2.44
1988	5.5	4.7	11.7	2.47
1989	5.3	4.5	11.5	2.56
1990	5.6	4.8	11.4	2.36
1991	6.9	6.1	12.5	2.05
1992	7.5	6.6	14.2	2.16
1993	6.9	6.1	13.0	2.13
1994	6.1	5.3	11.5	2.18
1995	5.6	4.9	10.4	2.12
1996	5.4	4.7	10.5	2.25
1997	4.9	4.2	10.1	2.39
1998	4.5	3.9	8.9	2.31
1999	4.2	3.7	8.0	2.18
2000	4.0	3.5	7.6	2.18
2001	4.7	4.2	8.7	2.08
2002	5.8	5.1	10.2	2.01
2003	6.0	5.3	10.8	2.05
2004	5.5	4.8	10.4	2.16
2005	5.1	4.4	10.0	2.29
2006	4.6	4.0	9.0	2.22
2007	4.6	4.1	8.3	2.01
2008	5.8	5.2	10.1	1.93
2009	9.3	8.5	14.8	1.74
2010 (*through April*)	9.8	8.8	16.3	1.85

Source: *U.S. Bureau of Labor Statistics.*

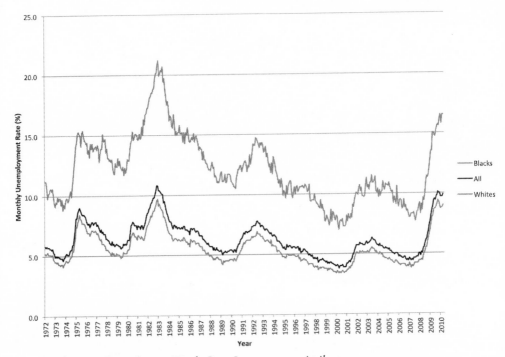

Figure 6.1. Unemployment Rate by Race, January 1972 to April 2010.
Source: U.S. Bureau of Labor Statistics.

the unemployment data for the *preceding* month, I lagged the *Times* coverage
behind the other variables by one month.[9] Predictably following the pattern
of unemployment, the coverage was the most concentrated in the early 1980s,
shooting up to 493 items in October 1982. Fluctuating around the median of
110 since the mid-1980s up to the most recent recession, the number of "unemployment" items dipped to its nadir of 37 in August 2007 (see Figure 6.3).

That the overall, white, and Black unemployment rates are all highly inter-
correlated comes as little surprise.[10] We would also expect each of them to be
significantly correlated with the level of coverage in the *Times*, although, given
the high correlations among the three unemployment rates, the independent
effect of each would be impossible to pull apart. But if the unemployment
coverage in the *Times* were to manifest relative indifference toward Blacks, we
would expect it to be less correlated to the unemployment rate of Blacks than
to that of whites or the general population.

To test the idea, I introduce a couple of control variables. First, even at the
same rate of unemployment, the *Times* may deal with unemployment more

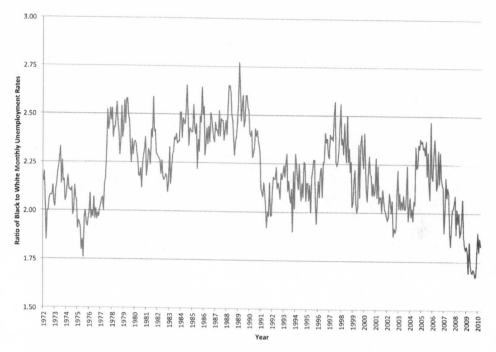

Figure 6.2. Ratio of Black to White Unemployment Rates, January 1972 to April 2010
Source: Calculated from U.S. Bureau of Labor Statistics data.

during periods of recession than those of expansion. Based on the National Bureau of Economic Research's determination of economic cycles, I include a dummy variable to differentiate periods of recession and expansion (NBER 2010a, 2010b). Second, because unemployment is a politically charged topic that is often invoked by politicians and, in turn, covered by the news media, and because the *Times*'s liberal lean and reputation may be related to how it reports on economic issues depending on which party is in power, a second dummy variable distinguishes between times of Democratic and Republican administrations.

Controlling for recessions and parties, all three rates of unemployment—over-all, white, and Black—are highly correlated with the level of "unemployment" coverage in the *Times* at a high degree of significance. But, consistent with the idea of depraved indifference toward Blacks, the correlation for Black unemployment is the weakest, at 0.688. Not only are the other two rates more tightly related to the *Times* coverage, but of the two, the white unemployment rate turns out to be slightly more predictive than the overall rate; the correlation for the

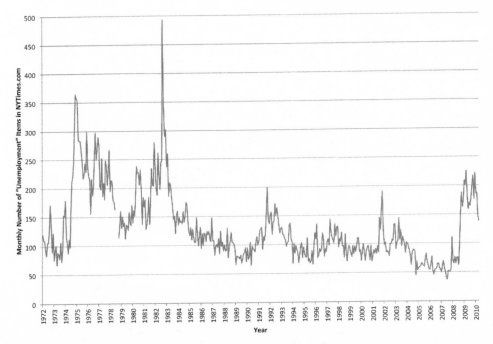

Figure 6.3. Number of "Unemployment" Items in the New York Times, *February 1972 to May 2010. Source: Compiled from NYTimes.com (retrieved September 3, 2010).*

former is 0.742, compared to 0.730 for the latter (see Table 6.2). A Hotelling's *t* score of 4.05 confirms that the correlation between the level of *Times* coverage and white unemployment is significantly higher than the correlation between the level of *Times* coverage and Black unemployment ($p < .001$, two-tailed test).[11]

To test more directly for symbolic perversity, I ran a regression using the aforementioned measure of racial inequality, the ratio of Black and white unemployment rates.[12] Looking at Table 6.3, we see that periods of recession and Democratic administration are associated with higher numbers of "unemployment" items in the *Times*. Controlling for these variables and the overall unemployment rate, if the *Times* were *not* depravedly indifferent to the inequality between white and Black unemployment, which is plainly visible to any passing glance at a BLS monthly press release, we would expect its coverage of unemployment to intensify with worsening inequality. But if the *Times* were depravedly indifferent—"depravedly" because of its ready access to the unemployment information produced by another dominant institution, the U.S. government—we would not anticipate a significantly positive relationship.

TABLE 6.2. PARTIAL CORRELATIONS BETWEEN THE NUMBER OF
"UNEMPLOYMENT" ITEMS IN THE *NEW YORK TIMES* AND OVERALL, WHITE, AND
BLACK UNEMPLOYMENT RATES, JANUARY 1972 TO APRIL 2010

	"Unemployment" Items in the New York Times *Partial r*
Overall Unemployment Rate	0.730*
White Unemployment Rate	0.742*
Black Unemployment Rate	0.688*
* p < .001 (two-tailed tests)	

Note: Controlling variables are periods of recession and Democratic administrations. The "unemployment" items in the *New York Times* lag the unemployment rates by one month. Of 460 total possible observations, 4 are removed: keyword search for "unemployment" items in NYTimes.com does not produce valid numbers for August, September, and October 1978, and September 1982 is an outlier.

Indeed, this is what we find. As the racial inequality faced by Blacks in relation to whites deepens, the *Times* is not more or less likely to publish articles on unemployment. To the *Times*, the longstanding racial inequality in unemployment lacks, statistically speaking, significance (*p* = 0.391, two tailed test).[13]

INCOMMENSURABLE AND INCOMPREHENSIBLE SUFFERING

One difficulty of comparing white and Black unemployment rates is that they are never comparable. When it is low for whites, it is high for Blacks. When it is high for whites, it is catastrophically high for Blacks. As a corollary rule, respective months of comparably high rates of white and Black unemployment tend to be far apart in time. In Figure 6.1, if we were to draw horizontal lines from the various peaks of white unemployment, some of the tangents would never cross even the deepest valleys of the Black graph line. For those that would, the intersecting points would be many months or years in the past or future. For example, the white unemployment rate reached its apex of 9.7 percent in December 1982, a below-average elevation for Blacks that they had not passed through since May 1974 and would not come across again until March 1995. These three moments would make for poor comparison, hailing from three different decades, economic cycles, and administrations.

The best months for comparison turn out to be from the recent past. In June 2008, Black unemployment stood at 9.4 percent, quickly soaring there-

TABLE 6.3. ORDINARY LEAST SQUARES REGRESSION PREDICTING THE NUMBER
OF "UNEMPLOYMENT" ITEMS IN THE *NEW YORK TIMES*, JANUARY 1972 TO
APRIL 2010

	Model 1	Model 2
Period of Recession	33.43*	32.56*
	(5.20)	(5.30)
Period of Democratic Administration	16.17*	16.00*
	(3.99)	(4.00)
Overall Unemployment Rate	28.48*	28.30*
	(1.26)	(1.27)
Ratio of Black and White Unemployment Rates		-8.00
		(9.32)
Constant	-59.95*	-40.96
	(8.31)	(23.65)
Observations	456	456

* p < .001 (two-tailed tests)

Note: Standard errors are in parentheses. On the one-month lag of the dependent variable and the number of observations, see the note to Table 6.2.

after, and white unemployment crested at the same figure in October 2009.[14] The sixteen months in between mark the shortest gap between a peak rate of white unemployment and a comparable rate of Black unemployment. Related to the minimal lapse in time, the two months belonged to the same upswing cycle in unemployment (see Figure 6.1), even if the most recent recession had technically ended a few months before October 2009. Further, according to Table 6.3, the expected bump in the *Times*'s coverage of unemployment during periods of recession, as in June 2008, is partially matched by a predicted uptick half as big for periods of Democratic administration, as in October 2009. Given the bigger anticipated boost in unemployment coverage for June 2008, the month indexed to Black unemployment, my comparative analysis should be, if anything, biased toward underestimating racial disparities. (Taking into account BLS's schedule of releasing the previous month's figures, I examine the *Times*'s coverage for July 2008 and November 2009.)

In July 2008, the *Times* published 67 items containing the word "unemployment."[15] A half-year into what would become the longest postwar recession, in the midst of the bubble burst in the housing market but before the meltdown on Wall Street, the overall outlook on the economy was negative but not overly alarmed. Since the beginnings and endings of recessions can only be determined retrospectively, whether a recession had commenced was still somewhat uncertain at the time. As economics columnist David Leonhardt speculated, "I'd say the odds that it's a true recession are about 75 percent." Writing on July 2, he anticipated bad news from the BLS the next day, when it would release the June employment figures: "a sixth straight month of job losses." He continued, "But whatever the report shows, the job market is likely to remain weak through the end of the year, because employment generally continues to fall for months after a downturn has ended."[16] A front-page piece by Peter Goodman on the same day noted that, as of May, unemployment had already risen a full percentage point to 5.5 percent in the past year and "the so-called underemployment rate" was at 9.7 percent. Worse yet, Goldman Sachs predicted that the overall unemployment rate would "peak at 6.4 percent late in 2009 before the picture improves, meaning that the painful process of shedding jobs may be only half-way complete."[17]

The next day, the BLS confirmed the dreary outlook. The overall unemployment rate showed no improvement, holding at 5.5 percent. For the rest of the month, the 5.5 percent figure appeared intermittently in the *Times*. As in Goodman's anticipatory piece, 5.5 percent was perceived as already high, but more important, it augured still higher numbers. The day after the BLS press release, a front-page article read,

The nation's employers eliminated tens of thousands of jobs in June for the sixth consecutive month in a steady chipping away of the work force that seems likely to leave the economy very weak through Election Day.

Responding quickly to the government employment report, issued Thursday, the presidential candidates called for action, beyond the recent stimulus package, to reverse the deterioration. . . .

Few teenagers and new college graduates found work, the bureau reported. What's more, the percentage of unemployed adult workers, 25 and over, ticked up for the second straight month, and various forecasters said that by Election Day, the unemployment rate would probably be 6 percent or more—a level last seen in the early 1990s, in the aftermath of a recession. . . .

Responding to the jobs report, Dana Perino, the White House press spokeswoman, acknowledged that the nation was "in a period of slow growth," which was having "an impact on employment."[18]

Later in the month, the paper reported, "Job losses will probably accelerate through this year and into 2009, and the job market will probably stay weak even longer. . . . Whatever it is called [recession or not], it is a painful time for tens of millions of people. . . . The unemployment rate still remains low by historical standards, at 5.5 percent. . . . But Goldman Sachs assumes unemployment will reach 6.5 percent by the end of 2009, which translates into several hundred thousand more Americans out of work."[19]

Right after the BLS issued the new numbers, the liberal columnist Bob Herbert detected "an undercurrent of anxiety in the land." He highlighted the fact that "the national employment rate for teens in June was the lowest in 60 years."[20] A couple of weeks later, the economist Paul Krugman, a fellow liberal in the Op-Ed pages, expressed a similarly dour outlook: "Home prices are in free fall. Unemployment is rising. Consumer confidence is plumbing depths not seen since 1980. When will it all end? The answer is, probably not until 2010."[21] Even John McCain, the Republican presidential candidate, found himself in the midst of busily, if ambivalently, tamping down his earlier optimism, telling a group of workers in Michigan, "America is hurting today. Michigan is hurting today. The automotive industry is hurting. And we've got big problems, and we've got big challenges."[22]

In light of the eventual severity of the economic downturn, the pessimistic numbers and prognostications may now discombobulate our sense of proportion, but let us not dismiss what the numbers meant for the *Times*, its informants, its readers, and politicians at the time. An unemployment figure of 5.5 percent was worrisome, and the worst-case scenario that they imagined and were bracing for at the time was unemployment in the 6.0 to 6.5 percent range, which, they knew, would be "painful" for many and unnerving for many more.

Times were already that painful and unnerving—actually much, much worse—for Blacks, however. The confirmatory evidence required no tenacious sleuthing by Pulitzer-hungry reporters, no Freedom of Information Act requests for classified documents. Just a scan five lines down on the BLS press release (see Figure 6.4). In plain sight, on the first table, on p. 2, in a font size no bigger or smaller than the much cited "5.5," the release reported the Black unemployment rate as 9.2 percent (later adjusted to 9.4 percent). One column over, for the previous month, the figure had been even higher, at 9.7 percent, equal to the highest unemployment rate of the past four decades for whites.[23] But such facts did not merit a single mention in the newspaper that proclaims

Table A. Major indicators of labor market activity, seasonally adjusted

(Numbers in thousands)

Category	Quarterly averages		Monthly data			May-June change
	I 2008	II 2008	Apr. 2008	May 2008	June 2008	
HOUSEHOLD DATA	Labor force status					
Civilian labor force	153,661	154,294	153,957	154,534	154,390	-144
Employment	146,070	146,089	146,331	146,046	145,891	-155
Unemployment	7,591	8,204	7,626	8,487	8,499	12
Not in labor force	79,146	79,117	79,241	c 78,871	79,237	c 366
	Unemployment rates					
All workers	4.9	5.3	5.0	5.5	5.5	0.0
Adult men	4.4	4.9	4.6	4.9	5.1	.2
Adult women	4.3	4.6	4.3	4.8	4.7	-.1
Teenagers	16.8	17.4	15.4	18.7	18.1	-.6
White	4.4	4.7	4.4	4.9	4.9	.0
Black or African American	8.8	9.1	8.6	9.7	9.2	-.5
Hispanic or Latino ethnicity	6.5	7.2	6.9	6.9	7.7	.8
ESTABLISHMENT DATA	Employment					
Nonfarm employment	137,917	p 137,702	137,764	p 137,702	p 137,640	p -62
Goods-producing [1]	21,820	p 21,569	21,628	p 21,574	p 21,505	p -69
Construction	7,384	p 7,245	7,284	p 7,247	p 7,204	p -43
Manufacturing	13,690	p 13,566	13,592	p 13,570	p 13,537	p -33
Service-providing [1]	116,097	p 116,133	116,136	p 116,128	p 116,135	p 7
Retail trade [2]	15,434	p 15,338	15,356	p 15,333	p 15,326	p -8
Professional and business service	18,063	p 17,981	18,031	p 17,982	p 17,931	p -51
Education and health services	18,664	p 18,796	18,757	p 18,801	p 18,830	p 29
Leisure and hospitality	13,660	p 13,704	13,690	p 13,699	p 13,723	p 24
Government	22,358	p 22,430	22,401	p 22,430	p 22,459	p 29
	Hours of work [3]					
Total private	33.7	p 33.7	33.8	p 33.7	p 33.7	p 0.0
Manufacturing	41.1	p 40.9	41.0	p 40.9	p 40.8	p -.1
Overtime	4.0	p 3.9	4.0	p 3.9	p 3.9	p .0
	Indexes of aggregate weekly hours (2002=100) [3]					
Total private	107.4	p 107.2	107.5	p 107.1	p 107.0	p -0.1
	Earnings [3]					
Average hourly earnings, total private	$17.81	p $17.95	$17.89	p $17.95	p $18.01	p $0.06
Average weekly earnings, total private	600.80	p 605.51	604.68	p 604.92	p 606.94	p 2.02

[1] Includes other industries, not shown separately.

[2] Quarterly averages and the over-the-month change are calculated using unrounded data.

[3] Data relate to private production and nonsupervisory workers.

p = preliminary.

c = corrected.

Figure 6.4. Employment Data for June 2008 Released by the U.S. Bureau of Labor Statistics.
Source: U.S. Bureau of Labor Statistics, "News Release," July 3, 2008, p. 2.

it publishes "all the news that's fit to print."[24] If they constituted a separate nation-state, Blacks in the United States, with 39.7 million people, would be the thirty-third largest in the world, between Spain and Kenya (CIA 2010; U.S. Census Bureau 2010). Yet while the *Times* utterly failed to notice Black unemployment, it published around twenty items with references to unemployment in various foreign countries, big and small, rich and poor.

By November 2009, the unemployment situation became what had been unthinkable a little over a year earlier, and the coverage in the *Times* reflected it. Many more articles, columns, and editorials documented how bad, *truly bad*, things were. In that month, when white unemployment reached the level that Blacks had been at sixteen months before, the *Times* printed 199—that is, three times as many—items on "unemployment." Though nominally out of the longest postwar recession, the labor force was facing the worst of the economic slump. The overall unemployment hit double digits for the first time since the early 1980s.

Leading up to the BLS press release, articles, columns, and editorials tended to look for and find a sliver of silver in the dark clouds gathered overhead—as exemplified by the headline "Through a Glass Less Darkly."[25] Though not yet official, the recession appeared to have ended, with the economy growing at a somewhat higher clip than expected. "The Great Recession is over," wrote Mark Zandi, an economist, in the Op-Ed pages. "Still, the recovery remains fragile," he continued, advocating additional policy measures to bolster hiring by small businesses.[26] Ben Bernanke, the head of the Federal Reserve, similarly "cautioned that the recovery was fragile and that unemployment would remain high through the end of next year."[27] A piece by the Associated Press read, "Unemployment hit a 26-year high of 9.8 percent in September, and the October report, due Friday, could show it topping 10 percent." It went on to quote Treasury Secretary Timothy Geithner as saying, "Unemployment is worse than almost everybody expected. But growth is back a little more quickly, a little stronger, than people thought."[28] On the same day, Krugman proffered his take, "The good news is that the American Recovery and Reinvestment Act, a.k.a. the Obama stimulus plan, is working just about the way textbook macroeconomics said it would. But that's also the bad news—because the same textbook analysis says that the stimulus was far too small given the scale of our economic problems. Unless something changes drastically, we're looking at many years of high unemployment." He noted that "last week's G.D.P.

report showed the economy growing again, at a better-than-expected annual rate of 3.5 percent." But he warned that this growth rate would produce jobs at an anemic pace and, "worse yet, it [was] far from clear that growth will continue at this rate."[29]

Lawmakers in Congress were less ambivalent and felt compelled to act immediately. On extending unemployment benefits for up to twenty additional weeks, "the Democrats feel an urgency to act now because the monthly labor report that comes out Friday is expected to show that the nation's unemployment rate in October continued to be at or above 10 percent." With many of their states already mired in double-digit unemployment, Republicans also fell in line. The Senate unanimously passed the bill, and the House was expected to approve it in quick order.[30] Wall Street, on the other hand, found hope in the news from the Department of Labor that "newly laid-off workers seeking unemployment benefits fell to 512,000 last week": "The Dow Jones industrial average jumped 200 points to its first close above 10,000 in two weeks." Apparently, the Labor Department's report on unemployment benefit filings "unleashed a wave of optimism" about the unemployment figures to be released the next day: "Analysts project that the unemployment rate rose to 9.9 percent in October."[31]

On November 6, the BLS released the new numbers. On November 7, the front page of the *Times* declared, "Jobless Rate Hits 10.2%, with More Underemployed." The top story placed the historic numbers in historical context, "The official jobless rate—10.2 percent in October, up from 9.8 percent in September—remains lower than the early 1980s peak of 10.8 percent." But, counting the discouraged and the underemployed, defined as part-time workers who want full-time positions, the combined 17.5 percent exceeded the 17.1 percent height of December 1982: "If statistics went back so far, the measure would almost certainly be at its highest level since the Great Depression."[32] For the remainder of the month, the 10.2 figure (later adjusted to 10.1) and the fact of its being a twenty-six-year high turned up frequently, to be made sense of in divers ways, and while the level of pessimism varied, Wall Street investors were certainly in the minority when they found a measure of hope in the probable rock-bottoming of the labor market.[33]

The *Times* devoted a large swath of their pages to unemployment and scrutinized it from assorted angles. The cumulative effect of the voluminous coverage was to convey a recognition of the seriousness of the situation and a sense of deep concern. Predictably, news articles that were narrowly economic in scope rarely strayed from dry prose and precise numbers, but unemployment figured variously in them, depending on their degree of separation. Those that focused on aspects of the economy that were linked less directly or exclusively to unemployment, like financial markets, tended to see unemployment as one indicator among others, a lagging one at that, and give a more mixed picture. For example, in an article on oil prices and the stock market, Javier C. Hernandez reported, "Wall Street stocks fell on Thursday as investors reacted with caution to a drop in the price of oil. An announcement by President Obama of a job creation initiative failed to motivate investors. . . . While the broader economy has shown signs of health since the near collapse of the financial system last year, the United States has continued to grapple with high levels of unemployment. Last month, the unemployment rate reached 10.2 percent, a 26-year high."[34] Stories on consumption, more closely tied to unemployment, sketched a more cautious picture: "Economists worry that high unemployment will slow the economic recovery as consumers keep a lid on spending, even as the government continues to inject billions into the economy. The unemployment rate reached 10.2 percent in October, the highest in 26 years."[35] A national survey on consumer confidence collected some of the lowest ratings in a quarter-century, and high unemployment appeared to be the main cause.[36] A story based on "anecdotal reports" of retailers and shoppers on the ground confirmed the wariness: "A year after an unfolding economic crisis sent consumers into shock, they ventured out Friday and opened their wallets a bit— still hunting bargains, but no longer quite so afraid to spend. . . . While the economy is showing signs of recovery, unemployment is the highest in decades and consumers are still deeply worried, which is likely to affect holiday shopping."[37] Similar apprehension characterized the news on the housing market.[38]

Articles on unemployment itself and its immediate effects portrayed a harsher reality. In the piece "Job Losses Mount, Enduring and Deep," Floyd Norris underscored the historic dimensions of the unemployment crisis. He noted that "the proportion of workers who have been out of work for a long time is higher now than it has ever been since the Great Depression. . . . Over the last three years—since October 2006—the overall unemployment rate has risen by 5.8 percentage points. That is the largest such increase since the Great Depression, providing another indication of the rapidity and severity of the current downturn."[39] Another article relayed the news from the Department of Labor that "joblessness rose in 29 states last month compared with 22 in September," four of which hit record levels.[40] As could be expected, demand for services like affordable mental health care grew.[41]

Politics over policy and elections, directly and indirectly related to unemployment, captured its share of column inches. Republicans cited unemployment as a reason not to pass a bill on health care. Ken Spain, the communications director of the National Republican Congressional Committee, was quoted as saying, "A vote for yet another job-killing expansion of government in the wake of newly released skyrocketing unemployment numbers would just be further proof of how politically tone-deaf the Democratic majority has become."[42] A year yet to go, there was already speculation about the effect of unemployment on the 2010 midterm elections:

If they crave comfort, Democratic candidates can grab onto this: political science research finds little historical connection between unemployment and midterm Congressional elections.

But neither the Obama White House nor outside Democratic strategists count on that evidence to protect them in the midterm elections of 2010. That is why, in a week when the Senate begins debating health care and President Obama reveals his new war strategy for Afghanistan, the White House "jobs summit" may be just as important politically. It represents the beginning of the Democratic effort to decide which new initiatives may be most effective in stimulating new hiring, and how aggressively to pursue them.[43]

President Obama's slipping approval ratings and Sarah Palin's continuing popularity in certain quarters owed their divergent fortunes in part to high unemployment, according to the *Times*.[44]

The effects of unemployment at state and local levels also received their share of attention. In the run-up to New York City's mayoral election, jobs and unemployment took center stage: "With the unemployment rate at a 16-year high, tens of thousands of homeowners facing foreclosure and the city's budget deficit topping $5 billion, Comptroller William C. Thompson Jr. and Mayor Michael R. Bloomberg offered strikingly different messages to an unsettled electorate."[45] In a small town in Maine, rising antagonism against Latinos, and a plan to build "a small apartment complex for farmworkers," seemingly tracked rising unemployment: "The county's unemployment rate is 10.4 percent, and 20 percent of its population lives in poverty. In a letter to a local newspaper, one resident pointed out that many native Mainers, not just immigrants, live in tumbledown trailers. 'When there is very little work,' the letter said, 'bringing more people in does not solve the problem.'"[46] Meanwhile, according to a front-page story, "unemployment has hit migrant communities in the United States so hard that a startling new phenomenon has been detected: instead of receiving remittances from relatives in the richest country on earth, some down-and-out Mexican families are scraping together what they can to support their unemployed loved ones in the United States."[47] Two articles on Thomson, a village in western Illinois, described the controversy and ambivalence roused by the possibility of converting a state prison to house Guantánamo "terrorism suspects," which "by some estimates . . . would provide 3,200 jobs and cut the local unemployment rate in half."[48]

Many articles, like those above, carried quotes and anecdotes of people whose lives were personally touched by unemployment. Others were more overtly "human interest" stories. "Job Woes Exacting a Heavy Toll on Family Life," published on November 12, detailed the strain of unemployment, especially male unemployment, on a few upper-middle-class, presumably heterosexual nuclear families in Texas, Kansas, and Indiana. Described as "on the brink," one family, a year after the husband's job loss, scraped by on his unemployment benefits and the wife's earnings from a part-time position. Their two daughters showed signs of distress, with the younger one "pulling out strands of her hair over the summer" and the older one "throwing tantrums." The couple was in therapy to "save their marriage." Unmentioned, not unusually, but visible in the accompanying photographs was the family's whiteness.[49]

Most human-interest stories were not depressing, in-depth looks at personal devastation or suffering. As if to balance the heaviness of the news, they favored a lighter touch. One contrasted the different mood in New York's financial district awaiting the victory parade of the Yankees, who just won the World Series, with that after the Giants' Super Bowl win twenty-one months earlier: "Sure, people will be cheering and the confetti will be flying. But the energy radiating from the offices that line the route may be more cathartic than triumphant. . . . Back then, the city's unemployment rate was 4.5 percent; now it is 10.3 percent and twice as many New Yorkers are out of work."[50] Another told stories of the "laptop brigade," the surge of unemployed in New York City, "where the unemployment rate remains at 10.3 percent," who congregate and job-hunt in "coffee shops and bookstores to get out of their tiny one-bedroom and away from their annoying roommates."[51] A number of even fluffier pieces likewise saw their way into print.

Unemployment occupied much of the opinion pages throughout the month. Two days after the BLS's release of the October numbers, an editorial in the Sunday paper detailed the ghastly state of joblessness:

Unemployment surged from 9.8 percent in September to 10.2 percent last month, its highest level since 1983. At the same time, the economy lost 190,000 more jobs. That means employers have eliminated 7.3 million positions since the recession began in December 2007.

As dreadful as they are, the headline numbers understate the severity of the problem. They also obscure an even grimmer fact: Unless there is more government support, it will take several years of robust economic growth—by no means a sure thing—to recoup the jobs that have been lost.

. . . The underemployment rate—which also includes jobless workers who have not recently looked for work and part-timers who need full-time work—reached 17.5 percent in October. And the long-term unemployment rate—the share of the unemployed population out of work for more than six months—also continues to set records. It is now 35.6 percent.

The official job-loss data also fail to take note of 2.8 million additional jobs needed to absorb new workers who have joined the labor force during the recession. When those missing jobs are added to the official total, the economy comes up short by 10.1 million jobs.

Taken together, the numbers paint this stark picture: At no time in post–World War II America has it been more difficult to find a job, to plan for the future, or—for tens of millions of Americans—to merely get by.

Making express note of the "record 27.6 percent" unemployment rate for teens, the editorial went on to endorse "more stimulus spending and government programs."[52]

The conservative columnist Ross Douthat staked out a blandly moderate position. He faulted the president not for the economic stimulus policy—"this dire [unemployment] figure isn't Barack Obama's fault"—but his insufficiently pessimistic unemployment projections earlier in the year in support of it: "This October, when Obama's advisers predicted that unemployment would stand at 8 percent with the stimulus and just under 9 percent without it, the actual jobless rate leaped to 10.4 percent."[53] In a sharper tone, but with a similar message, Charles M. Blow took Obama to task for not living up to his promise as a candidate to prioritize job creation: "On Friday, the Bureau of Labor Statistics released unemployment figures for October 2009. The official rate was 10.2 percent, up more than 50 percent from the time Obama gave that speech. Oops, nevermind."[54]

In "The Night They Drove the Tea Partiers Down," Frank Rich read the tea leaves of the November election results, delighting in the Tea Party Republicans' lackluster showing but also alerting Democrats of potential pitfalls for 2010. On the economy, he chided Wall Street: "The system is going back to the way it was with a vengeance, against a backdrop of despair. As the unemployment rate crossed the 10 percent threshold at week's end, we learned that bankers were helping themselves not just to bonuses as large as those at the bubble's peak but to early allotments of H1N1 vaccine." Citing a poll, Rich highlighted what Obama needed to do: "Unemployment ranked ahead of the deficit and health care as the No. 1 pocketbook issue in the survey, with 81 percent saying the Obama administration must take more action."[55] Wall Street, Goldman Sachs in particular, was also in Maureen Dowd's cross-hairs: "Now we have two economies. We have recovering banks while we have 10-plus percent unemployment and 17.5 percent underemployment. The gross thing about the Wall Street of the last decade is how much its success was not shared with society." With a humorous twist, she barbed, "Goldmine Sachs, as it's known, is out for Goldmine Sachs."[56]

In the fall of 2008, Paul Krugman won the Nobel Prize in economics, conferring unmatched authority upon his liberal opinions on the economy. He continually criticized and advocated from his Keynesian vantage point. Comparing the United States unfavorably with Germany in how it has reacted to the economic crisis, he reiterated his point that not enough was being done to address unemployment. He was especially concerned about long-term unemployment, "already at its highest levels since the 1930s and . . . still on the rise":

And long-term unemployment inflicts long-term damage. Workers who have been out of a job for too long often find it hard to get back into the labor market even when conditions improve. And there are hidden costs, too—not least for children, who suffer physically and emotionally when their parents spend months or years unemployed.

He preferred a "large enough conventional stimulus," but given the lack of political support, he was open to other options that might spur job growth— "something more than, and different from, what we're already doing."[57] Later in the month, he made the same point by underscoring the government's hitherto overly generous treatment of Wall Street. Consequently, although "the economy is still in deep trouble and needs much more government help" and "we desperately need more government spending on job creation," there was little voter support for more governmental action.[58] He surmised that Obama's administration was listening too intently to Wall Street's anxiety over the budget deficit. But even if there were legitimate concern, Krugman insisted that "this risk must be set against the certainty of mass suffering if we don't do more" to stimulate the economy.[59] He closed the month with his most direct appeal in a column titled "The Jobs Imperative." "If you're looking for a job right now, your prospects are terrible," he began, explaining that those seeking jobs outnumber openings six to one and that "the average duration of unemployment . . . is more than six months, the highest level since the 1930s." The expectation was that high unemployment would continue with destructive consequences, especially for some like the long-term unemployed and new graduates. "Failure to act on unemployment isn't just cruel, it's short-sighted," he declared. "So it's time for an emergency jobs program."[60]

Krugman's assessment was left of center, to be sure, but not far left. He was well within the mainstream. In November 2009, it was perfectly reasonable to argue that a failure to act was cruel and short-sighted and that the seriousness of the unemployment situation warranted emergency measures. With the white rate of unemployment at 9.5 percent (later adjusted to 9.4 percent), lower than the overall rate, the *Times* sensibly did not draw any explicit attention to how comparatively better off whites were. But we should be clear that without cruelty to whites, there would be little attention paid to the cruelties of unemployment. As seen above, neither Krugman nor anybody else at the *Times* had given *any* indication that Blacks in the summer of 2008 suffered what whites, the vast majority of the 10.2 percent, were suffering in the fall of 2009. No mention, let alone any calls for emergency programs.

The unemployment situation for Blacks had reached truly tragic propor-
tions: 15.7 percent of Blacks were out of work and were seeking jobs. To put
the number in perspective, this was six full percentage points above the absolutely worst rate of white unemployment of the postwar period. Yet *none* of the
articles, columns, and editorials on unemployment discussed so far, and many
undiscussed, mentioned Blacks at all. But the *Times* was not completely silent,
as it had been in July 2008. A handful of articles referred to Blacks, if mostly
in passing. A postmortem on the New York City mayoral race had Democrats
lamenting the opportunity they had squandered: "Registered Democrats outnumber Republicans by about five to one in New York City, and unemployment
is in the double digits, with joblessness among Black males near 50 percent."[61] A
detailed examination of the BLS release turned up the finding that the "unemployment rate for African-American men reached 17.1 percent."[62] Forecasting
ongoing high rates of unemployment, the head of the Federal Reserve observed
that the rate for young people, between the ages of 16 and 24, was at 19 percent
and for young Blacks at 30 percent.[63]

Three articles dealt with Blacks more substantively, but the depth of the
crisis for Blacks was clearly not the point of two of them. One was a peculiar
portrait of a suburb outside Atlanta, Georgia. It was peculiar by design, focused
as it was on a community that was demographically anomalous:

Across the country, there have been many reports about the recession's racial divide,
as blacks have lost their jobs and houses at far higher rates than whites. But Henry
County, about a 30-minute drive south of downtown Atlanta, has a very different
profile from the rest of the nation. In Henry, the median income of black families,
$56,715 in 2008, approaches that of whites, $69,728 (nationally, the average income
gap was $20,000). Blacks in Henry County, many of whom are retirees from the
North or professionals who work in Atlanta, are more likely than whites to have a
college degree.[64]

Although the influx of Blacks in the past two decades had led to "its share of racial
tension," the article argued, "the recession has begun to erase those differences."
The evidence presented on the equalizing effects of the recession, however, was
a confused jumble, requiring the exaggerated caveat, "That does not mean that
Henry County is a perfect laboratory of equality."[65] Even in the excerpt above, the
fact that whites were less likely to be college graduates but made 23 percent more

than Blacks prompted no pause or explanation; it was evidence of the county's relative *equality*. The other article discussed the flowing numbers of people who depend on food stamps and the ebbing stigma attached to them. Once having thought that "people on public assistance were lazy," as one interviewee put it, new recipients were now seeing things differently. A few times, the lengthy piece indicated that Blacks used food stamps at a higher rate than others, but the racial meanings, intended and received, went unexplored and were at best ambiguous. But certainly, the primary point of view was not that of Blacks.[66]

There was one article, among the nearly 200 items, that gave a sense of the misery Blacks were living through and what needed to be done. Titled "NAACP Prods Obama on Job Losses," the story relayed the civil rights organization's message:

African-American leaders say it makes sense to pressure the president on jobs because the unemployment rate for blacks has jumped to 15.7 percent, from 8.9 percent when the recession started 23 months ago. That compares with 13.1 percent for Hispanics and 9.5 percent for whites.

The black unemployment rate has climbed above 20 percent in several states, reaching 23.9 percent in Michigan and 20.4 percent in South Carolina.[67]

The NAACP, along with the AFL-CIO and the National Council of La Raza, planned to "call for increased spending for schools and roads, billions of dollars in fiscal relief to state and local governments to forestall more layoffs and a direct government jobs program, 'especially in distressed communities facing severe unemployment.'"[68]

On the opinion side, there were just two columns, both by Bob Herbert, that referred to Blacks at all. But those two did more than that. Although he did not focus exclusively on Black unemployment, Herbert clearly saw it as a central issue. The first made an appeal to President Obama: "Mr. President, you have two urgent and overwhelming tasks in front of you: to put Americans trapped in this terrible employment crisis back to work and to put the brakes on your potentially disastrous plan to escalate the war in Afghanistan." Herbert reminded Obama and the readers that the unemployment rate was at 10.2 percent overall and, "for blacks, . . . a back-breaking 15.7 percent." He concluded with heartbreaking numbers concerning children: "While we're preparing to pour more resources into Afghanistan, the Economic Policy Institute is telling us that one in five American children is living in poverty, that nearly 35 percent of African-American children are living in poverty, and that the unemployment crisis is pushing us toward a point in the coming years where more than half of all black children in this country will be poor."[69] Four days later, Herbert set his sights on the disparate impact of the recession and recovery on "elites" and "ordinary working people": "President Obama's strongest supporters during the presidential campaign were the young, the black and the poor—and they are among those who are being hammered unmercifully in this long and cruel economic downturn that the financial elites are telling us is over." The column was about "blue-collar workers of every ethnic and political persuasion," but Herbert also did not ignore the fact that certain populations were especially vulnerable: unmarried women, people of color, and children. Reiterating the 35 percent poverty rate for Black children and the 15.7 percent rate of Black unemployment, he added, "The underemployment rate for blacks in September . . . was a gut-wrenching 23.8 percent and for Hispanics an even worse 25.1 percent."[70]

To sum up, in November 2009, a month when Black unemployment exceeded 15 percent, the *Times* published one article and two columns that could be read as seriously acknowledging the issue. But for the NAACP, the venerable Black institution, and Bob Herbert, one of two Black columnists in the Op-Ed section, it would have published none.[71] And in July 2008, when Blacks faced what for whites would have been the highest level of unemployment in a quarter-century, it actually did publish none. To borrow from Kanye West's courageous indictment of George W. Bush, live before a national television audience, in the immediate aftermath of Hurricane Katrina, the *New York Times* doesn't care about Black people.[72]

CONCLUSION

In his 2010 memoir, Bush recalled that he was "deeply insulted by the suggestion that we allowed American citizens to suffer because they were black" and that West's accusation, along with those of Jesse Jackson and an unnamed member of the Congressional Black Caucus, marked "an all-time low. . . . the worst moment of [his] presidency" (2010: 299–300). On his book tour, he elaborated, "Nobody wants to be called a racist, if in your heart you believe in equality of race."[73] No doubt the *New York Times*, as a whole as well as its many constituent editorial and reportorial parts, would react in a similar—

though probably less melodramatic and self-pitying—fashion, insisting that the newspaper abides by the belief in equality of race. Liberal and even some leftist analysts of racism would corroborate: in the post-Civil Rights era, nearly all people and mainstream institutions report believing in racial equality in principle, however they may diverge in their definitions, practices, or opinions about how to bring it about.[74]

My contention is that they are all wrong. If *belief* and *principle* were to imply at least a modicum of depth and conviction, there is little evidence to suggest a dominant belief in racial equality, in principle or otherwise, least of all in relation to Blacks. Or, if racial equality *is* a dominant belief, it is belief in the sense that people believe in "world peace"—theoretically desirable perhaps but hopelessly utopian. Or, if racial equality *is* a dominant principle, it is a principle not in the sense of a "person of principle" but in the sense of "well, yes, in principle but . . . ": a principle without principle, which is to say no principle at all.

For the *New York Times*, in relation to employment, racial *equality* for Blacks is not on the table—as a goal, an ideal, or a dream. It is not even on the horizon. It does not structure in any significant or noticeable way how the paper handles evidence of enormous, persistent, *and* flagrantly conspicuous racial inequality among those who are actively seeking work, just as Al Gore had not dared to promise—nor likely given passing, much less serious, thought to—*eliminating* it. As in Gore's well-meaning, if self-aggrandizing, ballyhooing of "low" levels of unemployment to a Black audience that a white audience would have found bewildering and mean-spirited, implicit in the *New York Times*'s indifference is an unmistakable anti-Black racism—a deep, banal, unknowing acceptance of Black mass suffering that *is* known and knowable. And if we recognize that the *New York Times*, as but one dominant institution, and unemployment, as but one aspect of racial inequality and domination, are not the exception but the rule, we confront the disheartening reality that what we assume to have been a long abandoned racial logic of the ages of *Dred Scott* and *Plessy*, a blatant double standard of human value, prevails to an astonishing degree in the ages of *Brown* and Obama.

The only hope this country has is to turn overnight into a revolutionary country.

James Baldwin, "From *Nationalism, Colonialism, and the United States*"

CONCLUSION: DENATURALIZING RACISMS PRESENT AND FUTURE

In late November 2011, a flyer went out as an email attachment to about a dozen people, a mix of academics and nonacademics, in the Champaign-Urbana area. Ubuntu, a "Black Radical Work Group" associated with the Department of African American Studies at the University of Illinois, was announcing a panel discussion titled "Universalism and Particularity: The Occupy Movement and Race":

Over the last 90 days the Occupy Movement has focused attention on the capitalist class' 40 year devastation of the working and middle classes. In the 1960s, corporate executives made 26 times workers, by 1980 it rose to 32 times; and in 2009 it was 263 times. Led by young largely white college graduates Occupy is part of a worldwide movement that is challenging global class disparities. Yet, as inspiring as the Occupy movement has been, like previous U.S. radical movements it seems mired on the rocky shores of race. Is the Occupy movement doomed to repeat the errors of the past? Can it move beyond seemingly universal "colorblind" reformist proposals and engage the particularities of racialized oppression and chart a genuine struggle for a multiracial democracy?[1]

Given the seemingly unignorable but ignored devastation of the latest economic collapse for Blacks and other people of color, as well as the checkered history of the white left in relation to race, the questions warranted asking. At the time, in the early months of the Occupy Movement, I, for one, was trying to work out how race figured in it. The wording of the leaflet betrayed skepticism, but the panel's answers did not appear to be foregone conclusions, as at least two of the four panelists were white local activists from the labor movement.

One of the recipients forwarded the email to a left-leaning listserv in town.[2] The next day, a familiar figure on the local left sent an open reply:

This [event] seems to be an unfortunate "identity-politics" diversion.

Forty years ago, when it looked like issues of economics and inequality might actually penetrate the limits of allowable debate in American politics, liberals (and the Democrats—always a business party) hastily substituted diversity for equality as their announced goal.

Not that diversity isn't a good thing. But the U.S. political establishment was using it to take the place of demands for economic equality. (And in the meantime they launched neoliberalism, which enforced economic inequality at a rapid and accelerating rate—that's what the Occupy movement opposes.)

In subsequent years, we heard much about the "trinity of oppression"—class, race, and gender. But class is not like the other two. Conflicts of race and gender can in principle be solved by reconciliation, if not easily. But conflict between exploiter and exploited cannot—one or the other must be liquidated (the social role, if not the physical persons).

We all of course oppose racism, for political and personal reasons. But it's a great error to use that opposition to undercut the Occupy Movement.[3]

The circular about the event had not mentioned "diversity" or "identity politics," nor downplayed "economics and inequality," nor referred to gender, nor positioned itself as a liberal critique of the left, nor argued that class is "like" race or gender. Yet the author felt compelled to draft these points into relevancy in order to dismiss them as irrelevant. He not only thought that class was "not like the other two" but implied that class was more central and fundamental. He was sure that "conflicts of race and gender can in principle be solved by reconciliation, if not easily"; as signaled by the immediate follow-up "But . . . ," a principle only in principle. He was equally certain that "we all of course oppose racism," another principled stance undercut by another swift "But. . . ."

This line of argument among "the left" is hardly novel, though continually, forgetfully revived as if it were. Of recent incarnations, one might squint and make out the silhouette of the literary critic and public intellectual Walter Benn Michaels, a published interview of whom was attached to the writer's email, presumably to buttress his claims. What caught my attention in the piece, titled "Let Them Eat Diversity," is Michaels's assertion about the state of antiracism:

Today we're living in a deeply anti-racist society . . . officially committed to anti-racism . . . which you can tell when Glenn Beck thinks it's a good idea to couch his criticism of Obama by calling Obama a "racist." It's the killing word to say to anyone. That doesn't mean that there isn't still racism, it means that there is an important sense in which anti-racism is absolutely the official ideology because no one can imagine themselves to be committed to racism. (Sunkara 2011; ellipses in original)

In certain circles—academia being an outstanding, outlying case, trailed by mainstream media and politics—there is a sense in which "racist" is "the killing word to say to anyone." But this is obviously an exaggeration: whatever influence Beck might exert on the right, his name-calling has not had the general effect of metaphorically "killing" Obama. Another example would be Michaels's own retort to a leading question posed to him during the same interview. Referring to a blog entry on affirmative action by Richard Kim of *The Nation*, the questioner asked, "Do these rather explicit allegations of racism catch you off guard or . . . "?[4] Although Kim had not expressly labeled him a racist, Michaels took the bait to cavalierly, nay proudly, cast himself as a truth-telling iconoclast: "Are you kidding me, I've been called a racist for twenty years" (Sunkara 2011). A charge of racism, despite his contention, needed not be a fatal stigma. It could be flashed as a badge of indomitable courage and integrity.

There is also a sense in which "anti-racism," if understood as colorblindness or diversity, is the dominant racial ideology in the United States, though hardly "absolutely." But Michaels, like many, mistakes the officialness, or dominance, of an ideology for depth and commitment: "Today we're living in a deeply anti-racist society . . . officially committed to anti-racism." As I argue in chapter 2, ideologies are *reflective discourses*, and further, *dominant* ideologies are, in the main, reactionary discourses, discourses defending structures of inequality and domination in reaction to pressure from below—orthodoxy in Bourdieu's sense. Ideologies are relatively shallow, particularly when they are official and dominant. As a naturalized matter of course, agents that constitute structures of domination, like racism, do not consciously, discursively form thoughts and then act accordingly. There is little direct, controlling effect of dominant racial ideologies on racial structures of inequality and domination, which, at the risk of anthropomorphizing, prefer to hum along blithely without reflection. The inverse of Michaels's contention would follow: today, we live in a *thinly* antiracist society. It is this shallowness that renders possible and intelligible the emailer's solution to racism: if racism were, at base, a conflict of contrary opinions, "reconciliation"—and its hackneyed companion, the plea that we need to talk about race—might be the logical and sufficient politics of antiracism. But if racism were instead structural in the ways I have suggested in this book, reconciliation would be absurdly premature and impotent. In the final analysis, however Michaels's or the emailer's discourse may be seen as heterodoxy in relation to class, it should be seen for what it is in relation to race: left orthodoxy. To put it more oxymoronically, left conservatism: if the status quo is already "deeply anti-racist," what is to be done?[5] With antiracist friends like these. . . . [6]

TOWARD A BALDWINIAN SOCIOLOGY AND POLITICS OF RACE

While writing this very conclusion, I happened to re-read James Baldwin's "My Dungeon Shook: Letter to My Nephew on the One Hundredth Anniversary of the Emancipation," the first of two essays that compose *The Fire Next Time*. It was a re-revelation—of all the things I had forgotten and, frankly, had never picked up on the first time I read it some twenty-five years back. Published more than a half-century ago, in 1962, it has depressingly, but also invigoratingly, lost none of its immediacy and potency. Wading further into his nonfiction, I came upon the realization that what I had been unknowingly undertaking with this book has been in a sense Baldwinian sociology.

Baldwin himself would be aghast. He did not care much for sociology, which in his view not only failed to grasp Black oppression but contributed to it by pathologizing the oppressed (Baldwin 1955, 1961; Ferguson 2000). He was, and is, right, of course; for instance, consider something like the "Moynihan Report" (Moynihan 1965) and its many heirs, including those discussed in chapter 4. No love—or hate or interest—lost, sociology has found Baldwin beside the point: very few have engaged his ideas.[7] Sociology was, and is, wrong, of course: not many, if any, sociological theories of racism from the 1950s to the 1980s have fared as well in interpreting those particular or subsequent decades. Baldwin's prose was, needless to say, rhetorically powerful, but behind the words was the force of his ideas.

To close this book, I reflect on the preceding chapters in light of many points of convergence with, and two of divergence from, Baldwin. At the most basic level, what he saw as "part of the business of the writer" is what this book sets out to do: lamenting that race was "not only written about so widely . . . [but] so badly," Baldwin sought, and urged others, "to go beneath the surface, to tap the source" ([1955a] 1998: 7). The imperative is to denaturalize what is taken for granted in both how racism operates and how we analyze those operations— in other words, to denaturalize racism ontologically and epistemologically.

To denaturalize racism is, first, to denaturalize *race*, the mode of classifying humans "by some notion of stock or collective heredity of traits" (Anthias and Yuval-Davis 1992: 2), to deracinate it from the grounds of biology and nature. In other words, denaturalizing racism necessarily entails a social constructionist view of race. Of course, the idea that race is socially constructed is uncontroversial. It is by now a bedrock assumption in the social sciences, even among those who routinely violate it by never questioning the received categories they employ, and conventional wisdom imparted in introductory social science courses.[8] A social constructionist *avant la lettre*, Baldwin offers sagacious reminders about what has become an axiomatic cliché. His perspective differs from the overly discursive varieties of social constructionism that prevail today. As I discuss most explicitly in chapter 2, discourse matters, but more in what people do with words in situ than the words per se. For Baldwin, race is, above all, relational, historical, and political. "America became white" through "the necessity of denying black presence, and justifying the black subjugation" (Baldwin [1984] 2010: 167). In the process, "the American Republic" and "white people . . . invented the nigger" (Baldwin [1963] 2010: 60; [1971] 2010: 124). And "savage," "gook," "illegal," "terrorist," and so on. As previous chapters show in various ways, race or "color is not a human or a personal reality; it is a political reality" (Baldwin 1962: 139). To recognize that race is always political, in the comprehensive sense of being about power, is to see that race is always bound to *racism*, in the structural sense I outline in chapter 2. Racism is a vast web of unholy couplings, practical articulations of schemas and resources that instantiate domination and inequality. This is why Baldwin argues that "white is a metaphor for power" and that "the only thing that white people have that black people," or other racially oppressed peoples, "should want, is power" (Baldwin [1980a] 2010: 158, 1962: 130).

Racism is not only powerful but also runs deep. It cuts channels of durable schemas through individuals, institutions, and history. Take the schema of presuming Black inferiority, for instance: this precept courses through the Champaign Police Department, the Champaign City Council, the State's Attorney's office, and others in chapter 1, the U.S. Constitution and Supreme Court rulings in chapter 3, the scholarship on migrant settlement by liberal social scientists in chapter 4, and the *New York Times* in chapter 6. That a line could be drawn from Dred Scott to Kiwane Carrington bespeaks the renitent hold of the schema. It can be invoked consciously and explicitly, but much more prevalently and proficiently, it is embodied and put into practice through habituated dispositions of perception, interpretation, and action—*habitus* in Bourdieu's social theory. This anti-Black schema, like other schemas of racism, is not of nature but insidiously and most efficaciously works as second nature, even through agents that consciously, in good faith, may think and say otherwise. Again, ahead of his time, Baldwin recognizes the deep-seated dispositions that incorporate and alchemize history: "People are trapped in history and history is trapped in them" (Baldwin [1955] 1998: 119; see also Baldwin [1965] 1998).

Baldwin, like Bourdieu, trains his analysis of domination on the social unconscious: "habits of power are not only extremely hard to lose; they are as tenacious as some incurable disease" (Baldwin [1961a] 2010: 11). Unlike Bourdieu, however, he insists on what I refer to in chapter 5 as *doxic asymmetry*. Habits of domination are held more deeply among and, if challenged, clutched ever more tightly by the relatively powerful. It is not that the relatively powerless do not at all form bad habits in being subjected to domination, but the grip is looser, and they always, albeit to a greater or lesser degree, harbor freedom dreams, strategies, and tactics.[9] More than any sociologist of racism of his time, Baldwin names and indicts the galling "innocence" of whites: "it is not permissible that the authors of devastation should also be innocent. It is the innocence which constitutes the crime" (1962: 16; see also [1980b] 1998: 805). The innocence is not one of knowing prevarication or pretense but an "unconsciousness" (Baldwin [1961a] 2010: 11). It is the ignorance of the true believer—a true believer who stands, in a relation of dominance, over those beyond the pale: "ignorance, allied with power, is the most ferocious enemy justice can have" (Baldwin [1972] 1998: 445).

The unconscious dispositions of the oppressed are less at peace with the world, pushing questions and critiques into consciousness. The internalization of domination by the dominated is hardly ever complete. The ontological break with what is, which the dominant take for granted, lends the oppressed with not only a different but a more critical epistemological take on relations of domination. On this point, Baldwin is particularly incisive: "We have an edge over the people who think of themselves as white. We have never been deluded into knowing, into believing, what they believe"; "my life was in your hands, and I had to look at you. I know more about you, therefore, than you know about me. I've had to spend my life, after all—and all the other Negroes in the country have had to spend their lives—outwitting and watching white people. I had to know what you were doing before you did it" (Baldwin and Giovanni 1973: 21; Baldwin [1961a] 2010: 17; see also Baldwin [1976] 1998: 524–25, [1980a] 2010: 158).

Through the concepts of *symbolic coercion* and *symbolic perversity*, chapters 5 and 6 chart some of the depths and contours of the ignorance involved in racism. Chapter 5 considers a singular event, the 1924 massacre of Filipino sugar workers in Hawai'i, to illustrate a much more general feature of racism: legitimate state violence. Juxtaposing Bourdieu and Du Bois, I downsize the former's concept of symbolic violence and propose the complementary concept of symbolic coercion. Bourdieu's idea stresses what he calls the "paradox of doxa"—that so little of the existing order is questioned, by the dominant and the dominated alike. Through Du Bois, and others like Baldwin, we can appreciate that while the paradox always exists to an extent, relations of domination effect an unequal allocation not only of resources but also belief and heresy. The oppressed cannot afford to be, and are not, nearly as innocent. Symbolic coercion lies in the disjunction between the dominant's unconscious innocence and the dominated's conscious opposition: it is the dominant's *tacit nonrecognition* of subaltern dissent. When symbolic coercion is articulated to the coercive means of the state, physical coercion can be rendered implicitly and immediately legitimate through the implicit and immediate delegitimation of its sufferers, be they Filipino strikers in prewar Hawai'i or Kiwane Carrington and his friend in contemporary Champaign.[10] Bourdieu's favored metaphor of the conductorless orchestra is apt for this efficient, effortless legitimation process (1977: 72), but there is the all-important qualification that membership in the orchestra is racially restricted.

The deep, tacit ignorance of the dominant not only ordinarily runs roughshod over the critical discourse or knowledge of those they dominate. Paradoxically but nonetheless typically, the dominant also ignore their *own* knowledge of racial inequalities and domination—readily available knowledge produced and consumed by the relatively powerful themselves. The ignorance that I am interested in does not stem from conspiracy, arcaneness, or suppression. Rather it is "the apathy, the sleep, the unwillingness to know" (Baldwin [1961a] 2010: 11; see also Baldwin [1964b] 2010), even when the dominant can and do know. It is the unconscious will not to know what they know. This unknowing-knowing, what I label *symbolic perversity*, rests on unuttered double standards of human value and suffering that have survived fully intact the entire history of racism up to the present. We should therefore not overestimate the lasting effects of postwar decolonization around the world or the Civil Rights Movement in the United States on this score. We also should not overstate the difference between liberalism and conservatism, between Democrats and Republicans. The line that shows through most brightly in chapter 6 is not the one between Bill Clinton, Al Gore, and the *New York Times*, on the one hand, and George W. Bush, on the other, but the one enclosing them all. As Baldwin wryly observes, "What they care about is the continuation of white supremacy, so that white liberals who are with you in principle will move out when you move in" ([1961a] 2010: 15–16; see also Baldwin [1964a] 2010, [1976] 1998). Liberals, not only white ones, may tell you, in earnest, that they are in search of better, safer schools rather than people who are more like themselves, but they still move out.

What is the way forward? For this open-ended collective project, I merely suggest several guideposts based on the prior chapters. First, while its note of optimism may be tempting, as theory and as politics, we can rule out assimilation. Sanding some of the rough prescriptive edges of its intellectual forebears, neoclassical assimilation theory retells a familiar national narrative about immigrants, just with a more colorful cast. Segmented assimilation theory adds two parallel plots to complicate the story, one of which serves as a contrapuntal cautionary tale. Chapter 4 details the many pitfalls of assimilation theory of both varieties in relation to race, but I underscore two of them here. The most troubling is a distinct disregard, and even disdain, for native-born Blacks, academically reproducing what is already bountiful: assimilation theory either excludes them to make itself viable, while admitting their pivotal role in producing the conditions for others' "assimilation" through the Civil Rights Movement, or stereotypes poor African Americans, and sometimes other similarly positioned native-born peoples of color, as a source of cultural contamination that pulls migrants and their children downward. The other is that assimilation theory takes for granted the *nation*, often euphemized as "the mainstream," disabling its capacity to ask, much less answer, questions about the *politics of national belonging* that are, for the United States and many other states, inevitably linked to race and racism. Assimilation theory further takes for granted the desirability of assimilating into the nation, disabling its capacity to notice or appreciate more oppositional or otherwise alternative politics. As Baldwin advises his nephew, in *The Fire Next Time*, about the arrogance and "reality that lie[] behind the words *acceptance* and *integration*," "there is no reason for you to try to become like white people and there is no basis whatever for their impertinent assumption that *they* must accept *you*." The question for those of us who are, or identify with all who are, beyond the boundaries of national or state membership is, "Do I really want to be integrated into a burning house?" (Baldwin 1962: 19, 127; emphases in original).

   If racism as structure(s) exists at innumerable scales, from the interpersonal to the global, antiracism can be waged at each. The particular strategies and tactics would be historically contingent and context-specific, but if racism is structural, antiracism demands efforts to transform, more or less radically, the structure in question. At whatever scale, it is about disrupting racism's smooth reproduction, the routine articulation of schemas and resources. Who is to perform such acts of subversion? If the distribution of critical knowledge is inversely related to hierarchies of power and the distribution of ignorance, as I contend, the struggle against white supremacy, as in the past, will be led by people of color. This is not to say that whites cannot and will not join the fight, but it is less likely. It is harder for them to access and accept critical knowledge that is, on the whole, foreign to and at odds with their habitus and even harder to put into practice: "Many of them [whites], indeed, know better, but, as you will discover, people find it very difficult to act on what they know" (Baldwin 1962: 20). In other words, it is not enough to have a change of consciousness or an epiphany, the standard terminal point, for instance, of a heartfelt talk with a coworker, an enlightening exchange in a university seminar, or a screening of a moving film that is often mistaken for something more life-altering. As Baldwin notes, "People can cry much easier than they can change, a rule of psychology people like me picked up as kids on the street."[11] Antiracism is about *practice*. I mean practice in the sense that antiracist schemas cannot remain in the realm of ideology but must be put into practice through their articulations with resources, human and nonhuman. But I also mean practice in the sense that newly acquired practices of antiracism, as well as being open to acquiring new practices, need to be practiced, as one does in learning and mastering a sport or a musical instrument, until they become second nature (Bourdieu 2000: 172).

For those subjected to white supremacy, resistance is less at odds with their habitus, which is always, to a greater or lesser extent, in discord with the field of domination. Depending on a multitude of factors, including the magnitude and types of resources available and the level of repression, resistance manifests in a wide range of practical forms. Although large-scale structural change can happen as an unintended consequence or accumulation of small changes,[12] collective action is usually required. Here, mass social movements, like the Civil Rights Movement and decolonization, readily come to mind. Given the widespread sanitized view of the former, if not the latter, we need to remind ourselves that structural change typically necessitates disruptive, often unlawful, acts. However temporarily, acts of disobedience disarticulate the deeply naturalized coupling of certain schemas and resources: for example, occupying white-designated seats and boycotting to break the tight linkage between the Jim Crow schema of racial segregation and the resource of public transportation. Or, more contemporarily, we can think of something like the Umoja Village Shantytown that, for six months in 2006, "liberated a vacant lot" and housed the homeless in Miami, transgressing a host of schemas concerning race, poverty, and property through its takeover of a tangible resource, land (Rameau 2008: 7). Such acts, at minimum, lower the veil of naturalness

of practices of domination and, at times, can induce permanent rearticulations. As Baldwin puts it bluntly, "We have to begin a massive campaign of
civil disobedience. I mean nationwide. And this is no stage joke. *Some laws
should not be obeyed*" ([1963] 2010: 61; emphasis in original).

We can also be more open to recognizing "collective actions of noncol-
lective actors," what Asef Bayat refers to as *social nonmovements*, in bringing
about large transformations, particularly in contexts short on political opportunities and access to institutional resources. In contrast to social movements,
they involve large numbers of individuals carrying on parallel, everyday practices rather than relatively smaller groups united by ideology, leadership, and
organization carrying out planned, out-of-the-ordinary protests. For example,
whereas the Umoja Village was a consciously organized movement in the
global North, most shantytowns, particularly in the global South, exemplify
"the quiet encroachment of the ordinary": how the dispossessed "better their
lives by quietly impinging on the propertied and powerful, and on society at
large" by taking possession of land, building makeshift structures, tapping into
public utilities, and so on. Or, in the United States, as elsewhere, unauthorized
migrants embody and enact in their everyday lives uncoordinated informal,
including illegal, practices that cast alternative schemas of access and use over
resources, including space within state boundaries (Bayat 2010: 14–15, 19–20).
Social nonmovements are the conductorless orchestras of the dominated. Met
with repression, however, they can turn into social *movements*, as the formerly
individual actors defend their gains collectively in a more conscious, organized
fashion, as unauthorized, and authorized, migrants did en masse across the
United States in 2006 (Bayat 2010: 24).[13]

Of the two points on which I diverge from Baldwin, the lesser one is that
his thoughts on white supremacy centered first and foremost on Blacks. My
raising this issue does not mean that I think he, who was primarily involved
with the Black freedom movement, should have done otherwise, or that I
think he ignored altogether other peoples of color in the United States and
beyond, which he did not, as we can see in three counterexamples from three
separate decades:

A racist society can't but fight a racist war—this is the bitter truth. The assumptions
acted on at home are also acted on abroad, and every American Negro knows this, for he,
after the American Indian, was the first "Vietcong" victim. (Baldwin [1967] 2010: 248)

From this I want to point out a paradox: blacks, Indians, Chicanos, Asians, and that beleaguered handful of white people who understand their history are the only people who know who they are. (Baldwin [1979] 2010: 142)

The American innocence was unassailable, fixed forever, for it was not a crime to kill a black or a red or a yellow man. On the contrary, it might be, and was most often so considered, a duty. It was not a crime to rape a black or red or yellow woman—it was sport. (Baldwin [1980b] 1998: 805)

But when he discusses non-Black peoples of color, Baldwin tends to see only the commonalities they share with Blacks.[14] By contrast, most of the chapters in this book make the case that racisms against different peoples are inextricably linked but also qualitatively different, demanding our analyses and politics to reflect and make sense of this complexity. A corollary is, I would like to insist, that even when we happen to focus on one or another group, in scholarship or politics, we keep the larger structures of racial inequality and domination in mind. Critical analysis of racism and politics of antiracism cannot afford to be so tunnel-visioned as to be at the expense of those in more disadvantaged positions. Clearly, the new wave of assimilation theories intentionally and unintentionally fails Blacks, as well as American Indians and other colonized peoples; concerning the latter, note the dissonant, even opposite, meanings of "native" in immigration and indigenous studies. Likewise, antiracist movements that advocate on behalf of one particular constituency can set off unintended consequences on other oppressed groups whose relative positions in a given domain may already be worse off.[15] In this vein, as an Asian Americanist, I suggest that this entire book concerns Asian American racial politics, not just those parts that are directly about peoples of Asian origin. It is an implicit call to decenter "Asian Americans" in Asian American racial politics, the ultimate aim of which is to dismantle white supremacy, not to advance the position of Asians within it. I see no reason why, for Asians, the police killings of Kiwane Carrington, Aiyana Stanley-Jones, John Crawford III, and countless others should generate any less outrage, empathy, or involvement because they were Black and not Asian. In fact, in view of the incomparable anti-Black racism underlying "criminal justice," they should engender more.

The less reconcilable disagreement with Baldwin relates to the U.S. state, although it is at the same time rooted in an agreement: the need for radical change. Baldwin's denunciations of the United States could scarcely be more damning. He argues that genocidal racism cuts to the core of the U.S. state: "A very brutal thing must be said: The intentions of this melancholic country as concerns black people—and anyone who doubts me can ask any Indian— have always been genocidal" (Baldwin [1979] 2010: 141; see also Baldwin [1984] 2010: 167). Prophetically, at an early stage of the carceral state's astounding expansion in recent decades, Baldwin reports: "Death Row, like the ghetto, is dark with dark faces. . . . And finally, then, since I am an American discussing American Prisoners, we are also discussing one more aspect of the compulsive American dream of genocide" ([1983] 2010: 164–65). Connecting lethal racisms domestic and foreign, his thoughts on the U.S. war in Viet Nam still resonate today: "I want an answer: if I am to die, I have the right to know why. And the nonwhite population of the world, who are most of the world, would also like to know. The American idea of freedom and, still more, the way this free-dom is imposed, have made America the most terrifying nation in the world" (Baldwin [1967] 2010: 247; see also Baldwin [1980b] 1998).

Given his devastating appraisal of the United States, Baldwin's (1962: 115) call for a kind of revolution is unsurprising: "And today, a hundred years after his technical emancipation, he remains—with the possible exception of the American Indian—the most despised creature in his country. Now, there is simply no possibility of a real change in the Negro's situation without the most radical and far-reaching changes in the American political and social struc-ture." Against the "world's present economic arrangements," he even assents to Black Panther Huey Newton's belief in "the necessity of establishing a form of socialism in this country. . . . an indigenous socialism formed by, and respond-ing to, the real needs of the American people" (Baldwin [1972] 1998: 461; see also Boyd 2008: 109). But for all of his radicalism, Baldwin remains broadly within the American political project, albeit from the margins on behalf of the marginalized. He states straightforwardly, "I am an American" ([1963] 2010: 60), and this identity is the platform from which he critiques "America" and imagines its potential: "I love America more than any other country in the world, and, exactly for this reason, I insist on the right to criticize her perpetually" (Baldwin [1955] 1998: 9; see also Baldwin [1977] 1998, 1984). The vision of a more perfect Union, of a nation-state that lives up to its promise, tantalizes, but it is a mirage that cannot be otherwise. As all of the chapters suggest, and as chapter 3 argues most explicitly, the United States, an empire-state in nation-state's clothing, is constitutionally ill disposed to accommodate, let alone facilitate, the destruction of white supremacy. What would radical decolonization look like for indigenous peoples, for example, and would it be possible to achieve without abandoning "America" and "Americans"? Baldwin recalls, "It comes as a great shock around the age of 5, 6, or 7 to discover that the flag to which you have pledged allegiance, along with everybody else, has not pledged allegiance to you. It comes as a great shock to see Gary Cooper killing off the Indians and, although you are rooting for Gary Cooper, that the Indians are you" (Baldwin and Buckley [1965] 2007: 684). And once we realize that we are, or side with, Indians and Blacks, pledging allegiance to Old Glory is no longer an option. Instead it becomes incumbent on us to adhere to a variation on one of Baldwin's famous lines: As long as we think we're American, there's no hope for us.[16]

NOTES

CHAPTER 1

1. Aggie Noh, "Map of Champaign-Urbana-Savoy, Racial Diversity, U.S. Census 2010 Blocks," https://netfiles.uiuc.edu/wmbrown/CU_Maps/ (retrieved June 5, 2011). See also pdempsey, "Champaign-Urbana's Racial Divide," February 16, 2011, http://cu-citizenaccess. org/maps/content/champaign-urbanas-racial-divide (retrieved June 20, 2011).

2. Brian Dolinar, "Champaign Police Fatally Shoot Unarmed 15 Year-old African American Youth," *The Public i*, October 2009, p. 1; Paul Wood, "Home Renter: 15-Year-Old Who Was Shot Lived There," *News-Gazette.com*, October 13, 2009 (retrieved October 16, 2009); Paul Wood, "More Questions, Few Answers in Champaign Death," *News-Gazette.com*, October 13, 2009 (retrieved October 13, 2009); Champaign-Urbana Citizens for Peace and Justice (CUCPJ) interview of Deborah Thomas, December 11, 2009, http://timeline.chambana.net/ content/cucpj-interview-deborah-thomas-transcript (retrieved June 2, 2011); Illinois State Police (ISP) Investigative Report, interviews of Deborah Thomas, her two teenage children, and her boyfriend, October 9, 2009, transcripts.

Unless otherwise noted, I downloaded all documents from the ISP investigation on December 8, 2009, from the *News-Gazette* website; though on a different page on the site, the documents were still available there at http://www.news-gazette.com/news/courts-police-and-fire/2009–12–10/documents-kiwane-carrington-investigation.html, as of November 13, 2013. Thanks to the efforts of the Urbana-Champaign Independent Media Center and *Smile Politely*, they were also accessible at http://timeline.chambana.net (as of June 7, 2011).

3. ISP Investigative Report, second interview of Deborah Thomas, November 3, 2009, notes, p. 2. I refrain from using the full names of J.M. and I.T., who were minors at the time.

4. "History for Champaign, IL, Friday, October 9, 2009," http://www.wunderground.com/history/airport/KCMI/2009/10/9/DailyHistory.html (retrieved June 4, 2011).

5. ISP Investigative Report, interview of Everett Riley, October 9, 2009, transcript, pp. 2–3.

6. ISP Investigative Report, "Detailed History for Police Event #092820191 as of 10/09/2009 16:23:15," p. 2; Julia Rietz, "Report of the State's Attorney: October 7 [sic], 2009 Champaign Police Department Officer Involved Fatal Shooting," December 8, 2009, p. 3 (retrieved from the City of Champaign website on December 28, 2009; available at http://eblackcu.net/portal/archive/files/states-attorney-report-final-kiwane_0326cf7613.pdf as of November 13, 2013). The multijurisdictional investigation involved twenty-one police officers from Rantoul, Champaign county, Urbana, University of Illinois, and Illinois state police units (ISP Investigative Summary, November 9, 2009, pp. 1–2).

7. ISP Investigative Report, "Out of Hospital Care Report, Provena," October 9, 2009.

8. ISP Investigative Report, "Urbana Police Department Supplemental Report," October 13, 2009. ISP interviews of paramedics and nurses corroborated Carrington's lack of response to all treatments.

9. ISP Investigative Report, "Report of the Coroner's Forensic Pathologist to the Coroner of Champaign County, Illinois," October 31, 2009, p. 2.

10. A fifth person, the neighbor, remaining on the phone with the police up to the shooting, did not have a clear line of sight and could not provide visual details.

11. "[J.M.] Police Interview" video (watched at http://timeline.chambana.net on June 7, 2011); ISP Investigative Reports, "To document speaking with [J.M.]," "To document the Constitutional Rights and Waiver given to [J.M.]," "Statement of Constitutional Rights and Waiver Rights," October 9, 2009.

According to the notes of Lisa Crowder of the Illinois State Police, "S/A [Special Agent Clayton] Woodard left the room at approximately 3:11 p.m. to call [J.M.'s] guardian, [L.M.]" In the video recording, Woodard could be heard saying, "I'm gonna call her and let her know what's going on, o.k.? That way, if she wants to be here, she can be here with you, o.k.? We wanna, we wanna treat you fair, and we want you to know what's going on." There is then a break in the recording with the following explanation appearing on the screen: "[J.M.] is asked a series of questions consistent with standard booking procedures—none of them pertain to the shooting. He is then left alone for about 30 minutes." During this break, according to Crowder's notes, "At approximately 3:17 p.m., S/A Woodard entered the room. S/A Woodard said [L.M.] was en route to the police department and wanted to be present when officers spoke to [J.M.]" Yet, when Woodard and Tim Drake, also of the state police, administered the Miranda warning to J.M. after the recording resumed, his mother was not in the room.

12. See ISP Investigation, "Interview Caveat" of R.T. Finney, October 9, 2009, and "Interview Caveat" of Dan Norbits, October 13, 2009. The relevant case law is *Garrity v. New Jersey*, 385 U.S. 493 (1967).

13. ISP Investigative Report, Joseph Gallo, "Champaign Police Department Supplemental Report," October 15, 2009, p. 2.

14. ISP Investigative Report, Troy Daniels, "Champaign Police Department Supplemental Report," October 19, 2009, p. 2.

15. Ibid.; Gallo report, p. 2; ISP Investigative Summary, p. 5.

16. ISP Investigative Report, "Detailed History for Police Event #092820191 as of 10/09/2009 16:23:15."

17. ISP Investigation, "Photos of Chief Finney," http://timeline.chambana.net/content/photos-chief-finney (retrieved June 7, 2011). In contrast to those of Finney, photos of

Norbits were not taken at the scene but at the police department about an hour later (ISP Investigative Report, [Andrew] Good, "Champaign County Sheriff's Office Supplementary/ Continuation Report," October 9, 2009, p. 2; see ISP Investigation, "Photos of Officer Norbits," http://timeline.chambana.net/content/photos-officer-norbits [retrieved June 7, 2011]).

18. ISP Investigative Report, first interview of R.T. Finney, October 9, 2009, transcript, p. 2.

19. ISP Investigative Report, interview of Daniel Norbits, October 13, 2009, transcript, p. 4.

20. Ibid., p. 28.

Finney stated in an interview, several hours after the incident, "I identified myself, I yelled, police, get down" (First Finney ISP interview, p. 2, with Finney's correction). Ten days later, about a week after Norbits's own interview with investigators, Finney was asked specifically about his initial words. He reiterated having announced that he was police but conceded that "there is a possibility he said something to the effect of don't make me shoot . . . ha[ving] used this phrase in the past" (ISP Investigative Report, second interview of R.T. Finney, October 19, 2009, notes, p. 3).

The neighbor and the police staff person on the phone with him, as well as the third police officer on the scene, did not report hearing Finney identify himself as police or say "stop or I will shoot you." Although he did not see the shooting, the neighbor remembered, "Uh, I heard the police behind the house hollering 'get on the ground. Get on the ground' and then I heard a shot" (Riley interview, p. 4). Likewise, while still on the line with the neighbor, the police staffer, through the phone, "could hear one of the officers holler at the subjects to 'get down'" but noted no other utterances (ISP Investigation, "Champaign Police Department Supplemental Report" by Jamie R. Weidenburner, October 9, 2009). Similarly, Officer Steven Reynolds only made out the words "get down, get down" (ISP Investigative Report, interview of Steven Reynolds, October 9, 2009, transcript, pp. 3–4).

21. Norbits ISP interview, pp. 13–14.

22. At least two documents of the ISP investigation reported differing heights and weights, both on the date of the shooting: one listed "offender" Carrington at 5 ft. 2 in. and 110 lbs. and "offender" J.M. at 5 ft. 1 in. and 120 lbs. (ISP Investigative Report, University of Illinois Police coversheet to first Finney ISP interview, October 9, 2009, p. 1), whereas another logged them in as 5 ft. 5 in., 140 lbs., and 5 ft. 5 in., 160 lbs., respectively (ISP Investigative Report, Champaign County Sheriff's Office Suspect Form, October 9, 2009).

23. Deputy Chief John F. Murphy to Steve Carter, City Manager, Memorandum on "Shooting Review Board—Carrington Investigation," interview of R. T. Finney, April 7, 2010, transcript, p. 22, http://timeline.chambana.net/content/carter-report-released (retrieved June 1, 2011); Norbits ISP interview, p. 24; "photos of Chief Finney"; "photos of Officer Norbits."

24. Norbits ISP interview, p. 15.

25. First Finney ISP interview, p. 5; ellipsis in original.

26. Ibid.

27. Norbits ISP interview, pp. 24–25.

28. "Report of the Coroner's Forensic Pathologist," p. 2.

29. Norbits ISP interview, p. 6.

30. "Report of the Coroner's Forensic Pathologist," p. 2. The state's attorney asked the pathologist for clarification, and the doctor evidently defined "close range firing" as "less than 18 to 24 inches." Unfathomably, "no tests on Carrington's clothing to for [sic] the presence of soot or gunpowder residue" were performed or requested "to further determine the range of the weapon" ("Report of the State's Attorney," p. 7).

31. Norbits ISP interview, p. 22.

32. "Report of the State's Attorney," p. 5; ISP Investigative Report, laboratory reports for case #S09–008304, November 11 and 19, 2009.

33. First Finney ISP interview, p. 5.

34. Norbits ISP interview, pp. 6, 19. Six months later, in his interview with the Champaign Police Department (CPD) Shooting Review Board, Norbits's memory of the actual shooting had not improved. But there were a couple of notable changes. First, he now recalled that the original dispatch had erroneously indicated three suspects, in line with Finney's and others' accounts, although Norbits originally told investigators that there had been two (Norbits ISP interview, pp. 25–26; Deputy Chief John F. Murphy to Steve Carter, City Manager, Memorandum on "Shooting Review Board—Carrington Investigation," interview of Daniel Norbits, April 7, 2010, transcript, p. 9, http://timeline.chambana.net/content/carter-report-released [retrieved June 1, 2011]). Second, he now claimed multiple times that Carrington had moved toward him, depicting Carrington as more of an aggressor than previously; his extensive initial interview with the ISP, in which the incident was reviewed repeatedly, had no mention of such actions on the part of Carrington (Norbits CPD review board interview, pp. 8–11).

Finney's recollection also shifted over time, rendering Carrington a considerably more hostile figure. To the CPD review board, he now claimed that both J.M. *and Carrington,* not just J.M., moved toward *him* at the outset. Seemingly more vividly and certainly, Finney narrated Norbits's encounter with Carrington: "I could see Carrington resisting Officer Norbits. I could hear Officer Norbits yelling to Carrington to get down. I could hear Officer Norbits saying, 'Show me your hands,' and I could see out of the corner of my eye, and just briefly diverting side to side, Carrington and Norbits *fighting.* . . . I think Carrington was probably in a *more aggressive* mode than [J.M.]. I had [J.M.] come up almost to my weapon, and I shoved him back probably at least twice, and then grabbed him by the shoulder to pull him down to the ground. His resistance, I never, his hands never came up. He wasn't slapping around, and his resistance, I think, was probably less than Carrington. It seemed to me like there was *a lot of yelling* by Norbits for Carrington to show his hands, and they were engaged *much more aggressively* than I think I had with [J.M.]" (Finney CPD review board interview, pp. 17, 21; emphases added).

35. Author's notes, November 3, 2009.

36. "Report of the State's Attorney," p. 14.

37. See also "Illinois Pattern Criminal Jury Instructions" for "Homicide" and for "Mental State, Accountability, and Responsibility," http://www.state.il.us/court/circuitcourt/CriminalJuryInstructions/ (retrieved November 11, 2013).

38. On the interviewers' congeniality, we might take note that Norbits's union lawyer did not need to interject throughout her client's interview. She simply introduced herself, excused herself for almost coughing, and, at the end, asked the interviewers to contact Norbits through her (Norbits ISP interview, pp. 1, 27, 30).

39. "Report of the State's Attorney," p. 14.

40. Ibid.

41. Ibid.

42. Not seeing any such evidence, I contacted Rietz to confirm, and she unhelpfully referred me back to her report (emails from author to Rietz, January 13, 15, 20, and 22, 2010, and from Rietz to author, January 21, 2010).

43. Norbits ISP interview, pp. 6, 14, 15, 16, 18, 19, 22. Nobody else saw and talked about the shooting itself. Finney stated he did not see it, and J.M. did not say anything, perhaps because of the felony charge against him that Rietz was still refusing to drop.

44. WILL AM 580, "Rietz Rules 'Accidental' in Police Shooting Death of Kiwane Carrington," interview of Julia Rietz by Tom Rogers, December 8, 2009 (listened at http://will. illinois.edu/news/story/rietzfull1208091 on June 27, 2011).

45. Tim Mitchell, "Identity of Officer in Champaign Teen Shooting Released," *News-Gazette.com*, October 14, 2009 (retrieved June 21, 2011); Dolinar, "Champaign Police Fatally Shoot . . . ," p. 1.

46. Deborah Thomas CUCPJ interview, p. 30; ellipsis and parenthetical observation in original.

47. Mary Schenk, "Rietz Dismisses Charges against Second Youth in Kiwane Carrington Incident," *News-Gazette.com*, April 13, 2010 (retrieved July 6, 2011).

48. "Report of the State's Attorney," p. 8.

49. During the interviews, the Thomases began to receive word by phone that Carrington was the dead victim and became distressed, but the police refused to give information or confirm.

50. "Report of the State's Attorney," p. 11. See the first and second ISP, as well as CUCPJ, interviews of Deborah Thomas. On how welcome Carrington was at the Thomases', see the interview of Thomas's boyfriend (ISP Investigative Report, interview of Dennis Atkins, October 9, 2009, transcript).

51. "Report of the State's Attorney," p. 13.

52. For some more recent data, see Gabrielson, Jones, and Sagara (2014) and Eisen (2013).

53. The greater inequality in Champaign, calculated from 2006–2010 American Community Survey data, resulted from both a lower Black income—$31,458 vs. $41,675 for the United States—and a higher white income—$76,256 vs. $67,424 for the United States; these figures included those who checked off only one racial category (http://factfinder2.census. gov/, retrieved November 11, 2013).

It should be noted that overall economic inequality in cities (i.e., without regard to race) is not significantly related to police killings (Jacobs and O'Brien 1998).

54. Dan Petrella, "Local Police Departments Continue to Deny Open Records Requests," *CU-CitizenAccess*, June 7, 2010, http://cu-citizenaccess.org/content/local-police-departments-continue-deny-open-records-requests (retrieved June 26, 2011).

55. The figures are for those who identified with "one race." Including those who identified with "one or more other races," they are 17.1 percent and 70.3 percent for Blacks and whites, respectively (http://factfinder2.census.gov/, retrieved November 11, 2013).

56. Email from Belden Fields to CUCPJ, January 2, 2010, based on documents he acquired through the Freedom of Information Act (FOIA) from the Champaign police; CUCPJ, "Proposal That a Residency Requirement Be Incorporated into the Champaign Fraternal Order of Police Labor Contract," February 2010.

Brad Smith (2003) finds no relationship between "minority representation" on police forces and police homicides but does not examine the effects of residency or of the interaction between residency and minority representation.

57. Petrella, "Local Police Departments Continue to Deny Open Records Requests."

58. Champaign Police Department, "School Resource Officer Program, 2007–2008 School Year" and "School Resource Officer Program, 2008–2009 School Year," City of Champaign.

Over the objections of Black parents, Champaign schools adopted the School Resource Officer Program in 2006. The parents presciently feared that Black students would be targeted and criminalized (Jodi Heckel, "Unit 4: Proposal for Resource Officers Still Alive," *News-Gazette.com*, April 13, 2006; "Board OKs Resource Officers for Next Year," *News-*

Gazette.com, April 18, 2006; and "Black Parents Urge Boycott After School Board Action," *News-Gazette.com*, April 20, 2006 [retrieved July 1, 2011]).

59. Durl Kruse, "Juvenile Justice in Champaign County—A Racial Disparity," *The Public i*, January 2010, p. 2. Kruse's analysis is based on records of the state's attorney he requested through FOIA, covering the period from January 2008 to October 2009.

60. "An Angry Night at City Hall," *News-Gazette.com*, October 22, 2009 (retrieved June 29, 2011).

61. The first quote is of the reporter's paraphrase of Steve Carter, and the second is a quote of Harrison (Steve Bauer, "Champaign Council Willing to Wait for State Police Report," *News-Gazette.com*, October 25, 2009 [retrieved November 15, 2009]).

62. "No Charges No Surprise in Police Shooting," *News-Gazette.com*, December 9, 2009 (retrieved December 9, 2009).

63. For examples, see ibid.; Paul Wood, "Officials Promise Independent Probe into Teen's Death," *News-Gazette.com*, December 9, 2009 (retrieved December 9, 2009); Patrick Wade, "Champaign Police Trying to Increase Minority Police Hiring," *News-Gazette.com*, December 20, 2009 (retrieved July 6, 2011), "Forum to Tackle Police Relations in Light of Carrington Death," *News-Gazette.com*, February 23, 2010 (retrieved July 6, 2011); City of Champaign, "City Releases Community Forum Focus Questions," news release, March 5, 2010.

64. Illinois Fraternal Order of Police Labor Council, press release, April 23, 2010, http://ci.champaign.il.us/2010/04/23/fraternal-order-police-labor-council (retrieved June 28, 2011).

65. In its sense of tragic and absurd inevitability, the case felt like the slow-motion run-up to the 2003 U.S. invasion of Iraq, with various state and media actors playing out their roles as if scripted, to the disbelief of many but to the belief of many, many more.

66. There probably are a few words that most would agree are racist, but it is noteworthy that public figures who are "caught" using such words inevitably deny that they are racist, even as they apologize. For examples, see two items that appeared within a couple days of each other: http://www.nytimes.com/2013/03/07/opinion/coates-the-good-racist-people.html (retrieved March 13, 2013); http://espn.go.com/racing/nascar/nationwide/story/_/id/9047020/jeremy-clements-reinstated-sensitivity-counseling (retrieved March 13, 2013).

67. As quoted in Pat Wade, "Displeasure Expressed at Champaign Council Meeting," *News-Gazette.com*, December 9, 2009 (retrieved December 9, 2009).

The most active among the organizations involved, CUCPJ is a grassroots, "black-led, multi-racial group, which seeks to expose and remedy racial and class inequities in a number of areas of life in the Champaign-Urbana community" (see http://cucpj.org).

68. David Martin, "Defense of Young Man Raises Question," *News-Gazette.com*, December 16, 2009 (retrieved December 16, 2009). See also Linda Webb, "Police Critic Wrong in All Categories," *News-Gazette.com*, December 16, 2009 (retrieved December 16, 2009).

69. An example of the latter, the prosecutor office's legal practices are significantly responsible for producing the huge disparities in juvenile justice in Champaign county. At the same time, it produces and consumes the statistical knowledge of these inequalities. Yet this state agency evinces an evident indifference to this self-produced knowledge.

70. Of 81,055 Champaign residents identified by the 2010 census, 5,111 and 8,566 were Latinas/os and Asians, respectively (http://factfinder2.census.gov/, retrieved November 11, 2013).

71. For my brief take on this question, see Jung (2015).

72. There were 205 "American Indians and Alaska Natives" in 2010 (http://factfinder2.census.gov/, retrieved November 11, 2013).

CHAPTER 2

1. Bonilla-Silva deservedly received the Lewis A. Coser Award for Theoretical Agenda Setting in 2007 for this and related work, which indeed has been agenda-setting in sociology and beyond. My longstanding fondness for the theory derives almost, but not quite, entirely from its intellectual merits. A lifetime ago, I was a graduate student in a seminar taught by Bonilla-Silva, who shared an early draft of his 1997 article with the class. He and his theory made a lasting impression. I should also note that he supported my decision to write the present chapter.

2. Although his later research often exceeds it and intimates certain conceptual breaches, the theory has not undergone a thoroughgoing reevaluation and reconstruction.

3. The aspects of Bonilla-Silva's theory that have received the most critical attention relate to whether *race* is a legitimate analytical concept and whether there is a distinction to be drawn between *categories* and *groups*. In my opinion, the ratio of ink spilled on these criticisms to their significance has been too high. As explained later, *race*, in my work, does not refer to any categories or groups of people but to a mode of categorization.

4. Social networks' amenability to quantitative analysis indicates not the absence but the regularity of meaningful practices (Sewell 2005: ch. 10).

5. The concept of *articulation*, borrowed from structural Marxism, does not appear in Sewell's (1992) discussion of *structure* but is later central to his discussion of *language games* (Sewell 2005: ch. 10). I accept Sewell's exclusive focus on *human* agency for the purposes of this chapter and book, but I do not reject, nor wholly embrace, the idea of *nonhuman* agency.

6. Although schemas may be thought of as "effects of resources," Sewell's assertion that, in the reproduction of structures, schemas "must be validated by the *accumulation* of resources that their enactment engenders" does not hold (1992: 13; emphasis added). As Archer (1995: 111) points out, using philanthropy as an example, some structures may not accumulate resources but deplete them. To take another example, many personal relationships can drain energy, money, sanity, and other valuable resources.

A revised proposition would be that resources validate schemas, but not necessarily through accumulation. Validation without accumulation is made possible in part by what Sewell refers to as the *multiplicity* and *intersection* of structures, discussed below. Interconnected with each other, some structures may be net resource gainers, and others net losers. Moreover, within any given structure, certain resources may increase while others diminish. In addition, for both nonhuman and human resources, some are finite (e.g., fossil fuel, person-hours), and some are renewable (e.g., solar energy, rage). Finally, the resource effects of a structure may be historically variable.

7. The schema effects of resources can at first appear counterintuitive, as we are more prone to think that agents impose schemas on resources than that resources induce schemas in agents. But note, for instance, how the War on Drugs, declared by the Reagan administration during a period of declining drug use and crime, met initial resistance from police forces at state and local levels. Yet the infusion of massive resources (e.g., money, military weapons) conjured into being novel schemas, and novel applications of preexisting schemas (e.g., routine use of SWAT teams in police drug raids, arrests and incarceration for minor drug offenses), including predictably those of anti-Black racism (Alexander 2010). Or, more familiar to academics, we can observe how grant initiatives by government and other funding agencies or universities continually generate a multitude of schemas having to do not only with obtaining and using research funds but also with the content of research itself (i.e., discursive schemas of scholarly knowledge), often altering the career trajectories of ostensibly disinterested academics.

8. This relationship between depth and extension, however, is a tendency, not a necessity. For example, uncommon beliefs of small religious cults are no doubt deeply held by their adherents, but the extent of their influence is restricted.

Moreover, extensiveness may be positively related not only to the depth of schemas but also to the power of resources. Powerful structures tend to affect large numbers of agents, likely in a variety of ways and contexts. For example, it would be hard to deny that states, one of Sewell's examples of shallow but powerful structures, "are present in a relatively wide range of institutional spheres, practices, and discourses" (1992: 22).

9. Giddens's theory, which is vulnerable to similar criticism (Thompson 1984: 166–70) and serves as his point of departure, may be another source of Sewell's insufficient attention to structural constraint.

10. "Historical ontology" may be the appropriate label (Hacking 2002).

11. For a similar criticism, see Archer (1995: 109–10).

12. Bourdieu's concept of capital gives further support to this argument. The various noneconomic forms of capital (e.g., cultural capital) that he proposes, though in the materialist language of resources, are or entail, to varying degrees, knowledge of schemas.

I should also note here that material objects themselves set limits on which schemas can be applied to turn them into resources. For example, a pencil can be many things (e.g., writing tool, weapon, fuel) but cannot be far more things. For a discussion of *material agency*, see Pickering (1995).

13. At first glance, notions of racial "mixture" (e.g., multiracial, mestizo) may appear to present a counterexample. But the idea of combining or blending presupposes the past or present existence of "pre-mixed" categories and their continuing relevance *within* individuals.

14. I see *racism* and *white supremacy* as more or less interchangeable at most scales of analysis. As an articulated whole, the history of racism has been the history of white supremacy. However, there have been structures on less global scales (e.g., the Japanese empire) in which white domination has not been the most salient form of racism (Mills 2009).

15. For some examples, see Anderson (1990), Feagin (1991), and Waters (1999).

16. On whether the United States constitutes a nation-state at all, see chapter 3.

17. One effect of fixing the scale of analysis to the nation-state may be an ironic inattention to articulations of racism and nationalism.

18. Bonilla-Silva's (1997: 471) mention of Puerto Rico is both exceptional for its clearly not being a nation-state and unexceptional for its colonial status not bearing relevance.

19. Put differently, the "linchpin of the whole system of thought" and, I would add, practice is "the belief that 'races' exist at all" (Shelby 2003: 168).

20. In the modern era, "throughout Europe, states could take the lives of individuals, but enslavement was no longer an alternative to death; rather, it had become a fate worse than death and, as such, was reserved for non-Europeans" (Eltis 1993: 1409). In this light, the tendency to dismiss Black claims of genocide as ideological hyperbole is surely misguided. If anything, to the degree that it is seen as pertaining only to corporeal death, genocide underestimates the cruelty of slavery.

Paradoxically, the inclination to deny slavery as "a fate worse than death" in the present moment coexists with a general acceptance of the tenet, which is illustrated by a scenario posed by Jacqueline Stevens: "The public today would not tolerate slavery as a result of war but does not bristle at systemic death. If the Bush administration had acknowledged that despite their best intentions over twelve thousand Iraqi civilians had been enslaved by U.S. soldiers during the first months of the invasion, the outcry would be overwhelming.

But the same number of Iraqi civilians killed outright by the U.S. military provokes little reaction" (2010: 15).

21. An exemplary instance is laws on interracial marriage, Peggy Pascoe's (2009) book on which is appositely subtitled "miscegenation law and the making of race in America."

22. To pair, paraphrase, and, in the case of the first author, pervert Benedict Anderson (1991) and Jacqueline Stevens (1999), *race* and *nation* are closely related styles of imagining intergenerational communities. For Stevens (1999), race, nation, and their articulability derive from kinship rules constituted by the state; in contrast, Anderson (1991) conceives of the two as (nearly) inarticulable. For further discussion of the articulability of race and nation, as well as class, see Jung (2006: ch. 3).

In addition to schemas of national and state membership, the civic dimension of racism can be articulated to schemas of inclusion and exclusion of many other forms of communities, like neighborhoods, cities, regions, and religions.

23. Other schemas underwent similar transformations: the notion of "discrimination," originally referring to the unfair treatment of union members, took on an additional and quickly primary meaning of racial discrimination, and "divide and rule" went from a pat leftist explanation to a fully realized mnemonic schema that reinterpreted and aligned the workers' varied racial histories.

24. For an example of such rearticulations with regard to race, class, and gender, see Magubane (2005).

25. For a similar argument, in critical engagement with Judith Butler's work, see Hollywood (2003); for a Wittgensteinian rendition, see Richardson (2009).

26. My appropriation of Austin (1975) goes only so far as what I discuss here. For example, I do not focus narrowly on individual sentences or delve into the parsing of locutionary, illocutionary, and perlocutionary acts.

27. We might also include extra-textual representations in visual media, like photographs, cartoons, film, and so on.

28. For the psychological basis of this argument, see Bargh (1997a, 1997b), Hassin, Uleman, and Bargh (2006), Kahneman (2011), and Wilson (2002), and for its sociological importation, see Lizardo (2009) and Vaisey (2009). On the variability of tacitness and consciousness in practices, see Elder-Vass (2007).

29. Performative and reflective discourses are not mutually exclusive. There are certain performative discourses that are at the same time reflective. A paradigmatic example would be court rulings: deliberate opinions that instantiate what they pronounce (see chapter 3).

30. Findings in social psychology bear out the asymmetry of empathy, awareness, and attention in relations of power (e.g., Fiske 1993; Galinsky et al. 2006). For examples of such asymmetries in racial interactions, see Feagin (1991), Fleming, Lamont, and Welburn (2012), and Rawls (2000).

31. In such matters of discourse, "knowledge," as discussed earlier, exhibits the dual properties of schema and resource: it consists of enacting schemas of thought and speech and marshaling resources of preexisting ideas.

32. Note that if an ideology is being put forth by a social movement, the reflective-discursive schemas of the ideology may not necessarily be consonant with the performa-discursive and nondiscursive schemas, in articulation with resources, that structure the movement. Hence, an organization that consciously opposes racism may be, in practice, a structure of racial inequality and domination.

33. For an example of this dynamic, see Omi and Winant (1994) on the conservative reaction to the Civil Rights Movement and other progressive racial movements, including the co-optation of the notion of "equal opportunity."

34. It may secondarily propose ways to further exacerbate inequality and domination.

35. As the label implies, conservative ideologies seek to conserve what already is.

36. For critiques and alternatives, in relation to the cultural study of labor, see Biernacki (1997) and Richardson (2009).

37. To the extent that they present various "racial projects" as comparable, "competing possibles" (Bourdieu 1977: 169), Omi and Winant (1994) may be misleading, overlooking the overwhelming advantage of what already is over any alternatives. To borrow an imagery from Thompson (1984: 132), "mak[ing] a [new] meaning stick," to people and things, is much harder than defending a meaning that is already and therefore successfully stuck.

38. I allude to Bourdieu's clever turn of phrase: "what is essential *goes without saying because it comes without saying*" (1977: 167; emphasis in original). Given the conceptual distinction I draw between performative and reflective discourses, "comment" may be more appropriate, if rhetorically less pleasing, than "saying."

39. Overlapping with and, in some domains, trumping "colorblindness," discourse of "diversity" offers a more liberal, "dominated dominant" ideology of race (Bourdieu and Wacquant 1992: 81). Scarcely less compatible with or more critical of racial inequality and domination, it could be subjected to the present analysis with only minor modifications (Bell and Hartmann 2007). For an excellent analysis of how diversity functions as the dominant racial ideology in higher education, see Ahmed (2009).

40. In metropolitan areas with at least 1,000 Black residents, the index of Black isolation from whites was 0.77 in 1970, 0.68 in 1990, and 0.62 in 2005–09 (Iceland, Sharp, and Timberlake 2013: 120). The percentage of Black students attending majority-minority schools went from 76.6 percent in 1968–69 to 62.9 percent in 1980–81 to 74.1 percent in 2009–10 (Orfield, Kucsera, and Siegel-Hawley 2012: 19).

41. Calculated from data for Mishel et al. (2012) available at http://stateofworkingamerica. org/data/ (retrieved on May 18, 2013). Black median household wealth was $6,366 in 1983 and $4,890 in 2010. The comparable figures for whites were $95,709 and $97,000.

42. For a summary of more data on contemporary inequalities, see Smith and King (2009: 26–28).

43. Because of the dearth of public opinion data prior to the Civil Rights Movement, the onset of this attitude cannot be firmly dated, but it appears to have occurred earlier than is commonly assumed. A 1942 survey found that 47 percent of whites believed in the equal intelligence of Blacks and whites. By 1956, the figure had already climbed to 80 percent (Schuman et al. 1997: 353–54n37).

44. Concerning the enduring and implicit dehumanization of Blacks, see Goff et al. (2008).

45. In the Milwaukee study, Blacks with and without criminal records were called back 5 percent and 14 percent of the time, respectively. The comparable figures for whites were 17 percent and 34 percent (Pager 2003: 957–58).

46. In the survey, 61.9 percent of the employers stated that they were "very likely" or "somewhat likely" to hire a well-qualified white applicant with a criminal record. For an otherwise identical Black applicant, the percentage was 61.7 percent, although the percentage of "very likely" responses dropped more significantly (Pager and Quillian 2005: 364).

47. See also Moss and Tilly (2001), Neckerman and Kirschenman (1991), and Wilson (1996).

48. There are also a few cases of "categorical exclusion," in which the racial bias is more blatant and unambiguous. But even then, the bias is revealed only through comparison (Pager, Western, and Bonikowski 2009: 787–88).

49. For a vivid example of the disconnect between the reflective and the performative, see Moss and Tilly who report that "negative perceptions of black workers were linked to *increased* probability of hiring a black worker" (2001: 154; emphasis added).

50. Examining entry-level positions posted widely in classified ads, the studies by Pager and colleagues exclude the vast majority of jobs that are filled by other means. A study by William Julius Wilson and colleagues reveals that Chicago-area employers routinely engage in hiring practices for entry-level jobs—such as selective recruitment from certain neighborhoods and schools, limited and targeted newspaper advertisements, and avoidance of governmental referral agencies—that exclude, or fail to include, inner-city Blacks. The differences in the types of hiring practices by neighborhood and the higher percentage of Blacks in firms that employ standard skills tests show that race plays a significant role in these practices (Neckerman and Kirschenman 1991; Wilson 1996).

Deirdre Royster's detailed study of young Black and white working-class men in Baltimore, with similar backgrounds, skills, and performance at the same trade school, demonstrates how social networks create racial inequalities in employment. Whites consistently benefit from racially exclusive networks of teachers, families, friends, neighbors, and others, who repeatedly help them land good jobs. Taking this assistance for granted, they fail to notice its racialized character, presumably as do their benefactors. For example, giving "verbal support and encouragement" to promising Black students, white shop teachers do not need to see themselves as racially biased, even if they, most likely without any or much conscious reflection, "active[ly] and frequent[ly]" draw on their "personal resources to assist white students in getting within-trade jobs and work opportunities, particularly in teachers' own small businesses" (Royster 2003: 142).

51. As Bourdieu (1977: 109) notes, "practice has a logic which is not that of logic."

52. Here, an analogy to Edward Said's concept of Orientalism may be useful: "In a quite constant way, Orientalism depends for its strategy on this flexible *positional* superiority, which puts the Westerner in a whole series of possible relationships with the Orient without ever losing him the relative upper hand" (1978: 7; emphasis in original).

53. Drawing attention to this open secret, Vargas (2005, 2008) calls for the revival of the concept of *genocide* in the study of the African diaspora.

In particular contexts—in postcolonial Guyana (Jackson 2012) or among Mexican adolescents in contemporary New York City (Smith 2014), among other exceptional examples—Blackness may not be the most debased racial category.

54. On the principally noneconomic origin of chattel slavery's inapplicability and unthinkability in relation to Europeans, see Eltis (1993, 2000).

55. Stoler (1997) makes a similar point with regard to Dutch racism in colonial Indonesia.

56. For overviews, see Eberhardt (2005), Greenwald et al. (2009), Quillian (2006, 2008), and Kubota, Banaji, and Phelps (2012).

57. "The philosophers have only *interpreted* the world in various ways; the point is, to *change* it" (Marx [1845] 1994: 101; emphases in original). Thanks to Sara Farris for alerting me to the stray "however" that often finds its way between "is" and "to" in English translations.

58. This inversion of the familiar term "participant observation" appears in Vargas (2006a).

CHAPTER 3

An earlier version of this chapter appeared as "White Supremacist Constitution of the U.S. Empire-State: A Short Conceptual Look at the Long First Century," *Political Power and Social Theory* 20 (2009): 167–200.

1. *Boumediene v. Bush*, 553 U.S. 723 (2008) at 826–27.

2. Mark Perelman, "From Sarajevo to Guantanamo: The Strange Case of the Algerian Six," *Mother Jones*, December 4, 2007, http://www.motherjones.com/politics/2007/12/sarajevo-guantanamo-strange-case-algerian-six (retrieved July 23, 2013); Steven Erlanger, "Ex-Detainee Describes His 7 Years at Guantánamo," May 27, 2009, http://www.nytimes.com/2009/05/27/world/europe/27paris.html (retrieved July 25, 2013); Lakhdar Boumediene, "My Guantánamo Nightmare," *New York Times*, January 7, 2012, http://www.nytimes.com/2012/01/08/opinion/sunday/my-guantanamo-nightmare.html (retrieved July 16, 2013); Scott Sayare, "After Guantánamo, Starting Anew, in Quiet Anger," *New York Times*, May 25, 2012, http://www.nytimes.com/2012/05/26/world/europe/lakhdar-boumediene-starts-anew-in-france-after-years-at-guantanamo.html (retrieved July 28, 2013); Edward Cody, "Algerian Lakhdar Boumediene Tells of Struggle After 7 Years at Guantanamo Bay," *Washington Post*, May 26, 2009, http://www.washingtonpost.com/wp-dyn/content/article/2009/05/25/AR2009052502263.html (retrieved July 28, 2013).

3. *Boumediene v. Bush*, 553 U.S. 723 (2008) at 755, 769. In other words, when the United States "exercise[s] complete jurisdiction and control," should its purely *de jure* "recogni[tion of] the continuance of the ultimate sovereignty of the Republic of Cuba" define the border between the United States and Cuba (Article III, "Agreement between the United States and Cuba for the Lease of Lands for Coaling and Naval stations," February 23, 1903)?

4. *Boumediene v. Bush*, 553 U.S. 723 (2008) at 827.

5. *Boumediene* itself is rife with comparisons to the British empire of old.

6. Ibid. at 755.

7. Not surprisingly, *Boumediene* extensively discusses this earlier moment in U.S. empire.

8. The potential is particularly likely in my own discipline of sociology. Legal scholars, historians, cultural critics, and others substantially outpace sociologists in recognizing the full spatial and temporal scope of the U.S. colonial empire (e.g., Kaplan 2002; Kaplan and Pease 1993; Meinig 1986; W. A. Williams 1980; Wilson 2002).

9. Restricting the empirical purview to constitutional law of the long nineteenth century furnishes a measure of concision to this discussion, but the analysis could readily be brought to the present and cast a much wider empirical net.

10. "The constitutions of the last two centuries are monuments to an eminently modern enterprise. . . . Constitution-making is a deliberate attempt at institution-building at the fundamental level of laying down the normative and legal foundations of the political order" (Arjomand 1992: 39; see also Go 2003: 90).

11. "Save for a few notable (and notorious) exceptions, e.g., *Dred Scott v. Sandford*, 60 U.S. 393, 19 How. 393, 15 L.Ed. 691 (1857), throughout most of our history there was little need to explore the outer boundaries of the Constitution's geographic reach" (*Boumediene v. Bush*, 553 U.S. 723 [2008] at 755).

12. For a recent effort in political science that expands on and is mostly compatible with Omi and Winant (1994), see King and Smith (2005). They differ in a few ways. Whereas the former stresses the struggle between social movements and the state as the central dynamic in racial politics, the latter sees the opposing forces as *racial institutional orders*, rival political coalitions made up of both state and nonstate actors. As a consequence, King and Smith find the state to be less unitary in relation to race. They also do not share Omi and Winant's

view that the U.S. state is inherently racial and speculate that "someday the United States may transcend [racial institutional orders] entirely—though that prospect is not in sight" (King and Smith 2005: 75). As with Omi and Winant, however, the U.S. state is still conceptualized implicitly as a nation-state.

13. For example, though critical of Omi and Winant's theory of the racial state, Goldberg (2002: 4) affirms the nation-state as the primary object of analysis: "In *The Racial State* I seek to comprehend the co-articulation of race and the modern state. I argue that race is integral to the emergence, development, and transformations (conceptually, philosophically, materially) of the modern nation-state. Race marks and orders the modern nation-state, and so state projects, more or less from its point of conceptual and institutional emergence."

14. Although I use Anderson's definition of nation, I could substitute others without much consequence.

15. Weber defines the state as "a human community that (successfully) claims the *monopoly of the legitimate use of physical force* within a given territory" (1946: 78; emphasis in original).

16. On the concept of *empire-state*, see Cooper (2005), especially chapters 1 and 6. For an early usage of the term, see Francis (1954: 8–9).

17. Today, even outside the fifty states, all citizens of U.S. territories, except American Sāmoa, hold U.S. citizenship (Sparrow 2006).

18. The quotes are attributed to General Philip Sheridan, in 1869, and Captain Richard Pratt, in 1892. The former, however, is the popular rendering of what Sheridan might actually have said: "The only good Indians I ever saw were dead" (Hutton 1999: 180).

19. From the beginning of U.S. history to the present, amnesias and denials of empire have also been punctuated by moments of recognition, acceptance, celebration, and critique of empire. But as the cycle of forgetting and remembering may predict, most recognitions and critiques have been only too partial, in both senses.

20. Other exceptions include American Sāmoa, the Northern Mariana Islands, the Panama Canal Zone, and the Virgin Islands.

21. In this chapter I do not discuss nonterritorial imperialism and imperialistic activity (Go 2007, 2008; Mann 2008; Steinmetz 2005).

22. To be clear, I do not mean that comparisons cannot be useful or that empires are all equally different from each other.

23. I refer, of course, to James C. Scott's (1998) *Seeing Like a State*.

24. Certainly in sociology and, I am sure, in a number of other disciplines, the silence with regard to the Native peoples of North America and the Pacific Islands is shamefully nearly absolute.

25. *Limited*, but not *no*, utility. The boundedness of colonies and the existence and relative autonomy of colonial states within empire-states are variable.

26. Of the over 2 billion acres of indigenous land taken by the United States from its founding to 1900, only half was "purchased by treaty or agreement" (Barsh 1982: 7). Indian reservations within the contiguous United States totaled 84,199 square miles as of 1984 (Frantz 1999: 44), approximately the size of Utah or Idaho. See Biolsi (2005) for a range of mutually nonexclusive sovereignty claims made by Native Americans premised on different geographies.

27. Two states, North Carolina and Georgia, did so after the adoption of the Constitution.

28. Congress's power was complete in this regard as long as an admission did not involve areas under the jurisdiction of any existing states, in which case the legislative consent of the affected states was required.

29. Though all but forgotten, the ideas behind this and the previous paragraphs are not entirely novel. For example, despite his racist imperialism, political scientist Abbott Lawrence Lowell's characterization of the U.S. history of colonialism, in a popular forum in 1899, was on target: "Properly speaking, a colony is a territory, not forming, for political purposes, an integral part of the mother country, but dependent upon her, and peopled in part, at least, by her emigrants. If this is true, there has never been a time, since the adoption of the first ordinance for the government of the Northwest Territory in 1784, when the United States has not had colonies" (1899a: 145; see also Hart 1899; Thayer 1899). The ideology of U.S. exceptionalism and, after the *Insular Cases*, the close identification of the former Spanish colonies as the only true U.S. colonies were likely significant culprits for the collective memory loss.

30. Rather than whether the Constitution would "follow the flag" or whether U.S. citizenship would be conferred, Burnett and Marshall (2001a) see *indefiniteness* as the overriding defining feature of unincorporated territories. Burnett (2005) adds further that separability, the constitutional possibility of de-annexation, distinguishes unincorporated territories from states and incorporated territories.

The U.S. differentiation of overseas, unincorporated territories from mostly overland, incorporated territories prefigures the United Nations's postwar adoption of the so-called "salt water thesis," which, in effect, differentiates, among colonized peoples, those who can seek independence from those who cannot (see reference to "territory which is geographically separate" in U.N. Resolution 1541, December 14, 1960, http://www.un.org/ga/search/view_doc.asp?symbol=A/RES/1541(XV) (retrieved October 16, 2013). See also U.N. Resolution 1514, December 14, 1960, http://www.un.org/ga/search/view_doc.asp?symbol=A/RES/1514(XV) (retrieved October 16, 2013) and U.N. Declaration on the Rights of Indigenous Peoples, September 13, 2007, http://www.un.org/esa/socdev/unpfii/documents/DRIPS_en.pdf (retrieved October 16, 2013).

31. For an example, see Lowell (1899a). See Smith (2001) for a discussion of Lowell (1899a). Lowell's (1899b) legal scholarship anticipated the eventual doctrine of territorial incorporation developed in the *Insular Cases*.

32. For an example related to the law, see Perea (2001). For another that also takes anti-Native and anti-Black racisms into account, see Gómez (2005).

33. Hawaii's sugar-based economy depended on tariff-free access to the U.S. market, which had been established a quarter century prior, through the Reciprocity Treaty of 1876. Politically, the white elite, with the backing of the U.S. minister to Hawai'i and U.S. troops, had overthrown the Hawaiian monarchy in 1893 and set up a "republic" that actively invited U.S. annexation.

34. Similar dynamics prevailed for the territories of New Mexico and Oklahoma (Levinson and Sparrow 2005).

35. White supremacy was not, however, a sufficient condition for a short and smooth path to statehood. Utah, with its Mormon population, had a particularly long and rough ride.

36. Section 2 of Article I excludes "Indians not taxed" from enumeration for apportioning seats in the House of Representatives and "direct Taxes," which was later reproduced in the Fourteenth Amendment. In the same article, section 8 empowers Congress to "regulate Commerce with foreign Nations, and among the several States, and with the Indian Tribes."

37. *Johnson v. M'Intosh*, 21 U.S. (8 Wheat.) 543 (1823) at 573. What entitled the Europeans in their minds, according to the ruling, were "Christianity" and "civilization," which they possessed and the indigenous "heathens" and "fierce savages" lacked (ibid. at 573, 577, and 590).

38. Ibid. at 573–75.

39. Ibid. at 587. For recent discussions of the discovery doctrine, see Miller (2008), Newcomb (2008), Robertson (2005), and Williams (2005).

40. 30 U.S. (5 Pet.) 1 (1831) at 15.

41. The questions related to the Diversity Clause of the Constitution: "The judicial Power shall extend . . . to Controversies . . . between a State, or the Citizens thereof, and foreign States, Citizens or Subjects" (Article III, section 2, clause 1).

42. *Cherokee Nation v. Georgia*, 30 U.S. (5 Pet.) 1 (1831) at 16–17; emphasis added.

Even prior to the *Insular Cases* and the advent of unincorporated territories, "pupilage" and other cognate notions had appeared in Supreme Court cases in relation to U.S. overland territories (see Burnett and Marshall 2001a: 33n52).

It should be noted that tutelary metaphors had divergent meanings. For incorporated territories, they signified "growing" into being accepted as one of the several states on an equal footing. For unincorporated territories, they could mean eventual independence but not necessarily. And for the indigenous peoples of North America, they presaged neither equality nor independence.

43. *Worcester v. Georgia*, 31 U.S. (6 Pet.) 551 (1832) at 561.

44. Ibid. at 559.

45. "The whole intercourse between the United States and this nation, is, by our constitution and laws, vested in the government of the United States" (ibid. at 561).

46. 118 U.S. 375 (1886).

47. Robert A. Williams Jr. (2005: 72–75) points out that the congressional plenary power doctrine in relation to Indians was prefigured and outlined in *United States v. Rogers*, 45 U.S. (4 How.) 567 (1846).

48. Perhaps the most devastating was the General Allotment Act of 1887, which privatized reservation lands and distributed parcels to individual Indians. After such allotment, the remaining lands, often the choicest, were sold by the government to whites, the proceeds from which went toward programs for assimilating Indians. In this way, nearly two-thirds of Indian-held lands were taken between 1887 and 1934 (Frantz 1999; Newton 1984; O'Brien 1989).

49. 187 U.S. 553 (1903) at 565–67. Effectively self-abdicating, the court also declared, in relation to Indians, that congressional plenary "power has always been deemed a political one, not subject to be controlled by the judicial department of the government" (ibid. at 565).

50. The oft quoted passage from *Dred Scott v. Sandford* that Quey paraphrased is, "They [Blacks] had for more than a century before been regarded as beings of an inferior order, and altogether unfit to associate with the white race either in social or political relations, and so far inferior that they had no rights which the white man was bound to respect, and that the negro might justly and lawfully be reduced to slavery for his benefit" (60 U.S. [19 How.] 393 [1857] at 407).

51. They are not symmetrically related, however. The former implies the latter, but the reverse is not necessarily true.

52. Of the mentioned, the colonial status of Mexicans would be the most questionable, as a great majority of Mexican-origin people in the United States today are migrants or descendants of migrants, not descendants of those who had once lived under Mexican sovereignty in what is now the U.S. Southwest.

53. The boundary within the pairs is increasingly recognized, rightly, as having been variably motile, but colonialism is nonetheless "fundamentally dualistic" (Steinmetz 2008a: 593).

54. The sudden and fatal decline of *internal colonialism* as a theoretical framework in the social sciences has been lamentable. It did not get everything right; in fact, it probably got more things wrong than right. But it had enormous value in calling attention to

and critiquing U.S. racism and linking it to questions of colonialism. Although numerous factors led to the theories' precipitous decline, one of the major shortcomings was that many exponents, and nearly all of the critics, agreed that the theories, as applied to racism in the United States, took the notion of *colonialism* only metaphorically: the United States might have exhibited certain similarities to European colonialism in Africa and Asia but had not really engaged in colonialism proper. Thus the United States was, once again, seen as exceptional.

55. The bitter irony is that the Haitian defeat of the French enabled the purchase of Louisiana by the United States (Baptist 2008).

56. Mark Twain's ([1871] 1913) *Roughing It* would be a popular example from between the two turns of the century; for a discussion, particularly of Twain's treatment of Indians, see Blackhawk (2006).

57. With regard to Native Americans, Vine Deloria Jr. and David Wilkins (1999: 55) write, "Incisive and tedious review of Supreme Court decisions would show that this tendency to write law without reference to any doctrines or precedents is more the rule than the exception."

58. *Dred Scott v. Sandford*, 60 U.S. (19 How.) 393 (1857) at 418, 420.

59. Even in the absence of quotation marks around them, it should be obvious that these categories are shorthand anachronisms.

60. Ibid. at 403–04.

61. 45 U.S. (4 How.) 567 (1846) at 571–72. For an in-depth discussion, see Wilkins (1997: 38–51).

62. *Dred Scott v. Sandford*, 60 U.S. (19 How.) 393 (1857) at 419.

63. Ibid. at 578. As Smith (1997) suggests, Curtis's concession was rash and ultimately undermined his own argument.

64. *Dred Scott v. Sandford*, 60 U.S. (19 How.) 393 (1857) at 586. Curtis cited three treaties: "Treaties with the Choctaws, of September 27, 1830, art. 14; with the Cherokees, of May 23, 1836, art. 12; Treaty of Guadalupe Hidalgo, February 2, 1848, art. 8."

65. Ibid. at 533.

66. Ibid. at 419.

67. Ibid. at 418–19; emphases added. There is no acknowledgment here that he had noted earlier in the opinion that "the white race claimed the ultimate right of *dominion*" (ibid. at 403–04; emphasis added).

68. Ibid. at 417; emphasis added. *Dred Scott* does not appear to directly address foreign-born Blacks who migrated to the United States not as slaves. Smith (1997: 266) sees a contradiction, which may be. There is also the possibility that Taney was strictly insisting on, or fudging, the "class of persons" dealt with in the ruling, defined toward the beginning as "the descendants of Africans who were imported into this country and sold *as slaves*" (ibid. at 403; emphasis added).

69. *Dred Scott v. Sandford*, 60 U.S. (19 How.) 393 (1857) at 413–14, 416.

70. Also having been taken to Illinois, a "free" state, Dred Scott could have avoided the territorial issue altogether. However, a decision dealing only with the effect of residence in a "free" state would have been inapplicable to his wife, Harriet Scott, whom Dred Scott had met and wed at Fort Snelling.

71. Although two earlier rulings, including *Marbury v. Madison* (5 U.S. [1 Cranch] 137 [1803]), established the doctrine of judicial review, "*Dred Scott* was the only case in the eighty years of pre-Civil-War constitutional history in which the Supreme Court limited congressional power in any significant way" (Newman and Gass 2004: 8).

72. *Dred Scott v. Sandford*, 60 U.S. (19 How.) 393 (1857) at 432. With the last phrase "from a foreign Government," Taney rhetorically skirted around the thorny fact that two states, North Carolina and Georgia, had not yet ceded their trans-Appalachian lands when the Constitution was adopted. But since the cessions had been anticipated at the time, he could not have plausibly argued that the framers had not intended the Territorial Clause to be operative there.

73. Ibid. at 446, 449.

74. Ibid. at 451.

75. Of course, Levinson means "anti-imperialist" in a very restricted sense. Nobody on the court gainsaid the U.S. state's right to acquire the former Spanish colonies in the first place.

76. *Downes v. Bidwell*, 182 U.S. 244 (1901) at 384–85.

77. Ibid. at 360.

78. Ibid. at 251.

79. Ibid. at 279.

80. Ibid. at 274.

81. For an early statement on the issue, see *American Insurance Company v. Canter*, for which Chief Justice John Marshall wrote the opinion of the court: "Inhabitants of Florida. . . . do not, however, participate in political power; they do not share in the government, till Florida shall become a state. In the meantime, Florida continues to be a territory of the United States; governed by virtue of that clause in the Constitution, which empowers Congress 'to make all needful rules and regulations, respecting the territory, or other property belonging to the United States'" (6 U.S. 511 [1828] at 542). The influential ruling would feature significantly in *Dred Scott* and the *Insular Cases*, as well as *United States v. Kagama* and, most recently, *Boumediene v. Bush*.

For post-*Dred Scott* examples that appear in *Downes*, see *National Bank v. County of Yankton*, 101 U.S. 129 (1879), and *Shively v. Bowlby*, 152 U.S. 1 (1894), the latter of which also cites and is cited in Supreme Court cases dealing with American Indians.

82. *Downes v. Bidwell*, 182 U.S. 244 (1901) at 291–93. See Burnett and Marshall (2001a: 9–11) and Sparrow (2006: 91–93) for discussions of White's opinion.

83. *Downes v. Bidwell*, 182 U.S. 244 (1901) at 341–42.

Downes, like many of the *Insular Cases*, had to do with Article I, section 8, clause 1 of the Constitution: "The Congress shall have Power To lay and collect Taxes, Duties, Imposts and Excises, to pay the Debts and provide for the common Defence and general Welfare of the United States; but all Duties, Imposts and Excises shall be uniform throughout the United States." As the then recently former President Benjamin Harrison asked rhetorically, "It will be noticed that the descriptive term, 'The United States,' is twice used in the one sentence. . . . Is there any canon of construction that authorizes us to give to the words, 'The United States,' one meaning in the first use of them and another in the second" (1901: 14–15)?

84. As Burnett and Marshall (2001a: 11) note, the Constitution has never applied in full in any territory.

85. *Dorr v. United States*, 195 U.S. 138 (1904) at 142.

86. *Downes v. Bidwell*, 182 U.S. 244 (1901) at 279.

87. Ibid. at 287.

88. Ibid. at 280–81, 283. The cited cases involving the Chinese were *Yick Wo v. Hopkins*, 118 U.S. 356 (1886); *Fong Yue Ting v. United States*, 149 U.S. 698 (1893); *Lem Moon Sing v. United States*, 158 U.S. 538 (1895); and *Wong Wing v. United States*, 163 U.S. 228 (1896).

89. *Downes v. Bidwell*, 182 U.S. 244 (1901) at 306. In addition to *Johnson v. M'Intosh*, White's opinion appealed to *United States v. Kagama* (1886). In turn, the latter case (118 U.S.

375 [1886] at 379–380), which was key in establishing congressional plenary power in relation
to American Indians, had drawn on territorial precedents, *American Insurance Company v.
Canter*, 6 U.S. 511 (1828), and *Murphy v. Ramsey*, 114 U.S. 15 (1885).

On the whole, however, cases involving "territories" have had a largely separate legal
genealogy from those involving Indian sovereignty (Thomas 2001). But there have been
exceptions. In *Downes*, precedents dealing with American Indians lent support to White's
imperialist vision for the territories newly acquired from Spain. In contrast, *Cariño v. The
Insular Government of the Philippine Islands* (1909) spelled out the difference between overland colonization in North America and overseas colonization in the Philippines. Ruling in
favor of an Igorot plaintiff against the U.S. colonial state, the court contrasted U.S. colonial
rule over "inhabitants of the Philippines," including "savage tribe[s]," with U.S. colonial
rule over Native Americans: "The acquisition of the Philippines was not like the settlement
of the white race in the United States. Whatever consideration may have been shown to the
North American Indians, the dominant purpose of the whites in America was to occupy
the land. It is obvious that, however stated, the reason for our taking over the Philippines
was different. No one, we suppose, would deny that, so far as consistent with paramount
necessities, our first object in the internal administration of the islands is to do justice to
the natives, not to exploit their country for private gain" (212 U.S. 449 [1909] at 458). For
other examples, see *Shively v. Bowlby*, 152 U.S. 1 (1894), and *Tee-Hit-Ton Indians v. United
States*, 348 U.S. 272 (1955).

Beyond the courts, however, state actors and others at the turn of the twentieth century
readily compared and analogized the colonization of American Indians to that of Filipinos
(W. L. Williams 1980).

90. *Downes v. Bidwell*, 182 U.S. 244 (1901) at 279.

91. Ibid. at 286.

92. Also known as the *Chinese Exclusion Case*, 130 U.S. 581 (1889).

93. Congressional plenary power, however, has not meant absolutely unrestrained power
over aliens, particularly beyond the domain of "immigration" (Bosniak 2006).

94. "But, as with treaties made with foreign nations, *Chinese Exclusion Case*, 130 U.S.
581, 600, the legislative power might pass laws in conflict with treaties made with the Indians." (187 U.S. 553 [1903] at 566).

95. 169 U.S. 649 (1898) at 693. Exemplifying once again the interconnectedness of
noncolonial and colonial racial rule, this case dealing with the Chinese also addressed the
U.S. citizenship status of American Indians. The majority opinion invoked *Elk v. Wilkins*
(1884), the "only adjudication that ha[d] been made by this court upon the meaning of the
clause, 'and subject to the jurisdiction thereof,' in the leading provision of the Fourteenth
Amendment," to deny its applicability to "children born in the United States of foreign parents of Caucasian, African or Mongolian descent not in the diplomatic service of a foreign
country": the earlier decision had "concerned only members of the Indian tribes within the
United States" (ibid. at 680, 682). As quoted in *Wong Kim Ark*, the ruling in *Elk v. Wilkins*
had held that "Indians born within the territorial limits of the United States, members of,
and owing immediate allegiance to, one of the Indiana [sic] tribes, (an alien though dependent power,) although in a geographical sense born in the United States, are no more 'born
in the United States and subject to the jurisdiction thereof,' within the meaning of the first
section of the fourteenth amendment, than the children of subjects of any foreign government born within the domain of that government, or the children born within the United
States, of ambassadors or other public ministers of foreign nations" (112 U.S. 94 [1884] at
102). Further, both of these cases cited *Dred Scott*.

96. Residents of the Philippines were denied U.S. citizenship all the way through to independence in 1946.

97. For example, to this day, residents of Puerto Rico cannot elect representatives or senators to Congress or cast a vote for the presidency. They receive fewer and lower social welfare benefits. Puerto Rico's self-governance does not undermine but is enabled, and can be overridden, by congressional plenary power. Constitutional rights, including those enumerated in the Bill of Rights, do not apply in Puerto Rico of their own force but were extended there by Congress (Aleinikoff 2002). Legislatively granted by Congress, birthright citizenship itself of those born in Puerto Rico is "not equal, permanent, irrevocable citizenship protected by the Fourteenth Amendment" (H.R. Report No. 105–131, pt. 1, 1997, p. 19, as quoted in Román 1998: 3).

98. On the various ways Indians had become citizens before 1924, see Porter (1999: 123–24). Before the law, around 175,000 Indians had been U.S. citizens. The law encompassed the remaining 125,000 (Bruyneel 2004). Citizenship, however, hardly guaranteed enfranchisement (McGool, Olson, and Robinson 2007; McDonald 2004; McDonald, Pease, and Guest 2007; Svingen 1987; Wolfley 1991).

99. Stephen J. Field on *Plessy* was replaced by Joseph McKenna before the two later cases. Though on the court at the time, David J. Brewer did not participate in *Plessy*, nor did McKenna in *Wong Kim Ark*.

100. *Plessy v. Ferguson*, 163 U.S. 537 (1896) at 559–60. In a prelude of sorts, Harlan was also the sole dissenter in the *Civil Rights Cases* and similarly referenced *Dred Scott* in his opinion (109 U.S. 3 [1883] at 26–62).

101. *Plessy v. Ferguson*, 163 U.S. 537 (1896) at 559.

102. Ibid. at 561. The well-known majority opinion in *Plessy* also referred to the Chinese. In the second of the two instances, the present case was set against *Yick Wo v. Hopkins*, 118 U.S. 356 (1886). Ostensibly unlike *Plessy* in relation to Blacks, the earlier ruling had concerned "a covert attempt on the part of the municipality to make an arbitrary and unjust discrimination against the Chinese" (ibid. at 550).

103. How Harlan determined that "by the statute in question, a Chinaman can ride in the same passenger coach with white citizens of the United States" is unclear. The majority opinion's two references to the Chinese did not concern their treatment under the Louisiana statute. Among the briefs filed in the case, I found only one buried reference to the Chinese, which hardly necessitated and was unlikely to have triggered Harlan's disquisition. On behalf of the plaintiff Homer Adolph Plessy, his lawyer James C. Walker wrote:

The court [Supreme Court of Louisiana] is confident that the statute obviously provides that the passenger shall be assigned to the coach to which by race he belongs; but the trouble is the court takes for granted what is only assumed, and not granted or proved, that is to say the race to which the passenger belongs; when neither jurists, lexicographers, nor scientists, nor statute laws nor adjudged precedents of the state of Louisiana, enable us to say what race the passenger belongs to, if he be an "octoroon." We know that he is not of pure Caucasian type, neither can he be said to be of any of the colored races. Which race is the colored race referred to in the statute? There are Africans, Malays, Chinese, Polynesians; there are griffs and mulattoes. But which of all these is the colored race the statute speaks of? The legislature might have relieved us from this perplexity, but it has not done so. ("Brief for Plaintiff in Error," as reprinted in Kurland and Casper 1975: 78)

104. *Plessy v. Ferguson*, 163 U.S. 537 (1896) at 553.

105. Concurring with Fuller's dissent in *Wong Kim Ark*, Harlan did not draft his own. But he had addressed the issue at hand in his *Plessy* dissent: for him, the Reconstruction

amendments "established universal civil freedom, gave citizenship to all born or naturalized in the United States and residing there, obliterated the race line from our systems of
governments, National and State, and placed our free institutions upon the broad and sure
foundation of the equality of all men before the law" (*Plessy v. Ferguson*, 163 U.S. 537 [1896]
at 563). From the unqualified character of this statement, we can infer less a contradiction
to his opinion of the Chinese in *Plessy* and vote in *Wong Kim Ark* than the placement of
the Chinese beyond the pale of "universal civil freedom," "citizenship," and the "equality
of all men before the law."

Harlan had also been one of two dissenters in *Elk v. Wilkins*, the 1884 case that denied
U.S. citizenship to American Indians born on reservations even after leaving and severing
relations with their Native nations. One reason he put forth was that if the Fourteenth
Amendment had "confer[red] citizenship, national and State, upon the entire population in
this country of African descent (the larger part of which was shortly before held in slavery),"
it surely would not have "exclude[d] from such citizenship Indians who had never been in
slavery, and who, by becoming bona fide residents of States and Territories within the complete jurisdiction of the United States, had evinced a purpose to abandon their former mode
of life and become a part of the People of the United States" (112 U.S. 94 [1884] at 120–21).

106. This point is related to a more general caution: nationalisms, even hegemonic
ones, do not necessarily support or otherwise relate to nation-states. They can instead be
articulated to empire-states.

107. Although not discussed here, an empire-state approach to the United States would
facilitate studies of trans-state and interstate structures and processes. As the ripple effects of
Dred Scott suggest, the boundaries between what is domestic, colonial, imperial, and foreign
are blurry and contingent.

108. Sociologists of knowledge would find, I suspect, disquietingly correlated divides
of backgrounds, networks, and political and epistemological sensibilities between the two
subfields' practitioners.

CHAPTER 4

An earlier version of this chapter appeared as "The Racial Unconscious of Assimilation
Theory," *Du Bois Review* 6: 2 (2009): 375–95.

1. According to a keyword search in the Social Science Citation Index, research on
"assimilation" grew or held steady for most of the twentieth century and then skyrocketed
beginning in the early 1990s. The annual number of journal articles averaged 4.6, 11.9, 15.4,
and 15.0 in the 1950s, 1960s, 1970s, and 1980s, respectively, before rising steeply to 98.8, 234.2,
and 356.5 in the ensuing decades (calculated from data accessed at http://apps.webofknowl-
edge.com on May 29, 2013).

2. For an example of the debate between the two strands, see Haller, Portes, and Lynch
(2011a, 2011b) and Alba, Kasinitz, and Waters (2011), as well as Telles and Ortiz (2011) and
Waters et al. (2010).

3. Alba and Nee (2003: 60–61) identify three ideal-typical ways in which ethnic boundaries may decline: "boundary crossing," "boundary blurring," and "boundary shifting."

4. This is definition 7a for *assimilate* in the *Oxford English Dictionary*. The first definition listed in *Webster's New Collegiate Dictionary* is both transitive and organic: "to take in
and appropriate as nourishment: absorb into the system."

5. Some scholars attempt to shake free of the "assimilationist" senses of *assimilation*
by using the term *incorporation* instead, but it may be similarly weighted by organic and
transitive meanings: the word *incorporate* is etymologically derived from *corpus*, Latin for

body, and its primary definition is "to unite or work into something already existent so as to form an indistinguishable whole" (*Webster's New Collegiate Dictionary*). Thanks to Omar McRoberts for raising this point.

6. It is telling that *pluralism*—theorizing the persistence of ethnic difference—has been the primary "other" against which assimilation theories have argued and defined itself (e.g., Alba and Nee 2003; Brubaker 2004; Gans 1997; Zhou 1997).

7. For two well-known examples, see Bonilla-Silva (1997) and Omi and Winant (1994), but this point is axiomatic and uncontroversial.

8. Some scholars, such as Joel Perlmann and Roger Waldinger (1997), refute these arguments through a careful historical examination of the earlier migration (see also Waldinger 2007b). At the same time, they themselves engage in the same analytically suspect comparison.

9. According to Portes and Zhou (1993: 77–78), 85 percent of migrants' children in 1940 were of European ancestry, and 77 percent of migrants since 1960 have been of non-European ancestry.

10. Here, note the transformations wrought by World War I, the Great Depression, World War II, the postwar economic boom, the Civil Rights Movement, and deindustrialization, among others.

11. Another critical omission from their discussion of prewar migrants is Mexicans.

12. For a less optimistic interpretation of third- and fourth-generation Chinese and Japanese than is found in Alba and Nee (2003), see Tuan (1999).

13. Perlmann and Waldinger (1997) make a similar argument.

14. For a counterargument from within the historical scholarship on whiteness, see Guglielmo (2003).

15. This idea is not totally absent from Alba and Nee (2003: 119–20, 131–32), but its dissonance with their notion of assimilation is not acknowledged. See also Waldinger (2003: 266–68).

16. For a sense of this shift, compare Nathan Glazer's articles from 1971 and 1993. In the former, he advocates seeing Blacks as an ethnic group like any other—different in degree, not in kind. In the latter, he views Blacks as the great exception to the American story of assimilation.

17. Note that the subtitle of Alba and Nee's (2003) book is *Assimilation and Contemporary Immigration*.

18. Although recent Black *migrants* from the Caribbean and their children, like their other non-European counterparts, are studied, they form the bulk of those whom the authors fear are at the greatest risk of not becoming a part of the mainstream. For a counterexample to the exclusion of native-born Blacks, see Kasinitz et al. (2008).

19. Alba and Nee (2003: 58) write, "Immigrant minorities other than African Americans have derived considerably more benefit from institutional change, in part because their relationship to the mainstream is much less burdened by the legacies of the historic norms and etiquette governing race relations." Rather than actually elucidating why migrants of color have benefited more than native-born Blacks, this statement deflects the question, reformulating it into one of explaining the "legacies of the historic norms and etiquette," which they likewise do not take up.

20. Even among liberals and the left, Wilson was hardly alone. Nearly everyone writing on urban poverty in the 1980s and 1990s evidently felt compelled to comment unfavorably on the "culture" of the Black urban poor, although the empirical basis of such commentary was usually thin and speculative.

21. One difference is that segmented assimilation theorists recognize contemporary racial discrimination more prominently as a significant factor, whereas some "underclass" theorists downplay it.

22. The alignment is not perfect. Whereas Ogbu, in his later work, applies his argument to African Americans across class lines, segmented assimilation theory is concerned with the cultural influence of the "underclass."

23. Ogbu also refers to "involuntary" minorities as "subordinate" (1974) and "castelike" (1978, 1991a).

24. Ogbu (2003) continued with this line of research into the early 2000s. For a review of works on education that contend with his theory, see Downey (2008).

25. For a more detailed analysis, see Portes and Stepick (1993).

26. Inversely, contrary empirical findings appear to mute such assertions. With one mention of "underclass-like" in the whole article, Portes, Fernández-Kelly, and Haller report, "Less expected is the effect of school ethnic composition. This coefficient is now highly significant, but its direction is the opposite of that expected: junior-high schools with 60 per cent or more of minority students (coded higher) *reduce* downward assimilation, controlling for other variables" (2009: 1093; emphasis in original).

27. Alejandro Portes, "Homosexuality among Mariel Men," *Miami Herald,* September 8, 1991, p. 4C. For a detailed analysis of Portes's piece and the news article that he was responding to, see Peña (2005).

28. They continue, "These findings indicate that strong positive immigrant *cultural* orientations can serve as a form of *social* capital that promotes value conformity and constructive forms of behavior, which provide otherwise disadvantaged children with an adaptive advantage" (Zhou and Bankston 1994: 821; emphases added). More recently, Lee and Zhou (2014) turn to the concept of "cultural frames" to explain the academic achievements of children of Asian immigrants. On the false opposition of the cultural and the social, see chapter 2 and Sewell (1992).

29. As Waldinger (2003: 255) writes of Alba and Nee's research on assimilation, "I doubt that it would have been pursued with such intensity were it not for the normative and political issues at stake." See also Brubaker (2004).

30. In many other subfields of sociology concerned with inequality and domination, characterizing "oppositional culture" as wholly undesirable and counterproductive would be received with much more skepticism and even bafflement.

31. The productive and transformative potential of "oppositional culture" could also be seen in the participation of migrants and their children in the labor movement of the New Deal era (Waldinger 2003: 267–68). The revitalization of unions and other political organizations with traditionally African American bases by recent migrants of color and their children point in a similar direction (Kasinitz, Mollenkopf, and Waters 2002).

32. For example, in the 2004 presidential election, the last one before Barack Obama's first bid, a CNN exit poll revealed that only 11 percent of Blacks voted for George W. Bush, whereas 58 percent of whites did. (Asians and Latinas/os fell in between, both at 44 percent.) Similarly, only 36 percent of those earning less than $15,000 per year voted for Bush (http://www.cnn.com/ELECTION/2004/pages/results/states/US/P/00/epolls.0.html, accessed January 15, 2009).

33. In the first article of a five-part series on "social assimilation" in the *American Journal of Sociology,* Sarah E. Simons (1901: 790) cites Ludwig Gumplowicz's (1883) *Der Rassenkampf* as the primary inspiration for the turn-of-the-century surge of historical and social-scientific interest in assimilation.

34. In academia, the reprint in Park's (1950) *Race and Culture* is probably better known than the original publication.

35. Comprising the entire history of humanity, the temporal scope of Park's analysis was no less sweeping.

36. At the turn of the last century, whether the Constitution followed the flag was a common shorthand for the debate over U.S. imperialism.

37. Hyndman (2000) and Litzinger (2000) may have been the first to invoke the former term. The *politics of belonging* appears earlier and more frequently.

38. As Peter Spiro (2003: 1509) notes, "Questions at the constitutional margins, then, put the entire project into doubt."

39. See Bourdieu (1994: 1) on the state's capacity to inculcate and naturalize "categories of thought."

40. The distinction I draw between the *citizen* and the *national* is the one between membership to a state and membership to a nation. In the U.S. context, the terminology is confusing, for "national" has been one official, euphemistic category for certain colonized populations, such as Filipinas/os prior to independence and American Samoans today.

41. For several examples, see Das Gupta (2006, 2014), Fox (2013), Kretsedemas (2012), and Scott (2007).

CHAPTER 5

1. An early use of the term "Hanapepe Massacre" appears in Manlapit (1933: 67).

2. HSPA was the powerful decision-making body of the industry. Four of the seventy-six pled guilty and did not face trial ("Four Filipinos Plead Guilty in Kauai Riot," *Honolulu Star-Bulletin*, October 10, 1924, p. 1; "Four Plead Guilty, 72 Not Guilty in Recent Kauai Riot," *Honolulu Advertiser*, October 11, 1924, p. 11).

3. According to Lipold and Isaac (2009: 198), which, like other surveys, did not include the present case, there were 292 strike deaths during the two decades.

4. My intention is not to minimize the killing of the four police officers. Never deemed legitimate, their deaths lie outside the analytical ambit of this chapter.

5. The counterintuitiveness can be seen in the all too frequent misemployment of the concept, as something like physical violence that can be inflicted by an agent upon another.

6. For Weber's definition, see chapter 3.

7. But not fully redundant. Bourdieu (1994) finds doxic submission, or symbolic violence, as the source of legitimacy. Hence, in relation to physical violence, the presence of both "legitimate" and "symbolic violence" in his definition of the state appears redundant. In relation to symbolic violence, however, the definition's reference to its *legitimate* use seems to indicate not a redundancy but a symbolic violence of a second order: symbolically violent use of symbolic violence. But, exactly what that would be—or, negatively, exactly what an illegitimate use of symbolic violence would be—remains unclear.

8. See Lewis (2003) for a Bourdieuian analysis of education and the reproduction of racial domination.

9. Though not discussed or critiqued here, Jackman (2001) offers an approach to theorizing legitimacy and violence that differs from, but also overlaps with, both Bourdieu and Gramsci—greatly expanding the definitional scope of violence, somewhat like Bourdieu, and highlighting the ways in which the dominant's ideological construction of violence conceals their own preferred forms of violence, somewhat like Gramsci. For a normative analysis of legitimacy and violence, see Young (2002).

10. "Symbolic violence is the coercion which is set up only through the consent that the dominated cannot fail to give to the dominator (and therefore to the domination) when their understanding of the situation and relation can only use instruments of knowledge that they have in common with the dominator, which, being merely the incorporated form

of the structure of the relation of domination, make this relation appear as natural" (Bourdieu 2000: 170).

In one sense, *symbolic force* might better capture what Bourdieu means by symbolic violence, if force were understood less in terms of violence or violation and more in terms of force fields, akin to gravitational, electric, and magnetic fields in physics; Bourdieu often discusses his concept of *field* in this way. Though terminologically more apt, the conceptual issues discussed here would remain.

11. "The state does not necessarily have to give orders or to exercise physical coercion in order to produce an ordered social world, as long as it is capable of producing embodied cognitive structures that accord with objective structures and thus of ensuring the belief of which Hume spoke—namely, doxic submission to the established order" (Bourdieu 1994: 15).

12. "All the agents in a given social formation share a set of basic perceptual schemes" (Bourdieu 1984: 468).

13. As a thought experiment, imagine how bizarrely newspapers and magazines in the United States would read, especially to whites, if "white" were used as compulsorily as "black" or "African American" as an identifier.

14. But the datedness of *all* past writings—for example, their tacit assumption at the turn of the twentieth century that *race* was real in a biological sense—attests to Bourdieu's notion of doxa.

15. Using Du Bois's concept of double consciousness, Rawls's (2000) study of interactions shows how Blacks and whites often talk past each other in contentious discourse. She also finds that, particularly for whites, this unintelligibility is coupled with an unawareness of it.

16. Butler helpfully discerns "tacit distinctions among forms of illegitimacy." In addition to the legible, potentially legitimate illegitimacy that is subject to conscious consideration, judgment, and thereby possible conversion, she identifies, and is specifically interested in, the illegible *"the never will be, the never was"* illegitimacy that lies beyond the recognized terms of struggle between the consciously legitimate and the consciously illegitimate (Butler 2002: 18; emphasis in original). This chapter is concerned with a third form of illegitimacy that does not fit easily into either category: an illegible illegitimacy whose future legibility and convertibility are not foreclosed in advance.

17. "Crisis is a necessary condition for a questioning of doxa but is not in itself a sufficient condition for the production of a critical discourse" (Bourdieu 1977: 169). In this regard, Calhoun rightly points out that Bourdieu's theory of practice, relying on exogenous crises as precipitators of change, does not allow for endogenous social transformations (1995; see also Sewell 1992; Wacquant 1987).

18. By "conservative," I do not mean any narrowly political sense of the term.

19. Though convincing that the state holds *privileged* powers of effecting symbolic violence, Bourdieu (1989, 1994, 1996) is less persuasive in claiming the state's *monopoly* of its use—especially beyond the French case. Rather, the degree of state control would appear to be empirically variable.

20. On Cook's demise, see Obeyesekere (1992) and Sahlins (1985, 1995).

21. Merry (2000) also notes the lack of interest in violence in the study of Hawai'i. See Liu (1985) and Okihiro (1991) for critiques of the long dominant assimilationist framework.

22. In fact, the very prevalence of symbolic coercion may have had the enduring epistemological effect of reproducing Hawaii's pacific image.

23. The following discussion of the background to the massacre draws from Jung (2006).

24. Within the U.S. colonial scheme, *incorporated territories*, such as Hawai'i, were accorded the same tariff protection as states on the continent, protection that was denied *unincorporated territories*, such as the Philippines (Littler 1929: 40–41). See also chapter 3.

25. The total area under sugar cultivation expanded from 26,019 acres in 1880 to 254,563 acres in 1934 (Schmitt 1977: 357–60). The number of employees grew from 3,786 in 1874 to a peak of 57,039 in 1933 (*Hawaiian Annual* 1934: 20; Schmitt 1977: 359). Sugar production soared from 12,540 tons in 1875 to top 1 million tons three times in the 1930s (*Hawaiian Annual* 1940: 33; Taylor 1935: 166).

26. The "Big Five" were Alexander and Baldwin, American Factors (formerly H. Hackfeld and Company), C. Brewer and Company, Castle and Cooke, and T. H. Davies and Company. By 1930, the plantations controlled by these corporations produced 95.2 percent of Hawaii's sugar (*Hawaiian Annual* 1931: 132–35).

27. The total value of sugar exports was $74,896,568, and the total value of all exports, including sugar, was $108,632,223. The total value of pineapple exports was $28,292,485 (*Hawaiian Annual* 1925: 19, 21).

28. Both before and after U.S. annexation, migrants from Asia were excluded from naturalized citizenship and the franchise on racial grounds. The terms *issei* and *nisei* refer to the migrant generation from Japan and their U.S.-born children, respectively.

29. Immediate family members and returning migrants continued to arrive from Japan until the Immigration Act of 1924.

30. The numbers and percentage for 1924 were based on men only, as the 3,250 women counted were not broken down racially. The vast majority of women workers were likely Japanese.

31. John Waterhouse, presidential address, *Proceedings of the Fortieth Annual Meeting of the Hawaiian Sugar Planters' Association*, November 29–30, 1920, p. 8, Hawaiian Collection, University of Hawai'i at Mānoa.

32. After the 1920 strike, which the haole elite and mainstream press, all but ignoring the Filipinos, interpreted as an anti-American movement of the Japanese to take over Hawai'i, Japanese workers left the labor movement for over two decades. The primary factor for the interwar exodus was a redoubled, racist Americanization movement that relentlessly targeted the Japanese (Jung 2006; Okihiro 1991; Weinberg 1967).

33. Much that is known about the 1924 strike from the strikers' point of view is through Pablo Manlapit's *Filipinos Fight for Justice*. Prepared in 1924 but not published until 1933, it contains reprints of original documents as well as his personal recollections.

34. "Petition to Hawaiian Sugar Planters' Association" from signatories to president and board of directors of HSPA, [sent on April 10, 1923], as reprinted in Manlapit (1933: 35–36); see also Pablo Manlapit and George W. Wright to the public, "Manifesto of the High Wages Movement," January 2, 1924, pp. 1–2, Manuel Quezon Papers, Special Collections, University of Hawai'i at Mānoa.

35. "Manifesto of the High Wages Movement," p. 2.

36. Ibid., pp. 3–5.

37. Executive Committee of the HWM, "Strike Proclamation," March 14, 1924, as reprinted in Manlapit (1933: 62–64).

38. J. K. Butler to HSPA trustees and all plantation managers, May 11, 1928, PSC33/15, HSPA Plantation Papers, Special Collections, University of Hawai'i at Mānoa. In contrast, fewer than one-third of the Japanese remained sugar plantation residents.

39. A. W. T. Bottomley to John Watt, September 26, 1910, PSC25/13, HSPA Plantation Papers, Special Collections, University of Hawai'i at Mānoa.

40. "Sixteen of the judges were plantation managers while among the remainder of the group were head workers of social settlements, plantation doctors, and several educationists" (Porteus and Babcock 1926: 90). The judges' "race" went unremarked, which, in addition to their occupations, suggests that they were all haole.

41. Interviews of Cabico, de la Cruz, and Gueco; Anderson (1984: 12–14); Ariyoshi (2000: 14–15); Masuoka (1931); Reinecke (1979: 36); Sharma (1984: 601). The oral history interviews cited in this chapter are listed after the endnotes.

At least in part, the unshakable association with knives likely derived from Filipinos' occupational position on the plantations. Holding the most physically taxing and lowest paid jobs, they were predominantly the ones in the field actually cutting and handling cane.

42. Kramer (2006: 127–28); Roediger (1994: 117–18); de la Cruz interview, p. 141; Gueco interview, pp. 172–73. Note the casual, everyday, and widely assumed anti-Filipino racism of the 1920s in a personal recollection by Reinecke (1996: 144n10): "About Christmas 1927 the present author (JER) was joyriding with the young daughter of a prominent Kona rancher. Reaching out of the car window, she knocked off the hat of a Filipino pedestrian, then a bit shamefacedly explained her rudeness by saying, 'I don't like googoos.'" In the absence of a presumably disapproving passenger, her face would probably have been shameless, and her action free of explanation.

43. See also Kojiri interview, p. 585; Ogawa interview, p. 223. Oral history interviews of survivors and others linked to the Hanapēpē Massacre, conducted and collected by the Ethnic Studies Oral History Project (ESOHP) at the University of Hawai'i, form an invaluable resource. "Established by legislative appropriation in January, 1976," the ESOHP, now known as the Center for Oral History, is charged with "record[ing] and preserv[ing]" memories of Hawaii's residents, especially those of workers (Taniguchi et al. 1979: ix). *The 1924 Filipino Strike on Kauai* (ESOHP 1979) represents one of a number of such efforts carried out by the ESOHP. Audio recordings of interviews are available at the University of Hawai'i Library's Special Collections, and transcripts are available at a number of libraries in Hawai'i and around the continental United States.

44. *Hawaii Shinpo*, March 8, 1924, as quoted in Reinecke (1996: 36). *Hawaii Hōchi* also carried editorials in support of the strike (Reinecke 1996: 168). Filipino strikers on Kaua'i likewise remembered that some Japanese, and Chinese, businesses supplied food and money during the strike. See interviews of Agbayani, Anonymous A and Oroc, Cabinatan, Ganade, Lutao, P. Ponce, and Venyan and Juabot.

45. Kojiri interview, p. 585. The quotation is attributed to "SK," Kojiri's wife.

46. Behind the strikers' specific demands was a broader opposition to the lowly treatment of Filipinos, who were "treated like animals," according to a striker (Lagmay interview, p. 173). Recognition of their subordinated social position and resistance against it would be a persistent theme for Filipinos, in discourse and practice, throughout the prewar period and beyond (Jung 2006).

47. Executive Committee of the High Wage Movement, March 14, 1924, as reprinted in Manlapit (1933: 62–64).

48. Ibid.

49. Anonymous B interview, p. 848. See also Kerkvliet (2002: 48–49).

50. Anonymous A and Oroc interview, p. 779.

51. The strike up to that point had not been completely free of violence, but it had been probably less violent than other major strikes in Hawaii's history.

52. P. Ponce interview, p. 286.

53. Kojiri interview, p. 585; the second quotation is attributed to "SK," Kojiri's wife.

54. Beechert (1985: 220); Theo. H. Davies to John T. Moir, June 26, 1924, H. A. Walker to John T. Moir, June 27, 1924, and J. K. Butler to plantation managers on Hawaii, August 5, 1924, MKC1/8, HSPA Plantation Papers, Special Collections, University of Hawai'i at Mānoa.

55. Bulletin to plantation managers of Kauai, Maui, and Hawaii, April 17, 1924, as quoted in Beechert (1985: 220).

56. J. K. Butler to plantation managers on Hawaii and Maui, June 6, 1924, MKC1/8, HSPA Plantation Papers, Special Collections, University of Hawai'i at Mānoa. See also Kerkvliet (2002: 49).

57. Ibid.

58. J. K. Butler, as quoted in *Honolulu Times*, August 8, 1924, in Reinecke (1996: 3).

59. A vast majority of Filipino workers were recruited from the Visayas and Ilocos regions of the Philippines. Whether regional/ethnic difference played a role in the detention is not clear.

Oral history accounts of the strikers in Hanapēpē vary with regard to the two Ilocanos. They were plantation spies or passers-by; treated well or beaten; and convinced to stay and strike or frightened into silence. For examples, see interviews of Anonymous B, Ganade, Lagmay, and Venyan and Juabot.

60. Charles E. Hogue, "Officer Who Took Part in Rioting Gives Vivid Tale of Horror Clash," *Honolulu Advertiser*, September 11, 1924, p. 1. For the deputy sheriff's account, as told to his son, see Crowell interview, p. 223.

61. Acting Adjutant General E. M. Bolton to Farrington, September 22, 1924, as quoted in Reinecke (1996: 76).

62. *Honolulu Star-Bulletin*, September 10 and 11, 1924, as quoted in Reinecke (1996: 81). Included in the latter group were "Japanese language newspapers . . . preaching sympathy with the Filipinos" and "a heterogeneous group of 'reds,' 'pinks,' and yellows—'wobblies' and communists and crack-brained demagogues—who have aligned themselves with the strikers and are doing their bolshevik best to turn Hawaii into anarchy."

63. "17 Dead, Many Injured as Police, Strikers Clash," *Honolulu Advertiser*, September 10, 1924, p. 1; Charles Edward Hogue, "Revealing of Weapons Supports Theory That Riot Was Premeditated," *Honolulu Advertiser*, September 12, 1924, p. 1.

64. A. W. T. Bottomley, *A Statement Concerning the Sugar Industry in Hawaii; Labor Condition on Hawaiian Sugar Plantations; Filipino Laborers Thereon, and the Alleged Filipino "Strike" of 1924*, November 1924, pp. 43–44, Hawaiian Collection, University of Hawai'i at Mānoa. Bottomley wrote this pamphlet as the president of the HSPA.

65. A. W. T. Bottomley, presidential address, *Proceedings of the Forty-fourth Annual Meeting of the Hawaiian Sugar Planters' Association*, November 17–20, 1924, pp. 14–15, Hawaiian Collection, University of Hawai'i at Mānoa.

66. "Manlapit Mere Agitator, Declares Governor Wood," *Honolulu Advertiser*, September 14, 1924, p. 2.

67. Reinecke (1996: 79); Charles E. Hogue, "Truth Probe of Hanapepe Riot Starts," *Honolulu Advertiser*, September 13, 1924, pp. 1–2; C. Ponce interview, p. 308.

68. Kojiri interview, p. 585; the first sentence quoted is attributed to "SK," Kojiri's wife. Kojiri had been a taxi driver who, on September 9, 1924, took to Hanapēpē some of the police later involved in the violence.

69. *Honolulu Advertiser*, September 11, 1924, p. 1; Reinecke (1996); Cortezan interview, p. 431; ESOHP (1979: A-6); Fern interview, p. 526.

70. There is a bias to ESOHP's (1979) interview sample: "It does not include those convicted and later deported or those who became dissatisfied with plantation life on Kauai and

left. It includes those found not guilty and released, by definition only peripherally involved in the strike organization and decision making, and those who for whatever reasons elected to stay on Kauai" (Taniguchi et al. 1979: xi). In all likelihood, then, the discourse of Filipino strikers on Kauaʻi as a whole was even more in conflict with the dominant discourse than presented here.

71. P. Ponce interview, p. 287. He added, "That's what made it so difficult, when we were on strike before. Because our enemies were not only the plantations, but the police themselves" (Ponces interview, p. 323).

72. Anonymous A and Oroc interview, p. 771; Anonymous B interview, p. 851; Cabinatan interview, p. 65; Ganade interview, p. 104; Lagmay interview, p. 195; Plateros interview, pp. 355–56, 360; Venyan interview, p. 811.

73. Oroc in Anonymous A and Oroc interview, p. 795. See also C. Ponce interview, pp. 307–08; P. Ponce interview, p. 294.

74. Anonymous A in Anonymous A and Oroc interview, p. 795.

75. Ganade interview, p. 104.

76. Anonymous B interview, p. 849. See also Ganade interview, p. 85; Lagmay interview, p. 171.

77. Anonymous A in Anonymous A and Oroc interview, p. 771.

78. Runes interview.

79. Faye interview, pp. 470–73.

80. Fern interview, pp. 523–25.

81. Ibid., p. 526. Charles Fern attributed his lack of shock in 1924 to professional focus.

82. Fern interview, p. 534.

83. Venyan and Juabot interview, p. 825; Bakiano interview, p. 621; Heller (1951).

84. Bakiano interview, p. 608. See also Fern interview, p. 534.

85. Determining that those who killed the four police officers were themselves killed in the conflict, the authorities did not charge anyone with homicide.

86. The *Honolulu Star-Bulletin* was particularly inclined toward this view (Reinecke 1996: 81–83).

87. Perhaps indicative of the "open-and-shut" nature of the case, newspaper reporting was "very scanty" (Reinecke 1996: 85).

88. "Hanapepe Riot Case Is Slow; Tales Unusual," *Honolulu Advertiser*, November 2, 1924, territorial section, p. 1.

89. "Rioters Get Four Years in the Pen," *Honolulu Advertiser*, November 11, 1924, p. 6; Anonymous B interview, p. 859; Ganade interview, pp. 90, 99; Plateros interview, p. 366; Rivera interview, p. 898. The exact number of deportations remains unclear.

90. In contrast, no haole was hanged between 1911 and 1944, and only one was ever executed in the entire post-Cook history of Hawaiʻi.

91. As Mae Gwendolyn Henderson writes about Black women, "It is not that black women . . . have had nothing to say, but rather that they have had no say" (1989: 24, as quoted in Collins 1998: 44).

92. For similar ideas about coalitions, see Roberts and Jesudason (2013).

93. Likewise, to recognize and engage tacitly unrecognized subaltern discourses and practices and to construct meaningful articulations across them are some of the key opportunities and responsibilities of critical scholarship. Recognition and engagement should not be confused with uncritical acceptance, however well-intentioned, for even a second sight leaves many blind spots.

ORAL HISTORY INTERVIEWS

The oral history interviews cited in this chapter can be found in collections by the Ethnic Studies Oral History Project (ESOHP) of the University of Hawai'i, as follows:

Agbayani, Felomina. Interview with Gael Gouveia, December 6, 1978. Transcript in ESOHP (1979), vol. 1.

Anonymous A and Gregario Oroc. Interviews with Ed Gerlock and Chad Taniguchi, October 31 and December 5, 1978. Transcript in ESOHP (1979), vol. 2.

Anonymous B. Interview with Chad Taniguchi, August 19, 1978. Transcript in ESOHP (1979), vol. 2.

Bakiano, Agapito. Interviews with Ed Gerlock, Chad Taniguchi, Gael Gouveia, and Yoshikazu Morimoto, November 2, 1978, December 7, 1978, and March 7, 1978. Transcript in ESOHP (1979), vol. 2.

Cabico, Emigdio. Interviews with Pablo Lazo, June and July 1976. Transcript in ESOHP (1977).

Cabinatan, Exequil. Interviews with Gael Gouveia and Ed Gerlock, September 11 and November 2, 1978. Transcript in ESOHP (1979), vol. 1.

Cortezan, Josefina. Interview with Gael Gouveia, November 1, 1978. Transcript in ESOHP (1979), vol. 1.

Crowell, Edwin Kapalikauohi. Interview with Chad Taniguchi, November 3, 1978. Transcript in ESOHP (1979), vol. 1.

De la Cruz, Justo. Interview with Perry Nakayama, June 1976. Transcript in ESOHP (1977).

Faye, Lindsay Anton. Interview with Chad Taniguchi, December 9, 1978. Transcript in ESOHP (1979), vol. 2.

Fern, Charles James. Interviews with Chad Taniguchi, December 14, 1978, and May 16, 1979. Transcript in ESOHP (1979), vol. 2.

Ganade, Isabel. Interviews with Gael Gouveia and Ed Gerlock, October 18, 1978, and January 8, 1979. Transcript in ESOHP (1979), vol. 1.

Gueco, Frank. Interview with Araceli Agoo, July 1976. Transcript in ESOHP (1977).

Kojiri, Junzo. Interviews with Chad Taniguchi, August 17, 1978, and May 16, 1979. Transcript in ESOHP (1979), vol. 2.

Lagmay, Ignacia. Interviews with Gael Gouveia and Chad Taniguchi, March 9 and August 16, 1978. Transcript in ESOHP (1979), vol. 1.

Lutao, Edward S. Interview with Chad Taniguchi, September 10, 1978. Transcript in ESOHP (1979), vol. 2.

Ogawa, Masako. Interview with Gael Gouveia, August 19, 1978. Transcript in ESOHP (1979), vol. 1.

Plateros, Mauro. Interviews with Gael Gouveia, October 12, 1978, and January 10, 1979. Transcript in ESOHP (1979), vol. 1.

Ponce, Crescencia. Interview with Ed Gerlock and Gael Gouveia, November 1, 1978. Transcript in ESOHP (1979), vol. 1.

Ponce, Crescencia and Pedro. Interview with Ed Gerlock and Gael Gouveia, December 7, 1978. Transcript in ESOHP (1979), vol. 1.

Ponce, Pedro. Interview with Ed Gerlock and Gael Gouveia, October 30, 1978. Transcript in ESOHP (1979), vol. 1.

Rivera, Dimitrio. Interview with Ed Gerlock and Chad Taniguchi, November 1, 1978. Transcript in ESOHP (1979), vol. 2.

Runes, Jacinto Relles. Interview with Chad Taniguchi, September 15, 1978. Transcript in ESOHP (1979), vol. 1.

Venyan, Sulpicio, and Laurano Juabot. Interviews with Ed Gerlock and Chad Taniguchi, December 6, 1978, December 7, 1978, and May 22, 1979. Transcript in ESOHP (1979), vol. 2.

CHAPTER 6

1. "The 2000 Campaign; Gore's Stump Speech: A Clear Choice, with Clear Visions for the Future," *New York Times*, October 24, 2000.

2. See below for a description of the unemployment data used in this chapter.

3. "The 1992 Campaign; In Their Own Words," *New York Times*, October 31, 1992.

4. See video footage of the speech at http://www.c-spanvideo.org/program/33853-1 (retrieved September 1, 2011).

5. Literature reviews by Mullings (2005) and Quillian (2006) provide a number of examples.

6. For the paper's own marketing research, see http://www.nytimes.whsites.net/mediakit/pdfs/newspaper/MRI_NYTreaderprofile.pdf; http://www.nytimes.whsites.net/mediakit/pdfs/newspaper/MRI_Influentials_Strong_Reach.pdf; http://www.nytimes.whsites.net/mediakit/pdfs/newspaper/Erdus_Morgan_Opinion_Leaders_Study.pdf; http://www.erdosmorgan.com/pr/pr_20081113-1.html (retrieved August 4, 2010).

7. Nate Silver, "A Note to Our Readers on the Times Pay Model and the Economics of Reporting," March 24, 2011, http://fivethirtyeight.blogs.nytimes.com/2011/03/24/a-note-to-our-readers-on-the-times-pay-model-and-the-economics-of-reporting (retrieved April 22, 2014).

8. See http://data.bls.gov:8080/PDQ/outside.jsp?survey=ln (retrieved June 3, 2010).

9. For the news releases from 1994 onward, see http://www.bls.gov/schedule/archives/empsit_nr.htm (retrieved August 22, 2010). The *New York Times* data were collected from http://www.nytimes.com on September 3, 2010.

10. From January 1972 to April 2010, the correlations between overall and white, overall and Black, and white and Black unemployment rates were 1.00, 0.94, and 0.91, respectively.

11. Under certain conditions, which are not applicable here, this statistic may not be an appropriate test. Less intuitive measures, such as Dunn and Clark's Z, Steiger's Z, and Williams's t, likewise returned similarly significant results (Meng, Rosenthal, and Rubin 1992; Steiger 1980). For obvious reasons, the overall unemployment is excluded from these comparisons. Thanks to Tim Liao for his help with the Hotelling's t-test and to Alan Pickering, and research assistant Jae Kim who corresponded with him, for the computer program that generated the other statistics.

12. For the correlations in Table 6.2 and the regression in Table 6.3, one outlier case, in which the number of "unemployment" items is at the extraordinary high of 493, is removed; in the regression, the case is the only one with the dependent variable more than five standard deviations from the predicted value.

13. Though statistically insignificant, the correlation's negative sign is interesting, for it indicates that more racial inequality entails *less* coverage of "unemployment" in the *Times*.

14. There was another possible comparison, between *July* 2008 and October 2009. In July 2008, Black unemployment was at 9.9 percent, the closest match to the peak overall unemployment rate of 10.1 percent in October 2009. Also, if we were to have used the BLS press release numbers rather than those with corrections supplied by the BLS later, once again either June or July 2008 could have been used. However, choosing one or the other would have made little substantive difference.

15. I obtained the full texts of the 67 items through LexisNexis (retrieved August 15, 2010). LexisNexis maintains a full-text database of the *New York Times* from June 1980 onward. Keyword searches in LexisNexis and NYTimes.com do not return the same totals. For July 2008, the latter's count is 75.

16. "Dispelling the Myths of Summer," *New York Times*, July 2, 2008, p. C1.

17. "Deepening Cycle of Job Loss Seen Lasting into '09," *New York Times*, July 2, 2008, p. A1. The BLS later adjusted the May 2008 unemployment figure downward, to 5.4 percent.

18. Louis Uchitelle, "Outlook Darker as Jobs Are Lost and Wages Stall," *New York Times*, July 4, 2008, p. A1.

19. Peter S. Goodman, "On Every Front, Anxious Questions and Uncomfortable Answers," *New York Times*, July 19, 2008, p. A10. See also "Prime Numbers, June 29–July 5," *New York Times*, July 6, 2008, p. WK2.

20. "Cause for Alarm," *New York Times*, July 5, 2008, p. A17.

21. "L-ish Economic Prospects," *New York Times*, July 18, 2008, p. A19.

22. Michael Cooper, "McCain Adviser Refers to 'Nation of Whiners,' Touching Off Rebukes," *New York Times*, July 11, 2008, p. A15. The only Pollyanna holdout was Ben Stein, "a lawyer, writer, actor and economist" who had a regular business column: "The economy isn't at its best. . . . But over all, it's not all that bad. Employment in June was considerably less than 1 percent below its all-time peak in November 2007. This is painful indeed for the people involved, but the numbers showed that 94.5 percent of the people who wished to be employed and were capable of work were employed" ("It's Bad, but Remember We're Dodging the Worst," *New York Times*, July 27, 2008, p. BU5).

23. U.S. Bureau of Labor Statistics, "News Release," July 3, 2008, p. 2, http://www.bls.gov/news.release/archives/empsit_07032008.pdf (retrieved September 21, 2010).

24. Given that whites were at 4.9 percent (later adjusted to 5.0 percent), considerably lower than the overall rate, it seems perfectly reasonable for the *Times* not to have mentioned how comparatively better off they were.

25. David Leonhardt, "Through a Glass Less Darkly," *New York Times*, November 4, 2009, p. B1.

26. "Help Small Businesses Hire Again," *New York Times*, November 3, 2009, p. A29.

27. Edmund L. Andrews, "Fed Signals a Rate Rise Is Far Away," *New York Times*, November 5, 2009, p. B1.

28. "Geithner Laments the Deficit, but Demurs on Tax Increases," *New York Times*, November 2, 2009, p. B11.

29. "Too Little of a Good Thing," *New York Times*, November 2, 2009, p. A21.

30. Jackie Calmes, "Senate Approves a New Extension of Jobless Benefits," *New York Times*, November 5, 2009, p. A22. President Obama signed the bill into law on November 6 (David Leonhardt, "Jobless Rate Hits 10.2%, with More Underemployed," *New York Times*, November 7, 2009, p. A1).

31. Associated Press, "Dow Soars Past 10,000 as New Unemployment Claims Fall," *New York Times*, November 6, 2009, p. B7.

32. David Leonhardt, "Jobless Rate Hits 10.2%," p. A1.

33. For example, see Javier C. Hernandez, "Seeing the Glass Half Full Despite the Day's Reports," *New York Times*, November 7, 2009, p. B6.

34. "Oil Slides, and Wall Street Pulls Back," *New York Times*, November 13, 2009, p. B8. See also Associated Press, "Data on Homes Sales and Jobless Claims Lift Markets," *New York Times*, November 26, 2009, p. B9.

35. Javier C. Hernandez, "Car Sales Help Spur 1.4% Increase in U.S. Retail Sales," *New York Times*, November 17, 2009, p. B3.

36. Floyd Norris, "Seeing the Glass as Mostly Empty," *New York Times*, November 28, 2009, p. B3.

37. Stephanie Rosenbloom and Christopher Maag, "Shoppers out in Force, but Most Are Sticking to Their Lists," *New York Times*, November 28, 2009, p. A1.

38. Javier C. Hernandez, "Home Building Surprises Analysts by Slowing Down," *New York Times*, November 19, 2009, p. B3; David Streitfeld, "As Delinquencies Soar, One in 10 Mortgages Is a Month or More Late," *New York Times*, November 20, 2009, p. B6; David Streitfeld and Javier C. Hernandez, "An Upturn in Housing May Be Reversing," *New York Times*, November 25, 2009, p. B1; Javier C. Hernandez, "New-Home Sales Rise, But Factory Orders Slip," *New York Times*, November 26, 2009, p. B3.

39. *New York Times*, November 14, 2009, p. B3.

40. Bloomberg News, "Jobless Rate Up in 29 States, Hitting Records in 4 of Them," *New York Times*, November 21, 2009, p. B6.

41. Lesley Alderman, "How to Find Mental Health Care When Money Is Tight," *New York Times*, November 21, 2009, p. B5.

42. Adam Nagourney, "On Health Care, Democrats Play Down Election Results," *New York Times*, November 7, 2009, p. A14. See also David M. Herszenhorn and Robert Pear, "Top Democrats Push for Votes before Health Debate," *New York Times*, November 7, 2009, p. A13.

43. John Harwood, "Unemployment and Midterms," *New York Times*, November 30, 2009, p. A21. See also Jeff Zeleny, "Vital Tests for Obama on Mandate for Change," *New York Times*, November 30, 2009, p. A14.

44. Adam Nagourney, "Reading the Tea Leaves in Obama's Sliding Numbers," *New York Times*, November 24, 2009, p. A24; Kate Zernike, "Enthusiasm for Palin, and Echoes of 2008 Divide," *New York Times*, November 22, 2009, p. A22.

45. Michael Barbaro, "Bloomberg and Thompson Make Final Pitches to Voters Worried about Their Wallets," *New York Times*, November 2, 2009, p. A25.

46. Abby Goodnough, "Town Once Known as Inclusive Is Riven by Housing Dispute," *New York Times*, November 15, 2009, p. A20.

47. Mark Lacey, "Money Starts to Trickle North as Mexicans Help Out Relatives," *New York Times*, November 16, 2009, p. A1.

48. Charlie Savage, "Illinois Site May Be Path to Closing Cuba Prison," *New York Times*, November 16, 2009, p. A12. See also Monica Davey, "Village Split on Detainees as Neighbors," *New York Times*, November 18, 2009, p. A18.

49. Michael Luo, "Job Woes Exacting a Heavy Toll on Family Life," *New York Times*, November 12, 2009, p. A1. This chapter does not systematically analyze photographs.

50. Patrick McGeehan, "For a District That's Short of Heroes, a Teamful," *New York Times*, November 6, 2009, p. A23.

51. Deirdre Dolan and Jennifer Daniel, "The Daily Grind," *New York Times*, November 28, 2009, p. A19.

52. "Jobless Recovery," *New York Times*, November 8, 2009, p. WK7.

53. "Off the Chart," *New York Times*, November 16, 2009 (website-only column). The column, ultimately interested in the political fallout, lacked a sharp edge, disappointing or baffling readers who, at the beginning of the piece, probably expected a harsher criticism of Obama than inadequately negative predictions. One reader, in a letter to the editor, complained, "It's hard to understand exactly what Ross Douthat is criticizing" (David Berman, "Obama and Jobs," *New York Times*, November 23, 2009, website-only).

54. "Obama's to Fix," *New York Times*, November 7, 2009, p. A23.

55. *New York Times*, November 8, 2009, p. WK8.

56. "Virtuous Bankers? Really!?!" *New York Times*, November 11, 2009, p. A31.

57. Paul Krugman, "Free to Lose," *New York Times*, November 13, 2009, p. A31.
58. Paul Krugman, "The Big Squander," *New York Times*, November 20, 2009, p. A35.
59. Paul Krugman, "The Phantom Menace," *New York Times*, November 23, 2009, p. A27.
60. Paul Krugman, "The Jobs Imperative," *New York Times*, November 20, 2009, p. A31.
61. Michael Powell, "Morning After, Democrats Regret Lost Chances to Win," *New York Times*, November 5, 2009, p. A29.
62. Peter S. Goodman, "Economists Scan Jobs Data, Seeking Signs of Hope," *New York Times*, November 7, 2009, p. B1.
63. Edmund L. Andrews, "Continuing Unemployment Is Predicted by Fed Chief," *New York Times*, November 17, 2009, p. B1.
64. Shaila Dewan, "A Racial Divide Is Bridged by Hard Times," *New York Times*, November 17, 2009, p. A14.
65. Ibid.
66. Jason DeParle and Robert Gebeloff, "Food Stamp Use Soars across U.S., and Stigma Fades," *New York Times*, November 29, 2009, p. A1. See also Jason DeParle, "49 Million Americans Report a Lack of Food," *New York Times*, November 17, 2009, p. A14.
67. Steven Greenhouse, "NAACP Prods Obama on Job Losses," *New York Times*, November 17, 2009, p. A22.
68. Ibid.
69. Bob Herbert, "A Word, Mr. President," *New York Times*, November 10, 2009, p. A35.
70. Bob Herbert, "A Recovery for Some," *New York Times*, November 14, 2009, p. A23.
71. Bob Herbert left the *New York Times* at the end of March 2011.
72. West's bravery then should not be diminished or dismissed by any subsequent developments, including his own apology for his statement upon the publication of Bush's memoir.
73. John Springer, "Bush Reacts to Apology from Kanye West," November 11, 2010, http://today.msnbc.msn.com/id/40108402/ns/today-today_people (retrieved May 5, 2011). It should be noted that West did not call Bush a "racist."
74. For example, Omi and Winant write, "In the aftermath of the 1960s, any effective challenge to the egalitarian ideals framed by the minority movements could no longer rely on racism of the past. Racial equality had to be acknowledged as a desirable goal. But the *meaning* of equality, and the proper means for achieving it, remained matters of considerable debate" (1994: 117; emphasis in original).

CONCLUSION
1. Email and PDF file, November 29, 2011, in author's possession. The event was postponed and then canceled for unknown reasons.
For another take on race and the Occupy Movement from around the same time, see Rinku Sen, "Race and Occupy Wall Street," *The Nation*, November 14, 2011, http://www.thenation.com/article/164212/race-and-occupy-wall-street (retrieved October 4, 2012).
2. Not being coy with the phrasing of this sentence, I was not the recipient who forwarded the email.
3. Email, November 30, 2011, in author's possession.
4. See Richard Kim, "Asian Americans for Affirmative Action," *The Nation*, January 8, 2007, http://www.thenation.com/blog/asian-americans-affirmative-action (retrieved August 6, 2012).
5. Another piece titled "Let Them Eat Diversity," published in the *National Review*, intimates a kind of convergence and symmetry between right and left conservatisms. Rich

Lowry, "Let Them Eat Diversity," *National Review*, September 2, 2003, http://old.nation-alreview.com/lowry/lowry090203.asp (retrieved August 4, 2012).

6. As James Baldwin wrote, "one dare hope for nothing from friends like these" ([1976] 1998: 521).

7. For exceptions, see Jones (1966) and Ferguson (2000). In political science, Lawrie Balfour (2001) provides a serious book-length treatment of Baldwin's political ideas.

8. By far not exclusively, quantitative analyses are probably the most prone to not questioning received racial categories. For an innovative counterexample, see Saperstein and Penner (2012).

9. I borrow "freedom dreams" from Kelley (2002).

10. As Baldwin called out the white public, following John F. Kennedy's assassination, "we all know that it has been many generations and it hasn't stopped yet that black men's heads have been blown off—and nobody cared" ([1964b] 2010: 82).

11. James Baldwin as quoted in Robert Coles, "James Baldwin Back Home," *New York Times*, July 31, 1977, http://www.nytimes.com/books/98/03/29/specials/baldwin-home.html (retrieved August 27, 2012).

12. In a critical response to Sewell (2005), George Steinmetz notes, "some structures may change due to the accretion of a kind of *sociocultural drift*, in which numerous microscopic changes finally give rise to a structural change" (2008b: 538; emphasis in original).

13. For another valuable take on politics of the everyday, see Cohen (2004).

14. Baldwin's comparison of his own and U.S. Blacks' situation with that of Algerians in France is an exception ([1972] 1998: 366–67).

15. An example would be efforts by Asian faculty and students on college campuses to fight for inclusion in affirmative action programs, a worthy goal in many cases, without taking into account the programs' hitherto woeful inadequacy and ineffectiveness for Blacks, Latinas/os, and Native Americans and the detrimental impact on them if the inclusion happened without increasing the size of the proverbial pie.

16. The line by Baldwin has been much repeated within whiteness studies, ever since David Roediger's groundbreaking *The Wages of Whiteness*: "As long as you think you're white, there's no hope for you" (as quoted in 1991: 6). Baldwin can be seen saying those words in Karen Thorsen's 1989 documentary *James Baldwin: The Price of the Ticket*.

REFERENCES

Ahmed, Sara. 2009. "Embodying Diversity: Problems and Paradoxes for Black Feminists." *Race Ethnicity and Education* 12(1): 41–52.

Alba, Richard. 1995. "Assimilation's Quiet Tide." *Public Interest* 119: 3–18.

Alba, Richard, Philip Kasinitz, and Mary C. Waters. 2011. "The Kids Are (Mostly) Alright: Second-Generation Assimilation." *Social Forces* 89(3): 763–74.

Alba, Richard, and Victor Nee. 1997. "Rethinking Assimilation Theory for a New Era of Immigration." *International Migration Review* 31(4): 826–74.

———. 2003. *Remaking the American Mainstream: Assimilation and Contemporary Immigration*. Cambridge, MA: Harvard University Press.

Aleinikoff, T. Alexander. 2002. *Semblances of Sovereignty: The Constitution, the State, and American Citizenship*. Cambridge, MA: Harvard University Press.

Alexander, Michelle. 2010. *The New Jim Crow: Mass Incarceration in the Age of Colorblindness*. New York: New Press.

Alliance for Audited Media. 2013. "Top 25 U.S. Newspapers for March 2013." Retrieved April 22, 2014 (http://www.auditedmedia.com/news/research-and-data/top-25-us-newspapers-for-march-2013.aspx).

Anderson, Benedict. 1991. *Imagined Communities: Reflections on the Origin and Spread of Nationalism*. New York: Verso.

Anderson, Elijah. 1990. *Streetwise: Race, Class, and Change in an Urban Community*. Chicago: University of Chicago Press.

Anderson, Robert N., with Richard Coller and Rebecca F. Pestano. 1984. *Filipinos in Rural Hawaii*. Honolulu: University of Hawai'i Press.

Archer, Margaret S. 1995. *Realist Social Theory: The Morphogenetic Approach*. Cambridge, England: Cambridge University Press.

Arias, Elizabeth. 2011. "United States Life Tables, 2007." *National Vital Statistics Reports* 59(9): 1–60.

Ariyoshi, Koji. 2000. *From Kona to Yenan: The Political Memoirs of Koji Ariyoshi*, edited by Alice M. Beechert and Edward D. Beechert. Honolulu: University of Hawai'i Press.

Arjomand, Saïd Amir. 1992. "Constitutions and the Struggle for Political Order: A Study in the Modernization of Political Traditions." *European Journal of Sociology* 33(1): 39–82.

Audit Bureau of Circulation. 2010. "Circulation Averages for the Six Months Ended: March 31, 2010." Retrieved August 4, 2010 (http://abcas3.accessabc.com/ecirc/newstitlesearchus.asp).

Austin, Algernon. 2009. "American Indians and the Great Recession: Economic Disparities Growing Larger." *Economic Policy Institute Issue Brief* 264 (November). Retrieved August 3, 2010 (http://epi.3cdn.net/1aaad254862c0b29b6_2em6bnkyh.pdf).

Austin, J. L. 1975. *How to Do Things with Words*. Cambridge, MA: Harvard University Press.

Ayres, Ian, and Peter Siegelman. 1995. "Race and Gender Discrimination in Bargaining for a New Car." *American Economic Review* 85(3): 304–21.

Azuma, Eiichiro. 2005. *Between Two Empires: Race, History, and Transnationalism in Japanese America*. New York: Oxford University Press.

Baldoz, Rick. 2011. *The Third Asiatic Invasion: Migration and Empire in Filipino America, 1898–1946*. New York: New York University Press.

Baldwin, James. [1955] 1998. *Notes of a Native Son*. In *Collected Essays*, pp. 1–129. New York: Library of America.

———. [1961a] 2010. "From *Nationalism, Colonialism, and the United States: One Minute to Twelve—A Forum*." In *The Cross of Redemption: Uncollected Writings*, pp. 10–18. New York: Vintage International.

———. [1961b] 1998. *Nobody Knows My Name*. In *Collected Essays*, pp. 131–285. New York: Library of America.

———. 1962. *The Fire Next Time*. New York: Dell.

———. [1963] 2010. "We Can Change the Country." In *The Cross of Redemption: Uncollected Writings*, pp. 59–64. New York: Vintage International.

———. [1964a] 2010. "The Uses of the Blues." In *The Cross of Redemption: Uncollected Writings*, pp. 70–81. New York: Vintage International.

———. [1964b] 2010. "What Price Freedom?" In *The Cross of Redemption: Uncollected Writings*, pp. 82–87. New York: Vintage International.

———. [1965] 1998. "The White Man's Guilt." In *Collected Essays*, pp. 722–27. New York: Library of America.

———. [1967] 2010. "The International War Crimes Tribunal." In *The Cross of Redemption: Uncollected Writings*, pp. 245–49. New York: Vintage International.

———. [1971] 2010. "Speech from the Soledad Rally." In *The Cross of Redemption: Uncollected Writings*, pp. 120–25. New York: Vintage International.

———. [1972] 1998. *No Name in the Street*. In *Collected Essays*, pp. 349–475. New York: Library of America.

———. [1976] 1998. *The Devil Finds Work*. In *Collected Essays*, pp. 477–572. New York: Library of America.

———. [1977] 1998. "Every Good-Bye Ain't Gone." In *Collected Essays*, pp. 773–79. New York: Library of America.

———. [1979] 2010. "On Language, Race, and the Black Writer." In *The Cross of Redemption: Uncollected Writings*, pp. 140–44. New York: Vintage International.

———. [1980a] 2010. "Black English: A Dishonest Argument." In *The Cross of Redemption: Uncollected Writings*, pp. 154–60. New York: Vintage International.

———. [1980b] 1998. "The House of Bondage." In *Collected Essays*, pp. 799–807. New York: Library of America.

———. [1983] 2010. "This Far and No Further." In *The Cross of Redemption: Uncollected Writings*, pp. 161–65. New York: Vintage International.

———. 1984. "The Art of Fiction No. 78." *Paris Review* 91: 48–82.

———. [1984] 2010. "On Being White . . . and Other Lies." In *The Cross of Redemption: Uncollected Writings*, pp. 166–70. New York: Vintage International.

Baldwin, James, and William F. Buckley. [1965] 2007. "Debate at Cambridge University." In *Classics of American Political and Constitutional Thought, Volume 2: Reconstruction to the Present*, pp. 684–89, edited by Scott J. Hammond, Kevin Hardwick, and Howard L. Lubert. Indianapolis, IN: Hackett.

Baldwin, James, and Nikki Giovanni. 1973. *A Dialogue*. Philadelphia: J. B. Lippincott.

Baldwin, James, Alfred Kazin, Lorraine Hansberry, Emile Capouya, and Langston Hughes, with Nat Hentoff. 1961. "The Negro in American Culture." In *The New Negro*, pp. 108–45, edited by Mathew H. Ahmann. New York: Fides.

Baptist, Edward E. 2008. "Hidden in Plain View: Haiti and the Louisiana Purchase." In *Echoes of the Haitian Revolution, 1804–2004*, pp. 1–27, edited by Martin Munro and Elizabeth Walcott-Hackshaw. Kingston, Jamaica: University of the West Indies Press.

Bargh, John A. 1997a. "The Automaticity of Everyday Life." In *The Automaticity of Everyday Life*, pp. 1–61, edited by Robert S. Wyer Jr. Mahwah, NJ: Lawrence Erlbaum.

———. 1997b. "Reply to the Commentaries." In *The Automaticity of Everyday Life*, pp. 231–46, edited by Robert S. Wyer Jr. Mahwah, NJ: Lawrence Erlbaum.

Barsh, Russel Lawrence. 1982. "Indian Land Claims Policy in the United States." *North Dakota Law Review* 58: 7–52.

Bartky, Sandra Lee. 2002. "Race, Complicity, and Culpable Ignorance." In *"Sympathy and Solidarity" and Other Essays*, pp. 151–67. Lanham, MD: Rowman & Littlefield.

Bean, Frank D., and Gillian Stevens. 2003. *America's Newcomers and the Dynamics of Diversity*. New York: Russell Sage Foundation.

Beechert, Edward. 1985. *Working in Hawaii: A Labor History*. Honolulu: University of Hawai'i Press.

Bell, Joyce M., and Douglas Hartmann. 2007. "Diversity in Everyday Discourse: The Cultural Ambiguities and Consequences of 'Happy Talk.'" *American Sociological Review* 71(6): 895–914.

Bell, Roger John. 1984. *Last among Equals: Hawaiian Statehood and American Politics*. Honolulu: University of Hawai'i Press.

Biernacki, Richard. 1997. "Work and Culture in Class Ideologies." In *Reworking Class*, pp. 169–92, edited by John R. Hall. Ithaca, NY: Cornell University Press.

Biolsi, Thomas. 2005. "Imagined Geographies: Sovereignty, Indigenous Space, and American Indian Struggle." *American Ethnologist* 32(2): 239–59.

Blackhawk, Ned. 2006. *Violence over the Land: Indians and Empires in the Early American West*. Cambridge, MA: Harvard University Press.

Blauner, Robert. 1972. *Racial Oppression in America*. New York: Harper & Row.

Bonilla-Silva, Eduardo. 1997. "Rethinking Racism: Toward a Structural Interpretation." *American Sociological Review* 62(3): 465–480.

———. 2001. *White Supremacy & Racism in the Post–Civil Rights Era*. Boulder, CO: Lynne Rienner.

———. 2003. *Racism without Racists: Color-Blind Racism and the Persistence of Racial Inequality in the United States.* Lanham, MD: Rowman & Littlefield.

Bosniak, Linda. 2006. *The Citizen and the Alien: Dilemmas of Contemporary Membership.* Princeton, NJ: Princeton University Press.

Bourdieu, Pierre. 1977. *Outline of a Theory of Practice.* Translated by Richard Nice. Cambridge, England: Cambridge University Press.

———. 1984. *Distinction: A Social Critique of the Judgement of Taste.* Translated by Richard Nice. Cambridge, MA: Harvard University Press.

———. 1989. "Social Space and Symbolic Power." *Sociological Theory* 7(1): 14–25.

———. 1994. "Rethinking the State: Genesis and Structure of the Bureaucratic Field." *Sociological Theory* 12(1): 1–18.

———. 1996. *The State Nobility.* Translated by Lauretta Clough. Stanford, CA: Stanford University Press.

———. 2000. *Pascalian Meditations.* Translated by Richard Nice. Stanford, CA: Stanford University Press.

———. 2001. *Masculine Domination.* Translated by Richard Nice. Stanford, CA: Stanford University Press.

Bourdieu, Pierre, and Jean-Claude Passeron. 1977. *Reproduction in Education, Society and Culture.* Translated by Richard Nice. London: Sage.

Bourdieu, Pierre, and Loïc J. D. Wacquant. 1992. *An Invitation to Reflexive Sociology.* Chicago: University of Chicago Press.

Bourdieu, Pierre, and Terry Eagleton. 1994. "Doxa and Common Life: An Interview." In *Mapping Ideology*, pp. 265–77, edited by Slavoj Žižek. New York: Verso.

Boyd, Herb. 2008. *Baldwin's Harlem: A Biography of James Baldwin.* New York: Atria Books.

Brubaker, Rogers. 2004. "The Return of Assimilation?" In *Ethnicity without Groups*, pp. 116–31. Cambridge, MA: Harvard University Press.

Brunson, Rod K. 2007. "'Police Don't Like Black People': African-American Young Men's Accumulated Police Experiences." *Criminology & Public Policy* 6(1): 71–102.

Brunson, Rod K., and Jody Miller. 2006. "Young Black Men and Urban Policing in the United States." *British Journal of Criminology* 46: 613–40.

Bruyneel, Kevin. 2004. "Challenging American Boundaries: Indigenous People and the 'Gift' of U.S. Citizenship." *Studies in American Political Development* 18: 30–43.

Burnett, Christina Duffy. 2005. "The Constitution and Deconstitution of the United States." In *The Louisiana Purchase and American Expansion, 1803–1898*, pp. 181–208, edited by Sanford Levinson and Bartholomew H. Sparrow. Lanham, MD: Rowman & Littlefield.

Burnett, Christina Duffy, and Burke Marshall. 2001a. "Between the Foreign and the Domestic: The Doctrine of Territorial Incorporation, Invented and Reinvented." In *Foreign in a Domestic Sense: Puerto Rico, American Expansion, and the Constitution*, pp. 1–36, edited by Christina Duffy Burnett and Burke Marshall. Durham, NC: Duke University Press.

———, eds. 2001b. *Foreign in a Domestic Sense: Puerto Rico, American Expansion, and the Constitution.* Durham, NC: Duke University Press.

Bush, George W. 2010. *Decision Points.* New York: Random House.

Butler, Judith. 2002. "Is Kinship Always Already Heterosexual?" *differences* 13(1): 14–44.

Calhoun, Craig. 1995. *Critical Social Theory.* Cambridge, MA: Basil Blackwell.

Central Intelligence Agency. 2010. "The World Fact Book: Country Comparison by Population." Retrieved September 28, 2010 (https://www.cia.gov/library/publications/the-world-factbook/rankorder/2119rank.html).

Chapin, Helen Geracimos. 1996. *Shaping History: The Role of Newspapers in Hawai'i.* Honolulu: University of Hawai'i Press.

Chatterjee, Partha. 1993. *The Nation and Its Fragments.* Princeton, NJ: Princeton University Press.

Chin, Gabriel. 1996. "The *Plessy* Myth: Justice Harlan and the Chinese Cases." *Iowa Law Review* 82: 151–82.

Cohen, Cathy J. 2004. "Deviance as Resistance: A New Research Agenda for the Study of Black Politics." *Du Bois Review* 1(1): 27–45.

Cole, David. 2003. *Enemy Aliens: Double Standards and Constitutional Freedoms in the War on Terrorism.* New York: New Press.

Coles, Robert. 1977. "James Baldwin Back Home." *New York Times* (July 31). Retrieved August 27, 2012 (http://www.nytimes.com/books/98/03/29/specials/baldwin-home.html).

Collins, Patricia Hill. 1991. *Black Feminist Thought.* New York: Routledge.

———. 1998. *Fighting Words: Black Women and the Search for Justice.* Minneapolis: University of Minnesota Press.

Cook, Katherine M. 1934. "Education among Native and Minority Groups in Alaska, Puerto Rico, Virgin Islands, and Hawaii." *Journal of Negro Education* 3(1): 20–41.

Cooper, Frederick. 2005. *Colonialism in Question: Theory, Knowledge, History.* Berkeley: University of California Press.

Cullen, Francis T., Liqun Cao, James Frank, Robert H. Langworthy, Sandra Lee Browning, Renee Kopache, and Thomas J. Stevenson. 1996. "'Stop or I'll Shoot': Racial Differences in Support for Police Use of Deadly Force." *American Behavioral Scientist* 39(4): 449–60.

Das Gupta, Monisha. 2006. *Unruly Immigrants: Rights, Activism, and Transnational South Asian Politics in the United States.* Durham, NC: Duke University Press.

———. 2014. "'Don't Deport Our Daddies': Gendering State Deportation Practices and Immigrant Organizing." *Gender & Society* 28(1): 83–109.

Dean, Arthur L. 1950. *Alexander & Baldwin, Ltd. and the Predecessor Partnerships.* Honolulu: Alexander & Baldwin.

Deloria, Vine Jr., and David E. Wilkins. 1999. *Tribes, Treaties, and Constitutional Tribulations.* Austin: University of Texas Press.

Donato, Katharine M., Donna Gabaccia, Jennifer Holdaway, Martin Manalansan IV, and Patricia R. Pessar. 2006. "A Glass Half Full? Gender in Migration Studies." *International Migration Review* 40(1): 3–26.

Downey, Douglas B. 2008. "Black/White Differences in School Performance: The Oppositional Culture Explanation." *Annual Review of Sociology* 34: 107–26.

Du Bois, William E. B. [1903] 1965. *The Souls of Black Folk.* In *Three Negro Classics,* pp. 207–389, by Booker T. Washington, William E. B. Du Bois, and James Weldon Johnson. New York: Avon Books.

Dudley, William, ed. 1991. *Police Brutality.* San Diego, CA: Greenhaven Press.

Duus, Masayo Umezawa. 1999. *The Japanese Conspiracy: The Oahu Sugar Strike of 1920.* Translated by Beth Cary. Berkeley: University of California Press.

Eagleton, Terry. 1991. *Ideology: An Introduction.* New York: Verso.

Eberhardt, Jennifer L. 2005. "Imaging Race." *American Psychologist* 60(2): 181–90.

Eisen, Arlene. 2013. *Operation Ghetto Storm: 2012 Annual Report on the Extrajudicial Killings of 313 Black People by Police, Security Guards and Vigilantes.* Retrieved December 11, 2014 (http://www.operationghettostorm.org/uploads/1/9/1/1/19110795/new_all_14_11_04.pdf).

Elder-Vass, Dave. 2007. "Reconciling Archer and Bourdieu in an Emergentist Theory of Action." *Sociological Theory* 25(4): 325–46.

Eltis, David. 1993. "Europeans and the Rise and Fall of African Slavery in the Americas: An Interpretation." *American Historical Review* 98(5): 1399–1423.

———. 2000. *The Rise of African Slavery in the Americas.* New York: Cambridge University Press.

Ethnic Studies Oral History Project (ESOHP). 1977. *Waialua and Haleiwa: The People Tell Their Story.* Volume 3. Honolulu: Ethnic Studies Program, University of Hawaii.

———. 1979. *The 1924 Filipino Strike on Kauai.* Volumes 1 and 2. Honolulu: Ethnic Studies Program, University of Hawaii.

Fairlie, Robert W., and William A. Sundstrom. 1997. "The Racial Unemployment Gap in Long-Run Perspective." *American Economic Review* 87(2): 306–10.

Feagin, Joe R. 1991. "Continuing Significance of Race: Antiblack Discrimination in Public Places." *American Sociological Review* 56(1): 101–16.

Feagin, Joe R., Hernán Vera, and Pina Batur. 2001. *White Racism.* 2nd ed. New York: Routledge.

Ferguson, Roderick. 2000. "The Nightmares of the Heteronormative." *Cultural Values* 4(4): 419–44.

Fernández-Kelly, M. Patricia, and Richard Schauffler. 1994. "Divided Fates: Immigrant Children in a Restructured U.S. Economy." *International Migration Review* 28(4): 662–89.

Fiske, Susan T. 1993. "Controlling Other People: The Impact of Power on Stereotyping." *American Psychologist* 48(6): 621–28.

Fleming, Crystal M., Michèle Lamont, and Jessica S. Welburn. 2012. "African Americans Respond to Stigmatization: The Meanings and Salience of Confronting, Deflecting Conflict, Educating the Ignorant and 'Managing the Self.'" *Ethnic and Racial Studies* 35(3): 400–17.

Forman, Tyrone A., and Amanda E. Lewis. 2006. "Racial Apathy and Hurricane Katrina: The Social Anatomy of Prejudice in the Post–Civil Rights Era." *Du Bois Review* 3(1): 175–202.

Fox, Cybelle. 2012. *Three Worlds of Relief: Race, Immigration, and the American Welfare State from the Progressive Era to the New Deal.* Princeton, NJ: Princeton University Press.

Francis, E. K. 1954. "Variables in the Formation of So-Called 'Minority Groups.'" *American Journal of Sociology* 60(1): 6–14.

Frantz, Klaus. 1999. *Indian Reservations in the United States: Territory, Sovereignty, and Socioeconomic Change.* Chicago: University of Chicago Press.

Freehling, William W. 2005. "The Louisiana Purchase and the Coming of the Civil War." In *The Louisiana Purchase and American Expansion, 1803–1898*, pp. 69–82, edited by Sanford Levinson and Bartholomew H. Sparrow. Lanham, MD: Rowman & Littlefield.

Freeman, Catherine, and Mary Ann Fox. 2005. *Status and Trends in the Education of American Indians and Alaska Natives.* Washington, DC: National Center for Education Statistics, Institute of Education Sciences, U.S. Department of Education.

Friday, Chris. 1994. *Organizing Asian American Labor: The Pacific Coast Canned-Salmon Industry, 1870–1942.* Philadelphia: Temple University Press.

Fry-Johnson, Yvonne W., Robert Levine, Diane Rowley, Vincent Agboto, and George Rust. 2010. "United States Black:White Infant Mortality Disparities Are Not Inevitable: Identification of Community Resilience Independent of Socioeconomic Status." *Ethnicity & Disease* 20(1 Suppl 1): S1–131–5.

Fuchs, Lawrence. 1961. *Hawaii Pono: A Social History.* New York: Harcourt, Brace & World.

Fujita-Rony, Dorothy B. 2003. *American Workers, Colonial Power: Philippine Seattle and the Transpacific West, 1919–1941.* Berkeley: University of California Press.

Gabrielson, Ryan, Ryann Grochowski Jones, and Eric Sagara. 2014. "Deadly Force, in Black and White." *Pro Publica* (October 10). Retrieved November 26, 2014 (http://www.propublica.org/article/deadly-force-in-black-and-white).

Galinsky, Adam D., Joe C. Magee, M. Ena Inesi, and Deborah H. Gruenfeld. 2006. "Power and Perspectives Not Taken." *Psychological Science* 17(12): 1068–74.

Gans, Herbert J. 1992. "Second-Generation Decline: Scenarios for the Economic and Ethnic Futures of the Post-1965 American Immigrants." *Ethnic and Racial Studies* 15(2): 173–92.

———. 1997. "Toward a Reconciliation of 'Assimilation' and 'Pluralism': The Interplay of Acculturation and Ethnic Retention." *International Migration Review* 31(4): 875–92.

George, Lisa M., and Joel Waldfogel. 2006. "The 'New York Times' and the Market for Local Newspapers." *American Economic Review* 96(1): 435–47.

Gibson, Margaret. 1989. *Accommodation without Assimilation: Sikh Immigrants in an American High School.* Ithaca, NY: Cornell University Press.

Giddens, Anthony. 1979. *Central Problems in Social Theory: Action, Structure, and Contradiction in Social Analysis.* Berkeley: University of California Press.

Glazer, Nathan. 1971. "Blacks and Ethnic Groups: The Difference and the Political Difference It Makes." *Social Problems* 18: 444–61.

———. 1993. "Is Assimilation Dead?" *Annals of the American Academy of Political and Social Science* 530: 122–36.

Go, Julian. 2003. "A Globalizing Constitutionalism? Views from the Postcolony, 1945–2000." *International Sociology* 18(1): 71–95.

———. 2007. "Waves of Empire: U.S. Hegemony and Imperialistic Activity from the Shores of Tripoli to Iraq, 1787–2003." *International Sociology* 22(1): 5–40.

———. 2008. "Global Fields and Imperial Forms: Field Theory and the British and American Empires." *Sociological Theory* 26(3): 201–29.

Goff, Phillip Atiba, Jennifer L. Eberhardt, Melissa J. Williams, and Matthew Christian Jackson. 2008. "Not Yet Human: Implicit Knowledge, Historical Dehumanization, and Contemporary Consequences." *Journal of Personality and Social Psychology* 94(2): 292–306.

Goldberg, David Theo. 2002. *The Racial State.* Malden, MA: Blackwell.

Gómez, Laura E. 2005. "Off-White in an Age of White Supremacy: Mexican Elites and the Rights of Indians and Blacks in Nineteenth-Century New Mexico." *Chicago-Latino Law Review* 25: 9–59.

Gordon, Milton. 1964. *Assimilation in American Life: The Role of Race, Religion, and National Origins.* New York: Oxford University Press.

Gramsci, Antonio. 1971. *Selections from the Prison Notebooks.* Translated by Quintin Hoare and Geoffrey Nowell Smith. New York: International Publishers.

Greenwald, Anthony G., T. Andrew Poehlman, Eric Luis Uhlmann, and Mahzarin R. Bnaji. 2009. "Understanding and Using the Implicit Association Test: III. Meta-Analysis of Predictive Validity." *Journal of Personality and Social Psychology* 97(1): 17–41.

Groseclose, Tim, and Jeffrey Milyo. 2005. "A Measure of Media Bias." *Quarterly Journal of Economics* 120(4): 1191–1237.

Guglielmo, Thomas A. 2003. *White on Arrival: Italians, Race, Color and Power in Chicago, 1890–1945.* New York: Oxford University Press.

Gumplowicz, Ludwig. 1883. *Der Rassenkampf: Sociologische Untersuchungen.* Innsbruck, Austria: Universitäts-Verlag Wagner.

Hacking, Ian. 2002. *Historical Ontology.* Cambridge, MA: Harvard University Press.

Hagopian, Amy, Abraham D. Flaxman, Tim K. Takaro, Sahar A. Esa Al Shatari, Julie Rajaratnam, Stan Becker, Alison Levin-Rector, Lindsay Galway, Berq J. Hadi Al-Yasseri, William M. Weiss, Christopher J. Murray, and Gilbert Burnham. 2013. "Mortality in Iraq Associated with the 2003–2011 War and Occupation: Findings from a National Cluster Sample Survey by the University Collaborative Iraq Mortality Study." *PLOS Medicine* 10(10): 1–15.

Hall, Stuart. 1980. "Race, Articulation and Societies Structured in Dominance." In *Sociological Theories: Race and Colonialism*, pp. 305–45, edited by UNESCO. Paris: UNESCO.

Haller, William, Alejandro Portes, and Scott M. Lynch. 2011a. "Dreams Fulfilled, Dreams Shattered: Determinants of Segmented Assimilation in the Second Generation." *Social Forces* 89(3): 733–62.

———. 2011b. "On the Dangers of Rosy Lenses." *Social Forces* 89(3): 775–82.

Harrison, Benjamin. 1901. "The Status of Annexed Territory and of Its Free Civilized Inhabitants." *North American Review* 172(530): 1–22.

Hart, Albert Bushnell. 1899. "Brother Jonathan's Colonies: A Historical Account." *Harper's New Monthly Magazine* 98(January): 319–28.

Hassin, Ran R., James S. Uleman, and John A. Bargh, eds. 2006. *The New Unconscious.* New York: Oxford University Press.

Heller, Francis H. 1951. *The Sixth Amendment to the Constitution of the United States: A Study in Constitutional Development.* Lawrence: University of Kansas Press.

Henderson, Mae Gwendolyn. 1989. "Speaking in Tongues: Dialogics, Dialectics, and the Black Woman Writer's Literary Tradition." In *Changing Our Own Words: Essays on Criticism, Theory, and Writing by Black Women*, pp. 16–37, edited by Cheryl A. Wall. New Brunswick, NJ: Rutgers University Press.

Hirschman, Charles. 1983. "America's Melting Pot Reconsidered." *Annual Review of Sociology* 9: 397–423.

Hollywood, Amy. 2002. "Performativity, Citationality, Ritualization." *History of Religion* 42(2): 93–115.

Howard, Judith. 1994. "A Social Cognitive Conception of Social Structure." *Social Psychology Quarterly* 57(3): 210–27.

Hoxie, Frederick E. 2007. "What Was Taney Thinking? American Indian Citizenship in the Era of *Dred Scott*." *Chicago-Kent Law Review* 82: 328–59.

Hunt, Matthew O. 2007. "African American, Hispanic, and White Beliefs about Black/White Inequality, 1977–2004." *American Sociological Review* 72: 390–415.

Hurwitz, Jon, and Mark Peffley. 2005. "Explaining the Great Racial Divide: Perceptions of Fairness in the U.S. Criminal Justice System." *Journal of Politics* 67(3): 762–83.

Hutton, Paul Andrew. 1999. *Phil Sheridan and His Army.* Tulsa: University of Oklahoma Press.

Hyndman, Jennifer. 2000. *Managing Displacement: Refugees and the Politics of Humanitarianism.* Minneapolis: University of Minnesota Press.

Jackman, Mary R. 2001. "License to Kill: Violence and Legitimacy in Expropriative Social Relations." In *The Psychology of Legitimacy*, pp. 437–67, edited by John T. Jost and Brenda Major. New York: Cambridge University Press.

————. 2002. "Violence in Social Life." *Annual Review of Sociology* 28: 387–415.

Jackson, Shona N. 2012. *Creole Indigeneity: Between Myth and Nation in the Caribbean.* Minneapolis: University of Minnesota Press.

Jacobs, David, and Robert M. O'Brien. 1998. "The Determinants of Deadly Force: A Structural Analysis of Police Violence." *American Journal of Sociology* 103(4): 837–62.

Jacobson, Matthew Frye. 1998. *Whiteness of a Different Color: European Immigrants and the Alchemy of Race.* Cambridge, MA: Harvard University Press.

————. 2000. *Barbarian Virtues: The United States Encounters Foreign Peoples at Home and Abroad, 1876–1917.* New York: Hill and Wang.

Jacoby, Tamar, ed. 2004. *Reinventing the Melting Pot: The New Immigrants and What It Means to Be American.* New York: Basic.

James, David R., and Kent Redding. 2005. "Theories of Race and State." In *The Handbook of Political Sociology: States, Civil Societies, and Globalization,* pp. 187–98, edited by Thomas Janoski, Robert R. Alford, Alexander M. Hicks, and Mildred A. Schwartz. New York: Cambridge University Press.

Jenks, Albert Ernest. 1914. "Assimilation in the Philippines, as Interpreted in Terms of Assimilation in America." *American Journal of Sociology* 19(6): 773–91.

Jensen, Leif, and Tim Slack. 2003. "Underemployment in America: Measurement and Evidence." *American Journal of Community Psychology* 32(1/2): 21–31.

Johnson, Gloria Jones, and Cedric O. Herring. 1993. "Underemployment among Black Americans." *Western Journal of Black Studies* 17(3): 126–34.

Jung, Moon-Kie. 1999. "No Whites, No Asians: Race, Marxism, and Hawaii's Preemergent Working Class." *Social Science History* 23(3): 357–93.

————. 2003. "Interracialism: The Ideological Transformation of Hawaii's Working Class." *American Sociological Review* 68(3): 373–400, 967.

————. 2006. *Reworking Race: The Making of Hawaii's Interracial Labor Movement.* New York: Columbia University Press.

————. 2015. "The Problem of the Color Lines: Studies of Racism and Resistance." *Critical Sociology* 41(2).

Jung, Moon-Kie, and Yaejoon Kwon. 2013. "Theorizing the U.S. Racial State: Sociology since *Racial Formation.*" *Sociology Compass* 7(11): 927–40.

Kahneman, Daniel. 2011. *Thinking, Fast and Slow.* New York: Random House.

Kaplan, Amy. 2002. *The Anarchy of Empire in the Making of U.S. Culture.* Cambridge, MA: Harvard University Press.

Kaplan, Amy, and Donald E. Pease, eds. 1993. *Cultures of United States Imperialism.* Durham, NC: Duke University Press.

Kasinitz, Philip, John H. Mollenkopf, and Mary C. Waters. 2002. "Becoming American/Becoming New Yorkers: Immigrant Incorporation in a Majority Minority City." *International Migration Review* 36(4): 1020–36.

Kasinitz, Philip, John H. Mollenkopf, Mary C. Waters, and Jennifer Holdaway. 2008. *Inheriting the City: The Children of Immigrants Come of Age.* New York: Russell Sage Foundation.

Kazal, Russell A. 1995. "Revisiting Assimilation: The Rise, Fall, and Reappraisal of a Concept in American Ethnic History." *American Historical Review* 100(2): 437–71.

Kelley, Robin D. G. 2002. *Freedom Dreams: The Black Radical Imagination.* Boston, MA: Beacon.

Kerkvliet, Melinda Tria. 2002. *Unbending Cane: Pablo Manlapit, a Filipino Labor Leader in*

Hawai'i. Honolulu: Office of Multicultural Student Services, University of Hawai'i, Mānoa.

King, Desmond S., and Rogers M. Smith. 2005. "Racial Orders in American Political Development." *American Political Science Review* 99(1): 75–92.

Kivisto, Peter, ed. 2005. *Incorporating Diversity: Rethinking Assimilation in a Multicultural Age*. Boulder, CO: Paradigm.

Kochhar, Rakesh, Richard Fry, and Paul Taylor. 2011. *Twenty-to-One: Wealth Gaps Rise to Record Highs between Whites, Blacks and Hispanics*. Washington, DC: Pew Research Center.

Kramer, Paul A. 2003. "Empires, Exceptions, and Anglo-Saxons: Race and Rule between the British and U.S. Empires, 1880–1910." In *The American Colonial State in the Philippines: Global Perspectives*, pp. 43–91, edited by Julian Go and Anne L Foster. Durham, NC: Duke University Press.

———. 2006. *The Blood of Government: Race, Empire, the United States, and the Philippines*. Chapel Hill: University of North Carolina Press.

Kretsedemas, Philip. 2012. *The Immigration Crucible: Transforming Race, Nation, and the Limits of Law*. New York: Columbia University Press.

Kubota, Jennifer T., Mahzarin R. Banaji, and Elizabeth A. Phelps. 2012. "The Neuroscience of Race." *Nature Neuroscience* 15(7): 940–48.

Kurland, Philip B., and Gerhard Casper, eds. 1975. *Landmark Briefs and Arguments of the Supreme Court of the United States: Constitutional Law*. Volume 13. Arlington, VA: University Publications of America.

Lee, Jennifer. 2000. "The Salience of Race in Everyday Life: Black Customers' Shopping Experiences in Black and White Neighborhoods." *Work and Occupations* 27(3): 353–76.

Lee, Jennifer, and Min Zhou. 2014. "The Success Frame and Achievement Paradox: The Costs and Consequences for Asian Americans." *Race and Social Problems* 6(1): 38–55.

Levinson, Sanford. 2001. "Installing the *Insular Cases* into the Canon of Constitutional Law." In *Foreign in a Domestic Sense: Puerto Rico, American Expansion, and the Constitution*, pp. 121–39, edited by Christina Duffy Burnett and Burke Marshall. Durham, NC: Duke University Press.

Levinson, Sanford, and Bartholomew H. Sparrow. 2005. "Introduction." In *The Louisiana Purchase and American Expansion, 1803–1898*, pp. 1–18, edited by Sanford Levinson and Bartholomew H. Sparrow. Lanham, MD: Rowman & Littlefield.

Lewis, Amanda E. 2003. *Race in the Schoolyard: Negotiating the Color Line in Classrooms and Communities*. New Brunswick, NJ: Rutgers University Press.

———. 2004. "'What Group?' Studying Whites and Whiteness in the Era of 'Color-Blindness.'" *Sociological Theory* 22(4): 623–46.

Lichter, Daniel T. 1988. "Racial Differences in Underemployment in American Cities." *American Journal of Sociology* 93(4): 771–92.

Lind, Andrew W. 1938. *An Island Community: Ecological Succession in Hawaii*. New York: Greenwood.

———. 1980. *Hawaii's People*. 4th ed. Honolulu: University Press of Hawaii.

Lindqvist, Sven. 1992. *"Exterminate All the Brutes": One Man's Odyssey into the Heart of Darkness and the Origins of European Genocide*. New York: New Press.

Lipsitz, George. 1998. *The Possessive Investment in Whiteness: How White People Profit from Identity Politics*. Philadelphia: Temple University Press.

Lipold, Paul F., and Larry W. Isaac. 2009. "Striking Deaths: Lethal Contestation and the

'Exceptional' Character of the American Labor Movement, 1870–1970." *International Review of Social History* 54: 167–205.

Littler, Robert M. C. 1929. *The Governance of Hawaii.* Stanford, CA: Stanford University Press.

Litzinger, Ralph A. 2000. *Other Chinas: The Yao and the Politics of National Belonging.* Durham, NC: Duke University Press.

Lizardo, Omar. 2009. "Is a 'Special Psychology' of Practice Possible? From Values and Attitudes to Embodied Dispositions." *Theory & Psychology* 19(6): 713–27.

Liu, John M. 1985. "Cultivating Cane: Asian Labor and the Hawaiian Sugar Plantation System within the Capitalist World Economy, 1835–1920." Ph.D. dissertation, University of California, Los Angeles.

Loveman, Mara. 1999. "Is 'Race' Essential?" *American Sociological Review* 64: 891–98.

Lowell, Abbott Lawrence. 1899a. "The Colonial Expansion of the United States." *Atlantic Monthly* 83(496): 145–54.

———. 1899b. "The Status of Our New Possessions—A Third View." *Harvard Law Review* 13(3): 155–76.

MacLennan, Carol Ann. 1979. "Plantation Capitalism and Social Policy in Hawaii." Ph.D. dissertation, University of California, Berkeley.

Magubane, Zine. 2003. *Bringing the Empire Home: Race, Class, and Gender in Britain and Colonial South Africa.* Chicago: University of Chicago Press.

Manalansan, Martin, IV. 2006. "Queer Intersections: Sexuality and Gender in Migration Studies." *International Migration Review* 40(1): 224–49.

Manlapit, Pablo. 1933. *Filipinos Fight for Justice: Case of the Filipino Laborers in the Big Strike of 1924.* Honolulu: Kumalae Publishing.

Mann, Michael. 2008. "American Empires: Past and Present." *Canadian Review of Sociology* 45(1): 7–50.

Marable, Manning. 2000. *How Capitalism Underdeveloped Black America.* Updated ed. Boston: South End Press.

Marx, Karl. [1845] 1994. "Theses on Feuerbach." *Selected Readings*, pp. 98–101. Edited by Lawrence H. Simon. Indianapolis, IN: Hackett.

Massey, Douglas, and Nancy A. Denton. 1993. *American Apartheid: Segregation and the Making of the Underclass.* Cambridge, MA: Harvard University Press.

Masuoka, Jitsuichi. 1931. "Race Attitudes of the Japanese People in Hawaii: A Study in Social Distance." M.A. thesis, University of Hawaii.

Matute-Bianchi, Maria Eugenia. 1991. "Situational Ethnicity and Patterns of School Performance among Immigrant and Nonimmigrant Mexican-Descent Students." In *Minority Status and Schooling: A Comparative Study of Immigrant and Involuntary Minorities*, pp. 205–47, edited by Margaret Gibson and John U. Ogbu. New York: Garland.

Mauer, Marc, and Ryan Scott King. 2004. "Schools and Prisons: Fifty Years after *Brown v. Board of Education.*" Washington, DC: The Sentencing Project.

McCool, Daniel, Susan M. Olson, and Jennifer L. Robinson. 2007. *Native Vote: American Indians, the Voting Rights Act, and the Right to Vote.* New York: Cambridge University Press.

McDonald, Laughlin. 2004. "The Voting Rights Act in Indian Country: South Dakota, a Case Study." *American Indian Law Review* 29(1): 43–74.

McDonald, Laughlin, Janine Pease, and Richard Guest. 2007. "Voting Rights in South Dakota: 1982–2006." *Southern California Review of Law and Social Justice* 17(1): 195–247.

McKenzie, Fayette Avery. 1914. "The Assimilation of the American Indian." *American Journal of Sociology* 19(6): 761–72.

Meinig, D. W. 1986. *The Shaping of America: A Geographical Perspective on 500 Years of History.* Volume 1. New Haven, CT: Yale University Press.

———. 1993. *The Shaping of America: A Geographical Perspective on 500 Years of History.* Volume 2. New Haven, CT: Yale University Press.

Meng, Xiao-Li, Robert Rosenthal, and Donald B. Rubin. 1992. "Comparing Correlated Correlation Coefficients." *Psychological Bulletin* 111(1): 172–75.

Merry, Sally Engle. 2000. *Colonizing Hawai'i: The Cultural Power of Law.* Princeton, NJ: Princeton University Press.

Miller, Robert J. 2008. *Native America, Discovered and Conquered: Thomas Jefferson, Lewis and Clark, and Manifest Destiny.* Lincoln: University of Nebraska Press.

Mills, Charles W. 1997. *The Racial Contract.* Ithaca, NY: Cornell University Press.

———. 2007. "White Ignorance." In *Race and Epistemologies of Ignorance*, pp. 13–38, edited by Shannon Sullivan and Nancy Tuana. Albany: State University of New York Press.

———. 2009. "Critical Race Theory: A Reply to Mike Cole." *Ethnicities* 9(2): 270–81.

Mishel, Lawrence, Josh Bivens, Elise Gould, and Heidi Shierholz. 2012. *The State of Working America.* 12th ed. Ithaca, NY: Cornell University Press.

Morawska, Ewa. 1994. "In Defense of the Assimilation Model." *Journal of American Ethnic History* 13(2): 76–87.

Moss, Philip, and Chris Tilly. 2001. *Stories Employers Tell: Race, Skill, and Hiring in America.* New York: Russell Sage Foundation.

Moynihan, Daniel P. 1965. *The Negro Family: The Case for National Action.* Washington, DC: Office of Policy Planning and Research, U.S. Department of Labor.

Mullings, Leith. 2005. "Interrogating Racism: Toward an Antiracist Anthropology." *Annual Review of Anthropology* 34: 667–93.

Murphy, Erin. 2009. "Women's Anti-Imperialism, 'The White Man's Burden,' and the Philippine-American War: Theorizing Masculinist Ambivalence in Protest." *Gender & Society* 23(2): 244–70.

Murphy, Sherry L., Jiaquan Xu, and Kenneth D. Kochanek. 2013. "Deaths: Final Data for 2010." *National Vital Statistics Report* 61(4): 1–167.

National Bureau of Economic Research (NBER). 2010. "U.S. Business Cycle Expansions and Contractions," September 20. Retrieved March 29, 2013 (http://www.nber.org/cycles.html).

Neckerman, Kathryn M., and Joleen Kirschenman. 1991. "Hiring Strategies, Racial Bias, and Inner-City Workers." *Social Problems* 38(4): 433–47.

Neckerman, Kathryn M., Prudence Carter, and Jennifer Lee. 1999. "Segmented Assimilation and Minority Cultures of Mobility." *Ethnic and Racial Studies* 22(6): 945–65.

Neisser, Ulric. 1976. *Cognition and Reality: Principles and Implications of Cognitive Psychology.* New York: Freeman.

Nelson, Jill, ed. 2000. *Police Brutality: An Anthology.* New York: W.W. Norton.

Newcomb, Steven T. 2008. *Pagans in the Promised Land: Decoding the Doctrine of Christian Discovery.* Golden, CO: Fulcrum.

Newman, Nathan, and J. J. Gass. 2004. *A New Birth of Freedom: The Forgotten History of the 13th, 14th, and 15th Amendments.* New York: Brennan Center for Justice, NYU School of Law.

Newton, Nell Jessup. 1984. "Federal Power over Indians: Its Sources, Scope, and Limitations." *University of Pennsylvania Law Review* 132(2): 195–288.

Ngai, Mae. 2004. *Impossible Subjects: Illegal Aliens and the Making of Modern America.* Princeton, NJ: Princeton University Press.

Nobles, Gregory H. 1997. *American Frontiers: Cultural Encounters and Continental Conquest.* New York: Hill and Wang.

Nordyke, Eleanor C. 1977. *The Peopling of Hawaii.* Honolulu: East-West Center and University Press of Hawaii.

Obeyesekere, Gananth. 1992. *The Apotheosis of Captain Cook.* Princeton, NJ: Princeton University Press.

O'Brien, Sharon. 1989. *American Indian Tribal Governments.* Norman: University of Oklahoma Press.

Ogbu, John U. 1974. *The Next Generation: An Ethnography of Education in an Urban Neighborhood.* New York: Academic Press.

———. 1978. *Minority Education and Caste: The American System in Cross-Cultural Perspective.* New York: Academic Press.

———. 1991a. "Low School Performance as an Adaptation: The Case of Blacks in Stockton, California." In *Minority Status and Schooling: A Comparative Study of Immigrant and Involuntary Minorities,* pp. 249–85, edited by Margaret A. Gibson and John U. Ogbu. New York: Garland Publishing.

———. 1991b. "Minority Coping Responses and School Experience. *Journal of Psychohistory* 18: 433–56.

———. 2003. *Black American Students in an Affluent Suburb: A Study of Academic Disengagement.* Mahwah, NJ: Lawrence Erlbaum.

Ogletree, Charles J., Mary Prosser, Abbe Smith, William Talley Jr., and Criminal Justice Institute at Harvard Law School for the National Association for the Advancement of Colored People. 1995. *Beyond the Rodney King Story: An Investigation of Police Conduct in Minority Communities.* Boston: Northeastern University Press.

Okamura, Jonathan Y. 2010. "From Running Amok to Eating Dogs: A Century of Misrepresenting Filipino Americans in Hawai'i." *Ethnic and Racial Studies* 33(3): 496–514.

Okihiro, Gary. 1991. *Cane Fires: The Anti-Japanese Movement in Hawaii, 1865–1945.* Philadelphia: Temple University Press.

Omi, Michael, and Howard Winant. 1986. *Racial Formation in the United States: From the 1960s to the 1980s.* New York: Routledge.

———. 1994. *Racial Formation in the United States: From the 1960s to the 1990s.* Rev. ed. New York: Routledge.

Ong, Paul, and Tania Azores. 1994. "Asian Immigrants in Los Angeles: Diversity and Divisions." In *The New Asian Immigration in Los Angeles and Global Restructuring,* pp. 100–29, edited by Paul Ong, Edna Bonacich, and Lucie Cheng. Philadelphia: Temple University Press.

Orfield, Gary, John Kucsera, and Genevieve Siegel-Hawley. 2012. *E Pluribus . . . Separation: Deepening Double Segregation for More Students.* Revised October 18, 2012, edition. Los Angeles: The Civil Rights Project/Proyecto Derechos Civiles, University of California at Los Angeles.

Osorio, Jon Kamakawiwo'ole. 2002. *Dismembering Lāhui: A History of the Hawaiian Nation to 1887.* Honolulu: University of Hawai'i Press.

Pager, Devah. 2003. "The Mark of a Criminal Record." *American Journal of Sociology* 108(5): 937–75.

Pager, Devah, and Diana Karafin. 2009. "Bayesian Bigot? Statistical Discrimination, Stereotypes, and Employer Decision Making." *Annals of the American Academy of Political and Social Science* 621: 70–93.

Pager, Devah, and Lincoln Quillian. 2005. "Walking the Talk? What Employers Say versus What They Do." *American Sociological Review* 70(3): 355–80.

Pager, Devah, Bruce Western, and Bart Bonikowski. 2009. "Discrimination in a Low-Wage Labor Market: A Field Experiment." *American Sociological Review* 74(5): 777–99.

Park, Robert E. 1914. "Racial Assimilation in Secondary Groups with Particular Reference to the Negro." *American Journal of Sociology* 19(5): 606–23.

———. 1926. "Our Racial Frontier on the Pacific." *The Survey* 56(3): 192–96.

———. 1950. *Race and Culture.* Glencoe, IL: Free Press.

Park, Robert E., and Ernest W. Burgess. 1921. *Introduction to the Science of Sociology.* Chicago: University of Chicago.

Pascoe, Peggy. 2009. *What Comes Naturally: Miscegenation Law and the Making of Race in America.* New York: Oxford University Press.

Patterson, Orlando. 1982. *Slavery and Social Death: A Comparative Study.* Cambridge, MA: Harvard University Press.

Peña, Susana. 2005. "Visibility and Silence: Mariel and Cuban American Gay Male Experience and Representation." In *Queer Migrations: Sexuality, U.S. Citizenship, and Border Crossings*, pp. 125–45, edited by Eithne Luibheid and Lionel Cantú. Minneapolis: University of Minnesota Press.

Perea, Juan F. 2001. "Fulfilling Manifest Destiny: Conquest, Race, and the *Insular Cases*." In *Foreign in a Domestic Sense: Puerto Rico, American Expansion, and the Constitution*, pp. 140–66, edited by Christina Duffy Burnett and Burke Marshall. Durham, NC: Duke University Press.

Pew Research Center. 2013. *Second-Generation Americans: A Portrait of the Adult Children Immigrants.* Washington, DC: Pew Research Center.

Perlmann, Joel, and Roger Waldinger. 1997. "Second Generation Decline? Children of Immigrants, Past and Present—A Reconsideration." *International Migration Review* 31(4): 893–922.

Pickering, Andrew. 1995. *The Mangle of Practice: Time, Agency, and Science.* Chicago: University of Chicago Press.

Pierre, Jemima. 2004. "Black Immigrants in the United States and the 'Cultural Narratives' of Ethnicity." *Identities* 11(2): 141–70.

Porter, Robert B. 1999. "The Demise of the *Ongwehoweh* and the Rise of the Native Americans: Redressing the Genocidal Act of Forcing American Citizenship upon Indigenous Peoples." *Harvard BlackLetter Law Journal* 15: 107–83.

Portes, Alejandro, and Patricia Fernández-Kelly. 2008. "No Margin for Error: Educational and Occupational Achievement among Disadvantaged Children of Immigrants." *Annals of the American Academy of Political and Social Science* 620: 12–36.

Portes, Alejandro, Patricia Fernández-Kelly, and William Haller. 2005. "Segmented Assimilation on the Ground: The New Second Generation in Early Childhood." *Ethnic and Racial Studies* 28(6): 1000–1040.

———. 2009. "The Adaptation of the Immigrant Second Generation in America: A Theoretical Overview and Recent Evidence." *Journal of Ethnic and Migration Studies* 35(7): 1077–1104.

Portes, Alejandro, and Dag MacLeod. 1996. "Educational Progress of Children of Immigrants: The Roles of Class, Ethnicity, and School Context." *Sociology of Education* 69: 255–75.

Portes, Alejandro, and Rubén G. Rumbaut. 2001a. "Conclusion—The Forging of a New

America: Lessons for Theory and Policy." In *Ethnicities: Children of Immigrants in America*, pp. 301–17, edited by Rubén G. Rumbaut and Alejandro Portes. Berkeley and New York: University of California Press and Russell Sage Foundation.

———. 2001b. *Legacies: The Story of the Immigrant Second Generation.* Berkeley and New York: University of California Press and Russell Sage Foundation.

Portes, Alejandro, and Alex Stepick. 1993. *City on the Edge: The Transformation of Miami.* Berkeley: University of California Press.

Portes, Alejandro, and Min Zhou. 1993. "The New Second Generation: Segmented Assimilation and Its Variants." *Annals of the American Academy of Political and Social Science* 530: 74–96.

Porteus, S. D., and Marjorie E. Babcock. 1926. *Temperament and Race.* Boston: Gorham Press.

Poulantzas, Nicos. 1973. "On Social Classes." *New Left Review* 78: 27–54.

———. 1975. *Political Power and Social Classes.* London: New Left Books.

Przybyszewky, Linda. 1999. *The Republic According to John Marshall Harlan.* Chapel Hill: University of North Carolina Press.

Quillian, Lincoln. 2006. "New Approaches to Understanding Racial Prejudice and Discrimination." *Annual Review of Sociology* 32: 299–328.

———. 2008. "Does Unconscious Racism Exist?" *Social Psychology Quarterly* 71(6): 6–11.

Rameau, Max. 2008. *Take Back the Land: Land, Gentrification, and the Umoja Village Shantytown.* Miami, FL: Nia Interactive Press.

Ramos, Efrén Rivera. 2001. "Deconstructing Colonialism: The 'Unincorporated Territory' as a Category of Domination." In *Foreign in a Domestic Sense: Puerto Rico, American Expansion, and the Constitution*, pp. 104–17, edited by Christina Duffy Burnett and Burke Marshall. Durham, NC: Duke University Press.

———. 2005. "Puerto Rico's Political Status: The Long-Term Effects of American Expansionist Discourse." In *The Louisiana Purchase and American Expansion, 1803–1898*, pp. 165–80, edited by Sanford Levinson and Bartholomew H. Sparrow. Lanham, MD: Rowman & Littlefield.

Rawls, Anne Warfield. 2000. "'Race' as an Interaction Order Phenomenon: W. E. B. Du Bois's 'Double Consciousness' Thesis Revisited." *Sociological Theory* 18(2): 241–74.

Reed, Isaac, and Jeffrey Alexander. 2009. "Social Science as Reading and Performance: A Cultural-Sociological Understanding of Epistemology." *European Journal of Social Theory* 12(21): 21–41.

Reid, Ira de A. 1938. "Negro Immigration to the United States." *Social Forces* 16(3): 411–17.

Reinecke, John E. 1979. *Feigned Necessity: Hawaii's Attempt to Obtain Chinese Contract Labor, 1921–23.* San Francisco: Chinese Materials Center.

———. 1996. *The Filipino Piecemeal Sugar Strike of 1924–1925.* Honolulu: Social Science Research Institute, University of Hawai'i.

Revised Laws of Louisiana: Containing the Revised Statutes of the State (Official Edition, 1870) as Amended by Acts of the Legislature, from the Session of 1870 to that of 1896 Inclusive, and All Other Acts of a General Nature for the Same Period. 1897. Compiled and annotated by Solomon Wolff. New Orleans: F. F. Hansell & Bro.

Richardson, Peter. 2009. "Doing Things with Wood: Builders, Managers and Wittgenstein in an Idaho Sawmill." *Critique of Anthropology* 29(2): 60–182.

Roberts, Dorothy, and Sujatha Jesudason. 2013. "Movement Intersectionality: The Case of Race, Gender, Disability, and Genetic Technologies." *Du Bois Review* 10(2): 313–28.

Robertson, Lindsay G. 2005. *Conquest by Law: How the Discovery of America Dispossessed Indigenous Peoples of Their Lands.* New York: Oxford University Press.

Robinson, Joan. [1962] 2006. *Economic Philosophy*. New Brunswick, NJ: Transaction.

Rodríguez, Tomás D. 2002. "Oppositional Culture and Academic Performance among Children of Immigrants in the USA." *Race Ethnicity and Education* 5(2): 199–215.

Roediger, David R. 1991. *The Wages of Whiteness: Race and the Making of the American Working Class*. New York: Verso.

———. 2005. *Working toward Whiteness: How America's Immigrants Became White*. New York: Basic Books.

Román, Ediberto. 1998. "The Alien-Citizen Paradox and Other Consequences of U.S. Colonialism." *Florida State University Law Review* 26(1): 1–47.

Royster, Deirdre A. 2003. *Race and the Invisible Hand*. Berkeley: University of California Press.

Sabol, William J., and Heather Couture. 2008. *Prison Inmates at Midyear 2007*. Washington, DC: U.S. Department of Justice, Bureau of Justice Statistics.

Sahlins, Marshall. 1985. *Islands of History*. Chicago: University of Chicago Press.

———. 1995. *How "Natives" Think, about Captain Cook, for Example*. Chicago: University of Chicago Press.

Said, Edward. 1978. *Orientalism*. New York: Vintage.

———. 1993. *Culture and Imperialism*. New York: Vintage.

Saperstein, Aliya, and Andrew M. Penner. 2012. "Racial Fluidity and Inequality in the United States." *American Journal of Sociology* 118(3): 676–727.

Saxton, Alexander. 1971. *Indispensable Enemy: Labor and the Anti-Chinese Movement in California*. Berkeley: University of California Press.

Schmitt, Robert C. 1977. *Historical Statistics of Hawaii*. Honolulu: University Press of Hawaii.

Schuman, Howard, and Maria Krysan. 1999. "A Historical Note on Whites' Beliefs about Racial Inequality." *American Sociological Review* 64: 847–55.

Schuman, Howard, Charlotte Steeh, Lawrence Bobo, and Maria Krysan. 1997. *Racial Attitudes in America: Trends and Interpretations*. Cambridge, MA: Harvard University Press.

Scott, James C. 1998. *Seeing Like a State: How Certain Schemes to Improve the Human Condition Have Failed*. New Haven, CT: Yale University Press.

Scott, Joan Wallach. 2007. *The Politics of the Veil*. Princeton, NJ: Princeton University Press.

Seward, Zachary M. 2009. "Top 15 Newspaper Sites of 2008." *Nieman Journalism Lab* (February 17). Retrieved August 4, 2010 (http://www.niemanlab.org/2009/02/top-15-newspaper-sites-of-2008).

Sewell, William H. Jr. 1992. "A Theory of Structure: Duality, Agency, and Transformation." *American Journal of Sociology* 98(1): 1–29.

———. 2005. *Logics of History: Social Theory and Social Transformation*. Chicago: University of Chicago Press.

Sharma, Miriam. 1984. "Labor Migration and Class Formation among the Filipinos in Hawaii, 1906–1946." In *Labor Immigration under Capitalism: Asian Workers in the United States before World War II*, pp. 579–615, edited by Lucie Cheng and Edna Bonacich. Berkeley: University of California Press.

Shaw, Donna. 2006. "The Pulitzer Cartel." *American Journalism Review* 28(5): 32–39.

Shelby, Tommie. 2003. "Ideology, Racism, and Critical Social Theory." *Philosophical Forum* 34(2): 153–88.

Simons, Sarah E. 1901. "Social Assimilation: Part I. Principles." *American Journal of Sociology* 6(6): 790–822.

Smith, Brad W. 2003. "The Impact of Police Officer Diversity on Police-Caused Homicides." *Policy Studies Journal* 31(2): 147–62.

Smith, Robert Courtney. 2014. "Black Mexicans, Conjunctural Ethnicity, and Operating Identities: Long-Term Ethnographic Analysis." *American Sociological Review* 79(3): 517–48.

Smith, Rogers M. 1997. *Civic Ideals: Conflicting Visions of Citizenship in U.S. History.* New Haven, CT: Yale University Press.

———. 2001. "The Bitter Roots of Puerto Rican Citizenship." In *Foreign in a Domestic Sense: Puerto Rico, American Expansion, and the Constitution*, pp. 373–88, edited by Christina Duffy Burnett and Burke Marshall. Durham, NC: Duke University Press.

Smith, Rogers M., and Desmond S. King. 2009. "Barack Obama and the Future of American Racial Politics." *Du Bois Review* 6(1): 25–35.

Somerville, Siobhan B. 2005. "Notes toward a Queer History of Naturalization." *American Quarterly* 57(3): 659–75.

Sparrow, Bartholomew H. 2006. *The Insular Cases and the Emergence of American Empire.* Lawrence: University Press of Kansas.

Spiro, Peter J. 2003. "The Impossibility of Citizenship." *Michigan Law Review* 101(6): 1492–1511.

Steiger, James H. 1980. "Tests for Comparing Elements of a Correlation Matrix." *Psychological Bulletin* 87(2): 245–51.

Steinmetz, George. 2005. "Return to Empire: The New U.S. Imperialism in Comparative Historical Perspective." *Sociological Theory* 23(4): 339–67.

———. 2006. "Imperialism or Colonialism? From Windhoek to Washington, by Way of Basra." In *Lessons of Empire: Imperial Histories and American Power*, pp. 135–56, edited by Craig Calhoun, Frederick Cooper, and Kevin W. Moore. New York: New Press.

———. 2008a. "The Colonial State as a Social Field: Ethnographic Capital and Native Policy in the German Overseas Empire before 1914." *American Sociological Review* 73(4): 589–612.

———. 2008b. *"Logics of History* as a Framework for an Integrated Social Science." *Social Science History* 32(4): 535–53.

Stevens, Jacqueline. 1999. *Reproducing the State.* Princeton, NJ: Princeton University Press.

———. 2010. *States without Nations.* New York: Columbia University Press.

Stoler, Ann Laura. 1997. "Racial Histories and Their Regimes of Truth." *Political Power and Social Theory* 11: 183–206.

———. 2006. "On Degrees of Imperial Sovereignty." *Public Culture* 18(1): 125–46.

Sugrue, Thomas J. 1996. *The Origins of the Urban Crisis: Race and Inequality in Postwar Detroit.* Princeton, NJ: Princeton University Press.

Sunkara, Bhaskar. 2011. "Let Them Eat Diversity." *Jacobin* 1. Retrieved August 3, 2012 (http://jacobinmag.com/winter-2011/let-them-eat-diversity).

Tang, Eric. 2011. "A Gulf Unites Us: The Vietnamese Americans of Black New Orleans East." *American Quarterly* 63(1): 117–49.

Taniguchi, Chad, Gael Gouveia, Vivien Lee, and Henrietta Yee. 1979. "Introduction." In *The 1924 Filipino Strike on Kauai*, pp. ix–xix, by Ethnic Studies Oral History Project. Honolulu: Ethnic Studies Program, University of Hawaii.

Taylor, William. 1935. "The Hawaiian Sugar Industry." Ph.D. dissertation, University of California, Berkeley.

Telles, Edward, and Vilma Ortiz. 2011. "Racialization and Mexican American Incorporation: A Reply to Lawrence Bobo and José Itzigsohn." *Du Bois Review* 8(2): 506–10.

Thayer, James Bradley. 1899. "Our New Possessions." *Harvard Law Review* 12(7): 464–85.

Theroux, Joseph. 1991. "A Short History of Hawaiian Executions, 1826–1947." *Hawaiian Journal of History* 25: 147–55.

Thomas, Brook. 2001. "A Constitution Led by the Flag: The *Insular Cases* and the Metaphor of Incorporation." In *Foreign in a Domestic Sense: Puerto Rico, American Expansion, and the Constitution*, pp. 82–103, edited by Christina Duffy Burnett and Burke Marshall. Durham, NC: Duke University Press.

Thompson, John B. 1984. *Studies in the Theory of Ideology.* Berkeley: University of California Press.

Thompson, Lanny. 2002. "The Imperial Republic: A Comparison of the Insular Territories under U.S. Dominion after 1898." *Pacific Historical Review* 71(4): 535–74.

Tilly, Charles. 1990. *Coercion, Capital, and European States, AD 990–1990.* Cambridge, MA: Blackwell.

Tomlins, Christopher. 2001. "Legal Cartography of Colonization, the Legal Polyphony of Settlement: English Intrusions on the American Mainland in the Seventeenth Century." *Law and Social Inquiry* 26(2): 315–72.

Torpey, John. 1998. "Coming and Going: On the State Monopolization of the Legitimate 'Means of Movement.'" *Sociological Theory* 16(3): 239–59.

———. 2000. *The Invention of the Passport: Surveillance, Citizenship, and the State.* New York: Cambridge University Press.

Tuan, Mia. 1999. *Forever Foreigners or Honorary Whites?* New Brunswick, NJ: Rutgers University Press.

Turner, Margery Austin, Stephen L. Ross, George C. Galster, and John Yinger. 2002. *Discrimination in Metropolitan Housing Markets: National Results from Phase 1 HDS 2000.* Washington, DC: Urban Institute.

Turner, Margery Austin, Rob Santos, Diane K. Levy, Doug Wissoker, Claudia Aranda, Rob Pitingolo, and the Urban Institute. 2013. *Housing Discrimination against Racial and Ethnic Minorities 2012.* Washington, DC: U.S. Department of Housing and Urban Development.

Twain, Mark. [1871] 1913. *Roughing It.* Volumes 1 and 2. New York: Harper and Brothers.

Ugarte, Eduardo. 1992. "Running Amok: The 'Demoniacal Impulse.'" *Asian Studies Review* 16(1): 182–89.

United States Census Bureau. 1998. *Measuring 50 Years of Economic Change Using the March Current Population Survey.* Current Population Reports, P60–203. Washington, DC: Government Printing Office.

———. 2010. "Population by Sex and Age, for Black Alone or in Combination and White Alone, Not Hispanic: 2008." Retrieved September 28, 2010 (http://www.census.gov/population/www/socdemo/race/ppl-bc08.html).

United States Department of Labor, Bureau of Labor Statistics (USBLS). 1940. "Labor in the Territory of Hawaii, 1939." Bulletin No. 687. 76th Congress, 3rd session, House Document No. 848. Washington, DC: Government Printing Office.

———. 2009. "How the Government Measures Unemployment." Retrieved July 30, 2010 (http://www.bls.gov/cps/cps-htgm.pdf).

United States House of Representatives (USHR). 1940. "Report of E. J. Eagen on the Hawaiian Islands." In "Hearing before the Special Committee to Investigate the National Labor Relations Board," pp. 4524–4539, 4598–4624. 76th Congress, 3rd session, vol. 22, 2–3 May 1940, pp. 4485–4685. Washington, DC: Government Printing Office.

Vaisey, Stephen. 2009. "Motivation and Justification: A Dual-Process Model of Culture in Action." *American Journal of Sociology* 114(6): 1675–1715.

Vargas, João H. Costa. 2003. "The Inner City and the Favela: Transnational Black Politics." *Race & Class* 44(4): 19–40.

———. 2005. "Genocide in the African Diaspora: United States, Brazil, and the Need for a Holistic Research and Political Method." *Cultural Dynamics* 17(3): 267–90.

———. 2006a. *Catching Hell in the City of Angels: Life and Meanings of Blackness in South Central Los Angeles.* Minneapolis: University of Minnesota Press.

———. 2006b. "When a Favela Dared to Become a Gated Condominium: The Politics of Race and Urban Space in Rio de Janeiro." *Latin American Perspectives* 33(4): 49–81.

———. 2008. *Never Meant to Survive: Genocide and Utopias in Black Diaspora Communities.* Lanham, MD: Rowman & Littlefield.

Vedder, Richard K., and Lowell Gallaway. 1992. "Racial Differences in Unemployment in the United States, 1890–1990." *Journal of Economic History* 52(3): 696–702.

Wacquant, Loïc J. D. 1987. "Symbolic Violence and the Making of the French Agriculturalist: An Enquiry into Pierre Bourdieu's Sociology." *Australian and New Zealand Journal of Sociology* 23(1): 65–88.

———. 1997. "For an Analytic of Racial Domination." *Political Power and Social Theory* 11: 221–34.

———. 2001. "Deadly Symbiosis: When Ghetto and Prison Meet and Mesh." *Punishment & Society* 31(1): 95–134.

Wacquant, Loïc J. D., and William Julius Wilson. 1989. "The Cost of Racial and Class Exclusion in the Inner City." *Annals of the American Academy of Political and Social Science* 501: 8–26.

Waldinger, Roger. 2003. "Foreigners Transformed: International Migration and the Remaking of a Divided People." *Diaspora* 12(2): 247–72.

———. 2007a. "The Bounded Community: Turning Foreigners into Americans in Twenty-first Century L.A." *Ethnic and Racial Studies* 30(3): 341–74.

———. 2007b. "Did Manufacturing Matter? The Experience of Yesterday's Second Generation: A Reassessment." *International Migration Review* 41(1): 3–39.

———. 2007c. "Transforming Foreigners into Americans." In *The New Americans: A Guide to Immigration since 1965*, pp. 137–48, edited by Mary C. Waters and Reed Ueda. Cambridge, MA: Harvard University Press.

———. 2011. "Immigration: The New American Dilemma." *Dædalus* 140(2): 215–25.

Waldinger, Roger, and Cynthia Feliciano. 2004. "Will the New Second Generation Experience 'Downward Assimilation'? Segmented Assimilation Re-assessed." *Ethnic and Racial Studies* 27(3): 376–402.

Waters, Mary C. 1994. "Ethnic and Racial Identities of Second-Generation Black Immigrants in New York City." *International Migration Review* 28(4): 795–820.

———. 1999. *Black Identities: West Indian Immigrant Dreams and American Realities.* Cambridge, MA, and New York: Harvard University Press and Russell Sage Foundation.

Waters, Mary C., and Tomás Jiménez. 2005. "Assessing Immigrant Assimilation: New Empirical and Theoretical Challenges." *Annual Review of Sociology* 31: 105–125.

Waters, Mary C., Van C. Tran, Philip Kasinitz, and John H. Mollenkopf. 2010. "Segmented Assimilation Revisited: Types of Acculturation and Socioeconomic Mobility in Young Adulthood." *Ethnic and Racial Studies* 33(7): 1168–93.

Weber, Max. 1946. *From Max Weber: Essays in Sociology.* Translated by H. H. Gerth and C. Wright Mills. New York: Oxford University Press.

Weinberg, Daniel Erwin. 1967. "The Movement to 'Americanize' the Japanese Community in Hawaii: An Analysis of One Hundred Percent Americanization Activity in the Territory of Hawaii as Expressed in the Caucasian Press, 1919–1923." M.A. thesis, Department of History, University of Hawaii.

Weiner, Mark S. 2001. "Teutonic Constitutionalism: The Role of Ethno-Juridical Discourse in the Spanish American War." In *Foreign in a Domestic Sense: Puerto Rico, American Expansion, and the Constitution*, pp. 48–81, edited by Christina Duffy Burnett and Burke Marshall. Durham, NC: Duke University Press.

Wesling, Meg. 2011. *Empire's Proxy: American Literature and U.S. Imperialism in the Philippines*. New York: New York University Press.

Western, Bruce, and Katherine Beckett. 1999. "How Unregulated Is the U.S. Labor Market? The Penal System as a Labor Market Institution." *American Journal of Sociology* 104(4): 1030–60.

Western, Bruce, and Becky Pettit. 2005. "Black-White Wage Inequality, Employment Rates, and Incarceration." *American Journal of Sociology* 111(2): 553–78.

Whitmeyer, Joseph M. 1994. "Why Actor Models Are Integral to Structural Analysis." *Sociological Theory* 12(2): 153–65.

Wilkins, David E. 1997. *American Indian Sovereignty and the U.S. Supreme Court: The Masking of Justice*. Austin: University of Texas Press.

Williams, David R., and James S. Jackson. 2000. "Race/Ethnicity and the 2000 Census: Recommendations for African American and Other Black Populations in the United States." *American Journal of Public Health* 90(11): 1728–30.

Williams, Raymond. 1977. *Marxism and Literature*. New York: Oxford University Press.

Williams, Robert A. Jr. 2005. *Like a Loaded Weapon: The Rehnquist Court, Indian Rights, and the Legal History of Racism in America*. Minneapolis: University of Minnesota Press.

Williams, Walter L. 1980. "United States Indian Policy and the Debate over Philippine Annexation: Implications for the Origins of American Imperialism." *Journal of American History* 66(4): 810–31.

Williams, William Appleman. 1980. *Empire as a Way of Life*. New York: Oxford University Press.

Wilson, James G. 2002. *The Imperial Republic: A Structural History of American Constitutionalism from the Colonial Era to the Beginning of the Twentieth Century*. Burlington, VT: Ashgate.

Wilson, Timothy. 2002. *Strangers to Ourselves: Discovering the Adaptive Unconscious*. Cambridge, MA: Harvard University Press.

Wilson, William Julius. 1978. *The Declining Significance of Race: Blacks and Changing American Institutions*. Chicago: University of Chicago Press.

———. 1987. *The Truly Disadvantaged: The Inner City, the Underclass, and Public Policy*. Chicago: University of Chicago Press.

———. 1996. *When Work Disappears: The World of the New Urban Poor*. New York: Knopf.

Wimmer, Andreas. 2008. "The Making and Unmaking of Ethnic Boundaries: A Multilevel Process Theory." *American Journal of Sociology* 113(4): 970–1022.

Wimmer, Andreas, and Nina Glick Schiller. 2003. "Methodological Nationalism, the Social Sciences, and the Study of Migration: An Essay in Historical Epistemology." *International Migration Review* 37(3): 576–610.

Winant, Howard. 2001. *The World Is a Ghetto: Race and Democracy since World War II*. New York: Basic Books.

Wolfe, Patrick. 2006. "Settler Colonialism and the Elimination of the Native." *Journal of Genocide Research* 8(4): 387–409.

Wolfley, Jeanette. 1991. "Jim Crow, Indian Style: The Disenfranchisement of Native Americans." *American Indian Law Review* 16(1): 167–202.

Worcester, Dean C. 1898. *The Philippine Islands and Their People*. New York: Macmillan.

Yang, Caroline H. 2009. "Reconstruction's Labor: Racialized Workers in the Narratives of U.S. Culture and History, 1870–1930." Unpublished manuscript.

Yinger, John. 1986. "Measuring Racial Discrimination with Fair Housing Audits: Caught in the Act." *American Economic Review* 76(5): 881–93.

Young, Iris. 1994. "Gender as Seriality: Thinking about Women as a Social Collective." *Signs* 19(3): 713–38.

———. 2002. "Power, Violence, and Legitimacy: A Reading of Hannah Arendt in an Age of Police Brutality and Humanitarian Intervention." In *Breaking the Cycles of Hatred: Memory, Law, and Repair*, pp. 260–87, edited by Martha Minow. Princeton, NJ: Princeton University Press.

Zelizer, Vivian. 1994. *The Social Meaning of Money.* New York: Basic Books.

Zhou, Min. 1993. "Underemployment and Economic Disparities among Minority Groups." *Population Research and Policy Review* 12(2): 139–57.

———. 1997. "Growing Up American: The Challenge Confronting Immigrant Children and Children of Immigrants." *Annual Review of Sociology* 23: 63–95.

Zhou, Min, and Carl L. Bankston III. 1994. "Social Capital and the Adaptation of the Second Generation: The Case of Vietnamese Youth in New Orleans." *International Migration Review* 28(4): 821–45.

———. 1998. *Growing Up American: The Adaptation of Vietnamese Adolescents in the United States.* New York: Russell Sage Foundation.

Zhou, Min, and Yang Sao Xiong. 2005. "The Multifaceted American Experiences of the Children of Asian Immigrants: Lessons for Segmented Assimilation." *Ethnic and Racial Studies* 28(6): 1119–52.

INDEX

Stanford Studies in
COMPARATIVE RACE AND ETHNICITY

Published in collaboration with the Center for Comparative Studies in Race and Ethnicity, Stanford University

SERIES EDITORS

Hazel Rose Markus

Paula M.L. Moya

EDITORIAL BOARD

H. Samy Alim

Gordon Chang

Gary Segura

C. Matthew Snipp

This series publishes outstanding scholarship that focuses centrally on comparative studies of race and ethnicity. Rather than exploring the experiences and conditions of a single racial or ethnic group, this series looks across racial and ethnic groups to take a more complex, dynamic, and interactive approach to understanding these social categories.

Race on the Move: Brazilian Migrants and the Global Reconstruction of Race
Tiffany D. Joseph
2015

The Ethnic Project: Transforming Racial Fiction into Racial Factions
Vilna Bashi Treitler
2013

On Making Sense: Queer Race Narratives of Intelligibility
Ernesto Javier Martínez
2012

Made in the USA
Lexington, KY
18 October 2017